PENGUIN BOOKS

Iain Sinclair is the author of *Downriver* (winner of the James Tait Black Memorial Prize and the Encore Award); *Landor's Tower*; *White Chappell, Scarlet Tracings*; *Lights Out for the Territory*; *Lud Heat*; *Rodinsky's Room* (with Rachel Lichtenstein); *Radon Daughters*; *London Orbital*; *Dining on Stones*; *Hackney, that Rose-Red Empire* and *Ghost Milk*. He is also the editor of *London: City of Disappearances*.

D0182859

By the same author

American Smoke

Journeys to the End of the Light

A Fiction of Memory

IAIN SINCLAIR

PENGUIN BOOKS

PENGUIN BOOKS

Published by the Penguin Group
Penguin Books Ltd, 80 Strand, London WC2R 0RL, England
Penguin Group (USA) Inc., 375 Hudson Street, New York, New York 10014, USA
Penguin Group (Canada), 90 Eglinton Avenue East, Suite 700, Toronto, Ontario, Canada M4P 2Y3
(a division of Pearson Penguin Canada Inc.)
Penguin Ireland, 25 St Stephen's Green, Dublin 2, Ireland (a division of Penguin Books Ltd)
Penguin Group (Australia), 707 Collins Street, Melbourne, Victoria 3008, Australia
(a division of Pearson Australia Group Pty Ltd)
Penguin Books India Pvt Ltd, 11 Community Centre, Panchsheel Park, New Delhi – 110 017, India
Penguin Group (NZ), 67 Apollo Drive, Rosedale, Auckland 0632, New Zealand
(a division of Pearson New Zealand Ltd)
Penguin Books (South Africa) (Pty) Ltd, Block D, Rosebank Office Park,
181 Jan Smuts Avenue, Parktown North, Gauteng 2193, South Africa

Penguin Books Ltd, Registered Offices: 80 Strand, London WC2R 0RL, England

www.penguin.com

First published by Hamish Hamilton 2013
Published in Penguin Books 2014
001

Copyright © Iain Sinclair, 2013
All rights reserved

The moral right of the author has been asserted

Typeset by Jouve (UK), Milton Keynes
Printed in Great Britain by Clays Ltd, St Ives plc

ISBN: 978-0-241-95581-9

www.greenpenguin.co.uk

MIX
Paper from
responsible sources
FSC
www.fsc.org FSC® C018179

Penguin Books is committed to a sustainable
future for our business, our readers and our planet.
This book is made from Forest Stewardship
Council™ certified paper.

For Edith and Andrew, onwards and outwards

Contents

Contents

Ocean

I return to find secrets. I return to rob them.
                                      – Robert Duncan

Two Men Smoking

and sees all things and to him
are presented at night
the whispers of the most flung shores
from Gloucester out

– Ed Dorn

It was the season of autumn ghosts, a dampness in the soul. 2011 and London had lost its savour. A good step beyond midway through my dark wood of the world, I came to America, hoping to reconnect with the heroes of my youth. The largest, the most light-occulting of all the giants, that earlier race, was Charles Olson: poet, scholar and last rector of Black Mountain College. This establishment, a scatter of buildings beside a lake in North Carolina, now imploded, bankrupt, seemed to us a Valhalla of all the talents: Josef Albers, John Cage, Merce Cunningham, Willem de Kooning, Robert Rauschenberg, Buckminster Fuller, Robert Duncan, Robert Cree-ley, Ed Dorn. Pick up the traces anywhere you choose, through fugitive magazines or literary gossip, and they lead back to one man. Olson knew, better than most, that his chosen territory, the Eastern Seaboard, the whaling ports, was once connected to Scot-land. And long before Prince Henry Sinclair, the Earl of Orkney, crossed the Atlantic, island-hopping in 1398, to bring back stories of infinite forests and their natives, and to leave his mark stamped on a rock. The native Micmac Indians, according to some authorities, recognized the tall voyager as their man-god, Glooscap. 'Kulóskap was the first, first and greatest, to come into our land,' sang the tribal poet. He was 'sober, grave, and good'. The big man walked on the backs of whales. One of Olson's youthful disciples, Peter

5

Anastas, carried out proper research into Glooscap; his heritage, the archaeological scratchings, the subsistence life in shack and trailer park endured by the last of the first people in this unyielding place.

Glooscap the man becomes Gloucester the town. By sound, by sonar echo, by necessity. Olson, writing about his childhood and his father, the Worcester mailman, calls the story 'Stocking Cap'. With some hope of payment, he sent it to the *New Yorker* in February 1948. It was rejected. Glooscap, Stocking Cap. A nod to elective Swedish ancestors, to Vikings. Cutting holes in the ice, winter fishing: father and son. I loved the old photograph used on the cover of Olson's memoir, *The Post Office*: that stern, bulb-headed baby emerging from a sack of letters, hard against his father's racing heart. Two figures from a race of huge, raw-boned immigrants, studio-captured against a painted pond, a forest clearing. I wanted it to be so. I needed a new mythology to shield against the sense of loss and hanging dread inherent in the invasion and dissolution of my familiar London ground; forty years learning where to walk and a few months to lose it all. Go back then into uncertainty, ocean-venturing exchanges. Ed Dorn, one of the sharpest and most independent of Olson's Black Mountain students, and just about the only one who bothered to graduate, characterized Gloucester as somewhere settled by people from remote islands who knew how to build fences and stone walls. 'That's one reason why New England is really there,' he said.

'It's a tough one,' Olson replied, laying out the American West as Dorn's field of study. 'One thing's sure: economics as politics as money is a gone bird.'

All poetry, a now-obsolete (and stronger for that) form, Dorn suggested, derived from *The Iliad* or *The Odyssey*. Either we stay put, dig in, battle with our gods, or we move, drift, detour: move for the sake of moving. Jack Kerouac's *On the Road* is precisely what it says: it goes on as long as the roll of paper lasts. Olson was formidable in combining the two archetypal sources: he excavated the particulars of his adopted town and he contemplated the restless sea. Without leaving his high window, he would drive off spleen by charting the madness of those who ventured on the watery part of the world. He began with Herman Melville. Curse me with truth. *Call me Ishmael.*

Today, quite suddenly, the sun breaks through; I follow Olson's obliterated footprints. There is the long shadow of a drowned man on the beach. And he is walking, rolling heavy shoulders. You have to be dead yourself, more than a little, to register him. The Atlantic, on this precious morning, is blameless; every pebble visible, an invitation to stripping off and striking out. But it won't happen, not now. Not ever.

I come along the curve of the esplanade they call 'boulevard', from Fort Point, tramping in suspended excitement, with watering eyes, above a beach I know so well; this place I have never been, even in sleep: Gloucester, Massachusetts. Late October, season of perfect storms. Even the houses of the wealthy, set back from the shore, are not immune. Buffalo waves break free of the jet stream; steepling rollers, in a shatter of wet glass, spout and smash, upturning cars, rearing over breakfast bars, their panoramic windows crusted with salt, rattled by scouring grains of sand. You are embedded here, at a small table, with your squirting egg and crisped bacon, your coffee refill. A few, mid-morning, comfortably fleshed, warmshirted citizens stare out on the rain, the road, the shore, making desultory conversation. Some do not turn their heads. More politics, another dying year. The decline of the fishing fleet. Boarded-up computer-repair shops. Banks like temples from an earlier granite era. Barriers erected around City Hall, the civic centre. Tactful marine presentations in Cape Ann Museum. Safe rocks and secure objects: rescued boats, fading portraits. The original statue of Our Lady of Good Voyage, that draped and crowned votive figure brought in from the church roof, now shockingly out of scale in a dim chamber. Huge hands, this woman of wood: a fish-gutter supporting a model twin-masted vessel.

Olson's car didn't do reverse. When a friend, sent out from the upstairs apartment with the great view, on the point, right over the

Inner Harbor, to fetch cigarettes and whisky for another all-night session, sandwiches even, asked, with some trepidation, how Charles managed this thing, navigating the icy streets in a defective motor, the poet said: 'Never go backwards.' Arm raised – *so!* – gloved fist clamped to fence, Russian cap and trailing coat. '*That* way. Always that way now.' Inland, brother. At the end of the poem, of the long emphysemic drag of breath and tumult, the headaches, bunker fevers, heartsick losses, he turned away from the sea. Found a nest in which to die. They carried him, complaining, head first, to the ambulance; crabbed, harpooned. Strike out, stride forward. Then, over Brooklyn Bridge, quoting *Lear* until the hurt was too much and he gripped his companion's arm, white, asking for pain-killers, and they gave him water. The words on the wall of the hut, the Gloucester Writers Center, where I was now lodged: *my wife my car   my colour   my self.* Precisely scored gaps for taking breath.

In the town museum I discovered a painting, studio-posed, reconfiguring some forgotten classical tableau. Rocks. The virgin New England shore of green scrub, grey clouds. Three people: two women and a man. I don't want to know who painted it. A clothed girl, dark hair depending from a summer hat, props herself on her left arm; she sprawls, shoes off, confronting the bathing-suited figure of a conspicuously fit young man with rather effeminate tresses and supplicant lips. At the edge of the composition, clutching a thick black branch, is another woman, a little older perhaps, more obviously mythological; smooth, bare leg emerging from a long white wrap. Sexual tension, subdued but palpable, plays across the interval between the solitary standing figure and the transfixed couple. The gash dividing the spread of rocks is matted with pubic moss. The couple facing us, recovered from their swim, near-naked but bone dry, make-up intact, confront the clothed girl, whose elbow is scabbed and raw: an orgy postponed. And hung in a corner of a museum nobody visits. As competent and pointless as Augustus John.

★

Olson's wife, Betty, found the apartment. And fell in love, at once, with what she saw, inside and out. Romanticizing inconvenience, cold water, cold season, she wrote to Charles, summoning up, across hard-driven distance, his comforting bulk and warmth. 28 Fort Square. They were set down, mature orphans, among the Sicilian community, the working fishermen. And it did play, this fortunate accident. The opening of the poem, after false starts elsewhere, was brought home, earthed. The thrust of Fort Point, lighthouse blinking in the fog on Ten Pound Island. The Inner Harbor. Longline swordfish boats setting out. Olson had tried it, by way of research: crewing. With his size he was awkward. The sea was not, finally, so he said, his trade. Making a lovely phrase, as poets do, out of getting it all wrong. His trade was the sea. And looking at it. Marine charts curling on a clapboard wall. What that early apprenticeship gave him, way short of the reach of a Melville or Conrad, was archive; photographs of a big man in old light, on deck, beside a gaffed swordfish. He knew it was a lie, he was watching the watching. Learning the simplest things last, the jolt of pain going over the bridge. The thickening silence.

When we drove into Gloucester at night, in the rain, Henry Ferrini, Vincent's nephew, made a little detour to point out Fort Square. Vincent Ferrini had been Olson's first Gloucester correspondent: the argument, the male rutting in those letters, fired the opening of *The Maximus Poems*. Buildings torn down. History trashed. 'I liked him right off,' Ferrini said. Vincent was the town character, feisty and fast. The poet in the leather hat. 'Write to me,' Olson ordered, 'and tell me how my streets are.' Already he is laying claim to the territory, the reek of the fish-processing plants.

Damp fog, like a residue of H. P. Lovecraft's Innsmouth, coated everything outside the immediate warmth of the hut and seeped into my skin. I dodged busy traffic – gas tankers, red-and-white Coca-Cola rigs longer than my London street, muddy station wagons – and scuttled down to the harbour. Boat buildings. A chained fleet waiting on the weather. CATERINA GLOU MA. JANAYA JOSEPH

GLOU MA. Crosstree masts. Spars. Cables. Fishing lines spooled on giant thimbles at the stern. Impossible, when I try the roadside convenience store, to find fresh fruit or breakfast cereal. Profusion of jumbo crunch, biscuits and pillows of crisps. Racks of root beer. Coke ordnance. Toothpaste-bright sweeties. Local news is the only news. The habit of newsprint dirties the eye.

NAMING OF BULGER TIPSTER WORRIES FBI OBSERVER

A newspaper's revelation that the tipster who led the FBI to notorious gangster James 'Whitey' Bulger is a former Miss Iceland is raising concerns about her safety. Gloucester Times. Thursday, October 13, 2011.

REVISITING OLSON'S LEGACY

The authenticity of this small gritty city and its residents inspired Olson, like an intellectual fountain of youth. Olson left behind his Gloucester epic titled 'The Maximus Poems' as well as tens of thousands of scraps of paper and letters filled with his thoughts.

5-DAY FORECAST

Today: Cloudy with rain tapering off. Friday: Periods of rain, some heavy.

Melville's Ishmael, contemplating a whaling voyage, and the dark Fates who have him under 'constant surveillance', imagines newspaper headlines much like the ones I inscribe in my new notebook. GRAND CONTESTED ELECTION FOR THE PRESIDENCY OF THE UNITED STATES. BLOODY BATTLE IN AFGHANISTAN. 1851. Nothing changes. Inky-fingered printers' devils hit the same buttons. Metaphysical weather systems punctuate the centuries with indifferent rigour.

I explore the hill, noting the vodka bottles and crumpled beer cans arranged on the steps in the gaps between neat clapboard houses. I witness the only black man in town enter the Crow's Nest, the authentic set for the inauthentic fiction of *The Perfect Storm*; when George Clooney and the Hollywood caravan rolled into town. Sebastian Junger, who wrote the original story, settled here as a 'high climber' for a tree company. He spent many hours in the fishermen's bar, listening. There was one black sailor on the fated crew. Swordfishing is harsh labour, nobody but the skipper has any relish for the sea. On the morning of their departure, the boys take a pickup truck to one of those big sheds, hypermarkets, out by the highway. They spend $5,000 on steaks, cigarettes, chicken, booze. Anything but fish. Ten thousand Gloucester men, Junger wrote, have been lost to the sea. Names on church wall, year by year. I stop to read the sepulchral memorial on the boulevard, as I pass, following Olson's evening stroll along the shoreline. Comfortable buses decant sober American tourists. A war that will never be won. But witnessed, with bowed heads, and raised cameras.

Mediterranean Catholicism, in this place I had previously imagined as puritanical and dark, is a rush of colour. Our Lady of Good Voyage, the replica now, is perched on her pedestal, by the blue onion dome, behind a complexity of telegraph wires. Upraised arm, open hand. Halo welded to her shrouded head like a steering wheel. Blood-red candles glow beside the small shrine like Thermos flasks. Or stacked shells in a trench. Blue and gold: the dome, the cross.

Olson, like his fellow Massachusetts author Jack Kerouac, was a Catholic from a working family. His father a delivery man for the mail service in Worcester. Kerouac's father, in Lowell, ran a print shop. When I walked the beach in Sandymount, Dublin, as a twenty-year-old student, Kerouac was my main man: those bad journeys, the questing, the tedium, and the mortal tremor beneath the surface, which I had not then identified. My companion, Christopher Bamford, who would, after Ireland, take the boat to Boston, and not come back, was peddling Beckett and Genet, all those lettuce-green Olympia Press paperbacks. Footmarks tramped a noose in the grey sand, a prison circuit, as we conjured plays written in a single night and floated magazines that never got beyond the proof stage, the abandoned dummy. As we received our airmail correspondence from William Burroughs in Tangier.

By some weird serendipity, we both returned, the same afternoon, with a slim blue-green Grove Press publication, acquired from a department store on O'Connell Street. *The Distances: Poems* by Charles Olson. By that evening this poet, new and difficult, was an obsession. 'What does not change/is the will to change.' The markers and references and processed autobiographical fragments floated over us, attractive in their obscurity. The man as we learnt a little of him from magazines and visiting American professors became a mythological presence. 'Ego like a lantern,' said a pompous fellow, a Restoration drama specialist on tweedy sabbatical, when questioned about why he'd left Olson out of his summary of the landscape of contemporary US poetics. And that seemed to me just what we were looking for: a dark lantern against prejudice and lazy conformity.

Hearing Olson talk, years later, in archive film sampled by Henry Ferrini for his portrait *Polis is This: Charles Olson and the Persistence of Place*, you got the excitement of the expanding moment; a rumbling voice thick with smoke, sweat dripping, black eyebrows emphatic as that other alpha male, Robert Maxwell (press baron, litigant, whale-corpse found floating). The suffering blackboard, a negative window, slashed by chalk prompts, a blizzard of names and dates. Wild, punching semaphore. And the gleaming melon dome of that glistening skull. To surf all those lines of energy and catch it up, almost, in feverish talk, struggling for breath, dark patches on white shirt. A fresh cigarette, a Camel, fired from the stub of the last. 'I take SPACE to be the central fact to man born in America, from Folsom Cave to now. I spell it large because it comes large here. Large, and without mercy.'

★

The Sicilian quarter, the tight community on Fort Square, where Charles Olson found a safe branch on which to perch, with Betty, in August 1957, was still very much present when I walked there from my roadside hut in October 2011. First floor, balcony on the side, new names on mailboxes: *Frontiero*, *Sova*, *Borichevsky*. And a harbour view that hits home, both directions in time and space: the workaday shacks, rust running from metal fence into stone wall, fishing boats putting out, seasonal pleasure boats at anchor. In the last years, when the task went sour on him, and Olson was alone, it was an exile interrupted by visitors, New York poets or Warhol's acolyte Gerard Malanga with a thirsty camera.

Olson's son, another Charles, a Gloucester carpenter who shunned literary events and tributes, was proud to put his hand to the simple memorial plaque, pressing it into wet cement: CHARLES OLSON POET 1910–1970. He said a few words to the gathering of enthusiasts.

Below the apartments, in their brightly painted nonconformity, up against the fence, on the edge of the sea, was an abandoned blockhouse, a whitewashed post-industrial Alamo. The former packing plant of Clarence Birdseye, pioneer of the global frozen-food operation. So Olson becomes an alternative Captain Birdseye, commander of a ghost fleet, wacky admiral on the hill. Or Captain Iglo, neighbourhood eccentric, pipe and flapped Russian cap, sliding down steep steps in the snow, a foot and more taller than the men of the interlinked Sicilian families. Cold cartons of fish fingers no longer thump from the assembly line. There is talk of converting Clarence Birdseye's plant into a smart hotel. Even Gorton's, the big Gloucester employer, are cutting back. The paying product these days is cat food. Canned mush for America's kept-at-home pets. The pampered muses of writers.

At the end of the curve of the gracious marine boulevard, after crossing the bridge over Annisquam River, I arrive at Stage Fort Park. It is no difficult matter to identify the gap in the trees at Half Moon Beach, the bench where the young Olson stood listening to the two old men, as they smoked and talked. This is the pivotal point where, feeling the immense weight of the land behind you, the overriding impulse is to turn and face the sea. The boy, whose wrists were already too much for the sleeves of his tight jacket, said that he was spellbound by what he heard: that male need to talk the day down. He knew their names, Lou Douglas and Frank Miles. A lazy, companionable exchange, in the face of lengthening shadows, as they draw on pipe or cigarette. For Charles Olson, this is where it all begins. Unnoticed, he listens. Then he turns back, up through the deserted park, where earlier he had played baseball with his friends, and across Hough Avenue to the holiday cottage. To his family, the summer community.

Frozen Air

The force of Olson as a personality was so potent, back then, because our estrangement from the local product was absolute. We didn't buy English anger, which seemed to be nothing more than a media-friendly staging post on the way to peevish rural retirement, empty bottles on the porch, second wives in red fur nursing black eyes. We didn't buy class envy or class entitlement as a thesis. We didn't buy the campus (or any other form of convenient bureaucracy) as a setting, a vehicle for satire, or comforting murder mysteries. Which is to say, we were denim-and-corduroy puritans with Diggerish aspirations, overread, underused. Wide open to the enticement of the Other, emanations of prairie Spirit; charisma, vision, prophetic pronouncements. Peyote shamanism. Territorial adventures. Peru. New Mexico. The genealogy, laid out with intricate lines and boxes, ran from Ezra Pound and Wyndham Lewis to Olson and Ed Dorn. Which is why, with no inhibiting sense of contradiction, we sat on a train with cold, greasy windows, travelling the slow way, past reservoirs, pylons, waste-burning chimneys, reed beds, frosted fields and humps, from Liverpool Street to Cambridge.

1971. And the 1960s were hitting their straps, doing the hard graft, after those earlier Kodak-colour excesses, the not-so-free festivals and stalled revolutions. Chris Bamford, a little tighter, more sand-papered, nail-chewing over wide cups of black coffee in the upstairs kitchen, was back from New England on a flying visit. There was content here still to be unpacked, he said. Family to acknowledge. But there was also distance, now he had lived in those fictional places. There had been films with Ginsberg and Ed Sanders. Uncertainties were racked up, mystics and philosophers sampled, along with aspects of sacred geometry and architecture: Blake, Kathleen Raine, Gregory Bateson. The realization, so Chris asserted, of a new planetary culture. The man on these islands with whom he needed to make contact was a certain Mr Prynne, a poet. *The* poet. The bridge, as he insisted, with brisk cutting gestures, rattling the plates, printing a sticky line of burnt crumbs across the taut ridge of his hand, between the two countries, our soon-to-be-conjoined cultures. He projected some form of eighteenth-century correspondence, actual letters, between himself in Massachusetts and this unknown scholar in Cambridge.

Irregular bulletins from the Lindisfarne Association of West Stockbridge arrived in Hackney; packages were passed around the kitchen table. In the photograph of a conference ritual, whitefolk in loose shirts and tight jeans holding hands in a frowning circle around a Hopi Indian man wearing beads and a bandana, Chris is clearly visible, a head taller than Janet McCloud, a member of the Seattle tribes. For the consecration of ground, before a grail chapel could be constructed, the rind of Celtic spiritual traditions must demonstrate its affinity with Native American practice. 'I am the hill where poets walk. I am the tomb of every hope.' There were no known photographs of Mr Prynne. His books were text, pure. With, perhaps, a red-ink diagram. He avoided, as we discovered at the entrance to his stairs, in the labyrinth of his Cambridge college, extraneous academic distinctions. Like a surgeon, he was listed on the wall as a plain mister among congeries of black-lettered doctors and professors.

It had happened again, just like Dublin. Chris acquired a copy of *The White Stones*, ordered from the English publishers and shipped out, at the very moment when I, stopping to browse on a walk across London, picked up a copy in the bookshop on Primrose Hill, where, two years before, I had filmed an Allen Ginsberg signing session. I stood by the enticingly stocked poetry shelves reading those opening lines: 'The century roar is a desert carrying/too much away; the plane skids off/with an easy hopeless departure.' I was sold, instantly. I wasn't going anywhere, but I loved the idea of it. White stones, like the ones the military used to paint as borders around huts, confirming this transatlantic causeway, but in a powerful new European register. The landmasses had once been attached. The cover of Olson's *Maximus Poems IV, V, VI*, published by Jonathan Cape in London, celebrates Earth before she started to come apart at the seams, some 125 million years ago. The time of Gondwanaland, before the great divorce and migration of continents. 'A while back,' as the introductory note puts it. When Ireland kissed Greenland. And Brazil's shoulder dug into future slaving grounds. 'The war of Africa against Eurasia has just begun again,' Olson said.

One of the miracles of the late 1960s and early 1970s, in the old railway zone of Camden Town, before the strangling evolution of the leather-and-vinyl market, was the independent bookshop called Compendium. The success of this operation was remarkable. It grew, seemingly overnight, from a tall, sallow man hunched, in a wretched, holed-at-the-elbow, down-to-the-knees sweater, at a fold-out table with a dozen paperbacks, to an interconnected series of caves, one of them given over entirely to poetry. I bought Ed Dorn's *Gunslinger 1 & 2*, date inscribed: 17/2/70. This was a giant leap in the mental health of the metropolis; the confirmation of that unitary vision expressed at the 1967 conference, up the road at the Roundhouse, the old engine-turning shed. Suddenly, out of nowhere, we had an operation equal to Foyle's in Charing Cross Road – but where the salesfolk actually *knew* about books – parachuted into a convenient halt on a loop of the North London Line.

Anything was possible now. Stuart Montgomery, the publisher of Dorn's *Gunslinger*, a wispy-moustached medical man with a significant hobby, decided to do something about the sluggishness and indolence of the mainstream critics. He flew off to Las Vegas and took a cab to the hotel where Howard Hughes was rumoured to be sequestered in the penthouse, to present him with a copy of the poem in which Dorn shaped the pencil-moustached ghost's non-existence into a divine comedy of cocaine and virtual travel through high sierras and white deserts running to the horizon like the bad craziness of a Monte Hellman western. It was that craziness we used to call *the possible*: that an invisible London publisher could provoke a reaction from the richest hermit on the planet, an unbarbered Texan tool-bit weirdo guarded by Mormon goons; that Howard Hughes, a fabulous entity capable of impersonation by Leonardo DiCaprio, would sue a poet and a doctor with unsold paperbacks stacked in his North London garage. Oh yes, those were the days. The bibliographic cornucopia of Camden Town, with its US imports, its French theorists, its New Age primers, was a classic small-business model. Money-laundering to a purpose. The whole pre-Thatcherite, wild-dog enterprise was underwritten by the area's other growth industry: drugs. Arrest, incarceration, downsizing followed, with the shop taken over by a management committee of the workers.

Navigating the shelves, I pulled out *The Kitchen Poems*, on the strength of the publisher's name, Cape Goliard, and in irritation, because this was the title I had chosen, and now had to revise, for my own first book. J. H. Prynne's slimly elegant package invoked Olson; the cover design was an oil-exploration chart of the North Sea, produced, so it seemed, by Esso. I got, all at once, the common ground, but not how smartly and acerbically this English don bit down on economics, consumption and profit in the body of who and where we were. The tender address. 'The ground on which we pass, / moving our feet, less excited by travel.'

Mr Prynne had travelled, so he told us when we settled into our big chairs in his Cambridge rooms. He was at home, we were not. But he made us welcome, by staying within the gracious formality of the place where we found ourselves. The sort of unnerving geography we had both experienced in earlier interviews of rejection. He was a tall man, uniformed in pressed grey flannels, with polished black shoes, black cord jacket and white shirt heretically enlivened by an orange tie. The look was not accidental, like our own, nor was it subject to the fads and revisions of fashion. He spoke of a voyage to the ice fringe, the Northwest Passage. That haunting blankness, pictures with no frames. And Boston, he'd done a year there. Frank Knox Fellow at Harvard. Prynne investigated the university bookshop by starting at the left-hand corner of the top shelf, and ploughing on, with the occasional wince and whinny, until he reached Olson. So that connection was confirmed. We felt comfortable enough now, to make our risky suggestion: that Mr Prynne should become the rector, or guiding light, of a British version of Black Mountain College. How this might be funded, who else would be involved, where the premises were to be found, we did not explain. We knew, the three of us, that the proposition was entirely metaphorical.

We also knew that Charles Olson was much more than an outlaw enthusiasm, picked up in Ireland, supported by renegades in Bristol and communes along the Welsh borders; there was a deep engagement within the folds of Cambridge academia. And, more than that, Mr Prynne was a key supplier for *Maximus* research, a tireless raider of libraries. His relationship with Olson was personal, direct, acknowledged in interviews. Yes, he had heard the century's roar and visited Gloucester. 'I read that piece of Jeremy Prynne's,' Olson told the interviewer sent to bother him by the *Paris Review*, 'and he says everything right, accurately.'

The heaped rooms overlooking the harbour at Fort Square. The large poet has crawled from his bed, sick again, sick of winter, kitchen in chaos, and he gestures his interrogator to a hard chair. He threw a rug from the window, that morning, to signal that he was at home and receiving. America was asleep, he reckoned. The deadest sleep there ever was. Jeremy Prynne, in England, was the energy source.

While Chris, hot, raw, twisted in the depths of the collegiate furniture, teasing out the moral complexities of the questions he needed to frame (so much depended on this), I scanned the bookshelves, encouraged by a long line of Patrick White novels. Here, vividly, and in terms I understood, was a demonstration of Prynne's doctrine of value. These items were, I felt confident, all first editions (the bonus of originality, first touch), but, in the fashion followed by collectors in the 1930s, the dustwrappers had been removed. Prynne, clearly, had no truck with the recent fetish for book as object, for pretty embellishments by Roy de Maistre or

Sidney Nolan. The words spoke for themselves and the rest was some debased form of public relations. Knowing the premium on intact copies, basically those that have never been read, I was a little shocked. And impressed. I was also impressed, and alarmed, by the casual vehemence with which Prynne wrote off certain poets honoured in the alternative canon, legendary names that were supposed to be on our side. He sliced through the looseness of language of some unfortunate who wrote to him asking for a sample of his thought. 'Like a lump of basalt!'

The afternoon closed down around our conversation, it had run for several hours. Cambridge was wreathed in low-lying fenland mist, bands of frozen air. Every rasped breath a cancelled speech balloon. Anna, who had come along for the trip, the journey from Hackney, was out there, wandering the unwelcoming streets. I excused myself, to find her and bring her back. The novelty of this town soon exhausted itself, she said. After a cup of tea, she even ventured into a bookshop. Prynne was effortlessly courteous, brandy in hand, the chair closest to the fire. He must have wondered what this young woman, my wife, a glamorously chilled figure in a long suede coat with fur collar, was doing, keeping company with vagrant poets of absurd ambition and minimal resources.

I drove Chris to the airport, filming his departure (still scribbling into a black notebook), and he vanished once again, not to reappear for many years. The letters dried up. The correspondence with Prynne never began. Too much to say very easily becomes nothing, silence. From what I picked up as others who knew him passed through London, Chris was importing English artists and seekers. Keith Critchlow, a metaphysical geometer from the Research into Lost Knowledge Organization, delivered a series of lectures on the Platonic Tradition and the Nature of Proportion. And while the esoteric lessons of European cathedral builders were seeded in Massachusetts, Mr Prynne helped to secure passage for the Black Mountaineer, Ed Dorn, into Essex University at Colchester. Where an active American presence was being established under the patronage of Donald Davie, Prynne's early sponsor. There was a good deal of neurotic shuttling across the Atlantic, often, like Chris, on cargo boats out of Liverpool; the longer the voyage, the better the chance of adjustment. Poets traded in difference, exiling themselves for a season to Buffalo or Berkeley. Dorn repaid the favour, with interest, by publishing *The North Atlantic Turbine*, mirroring the cover of Prynne's *The White Stones* with an Olsonian map of the ocean and its voyagers. Dorn saw himself clearing his debt to geography and opening the way to 'spiritual address'. 'Off shore I have missed my country for the first time,' he said. Colchester offered mornings walking to the Roman wall as the most casual of excursions. If he checked out *The Magnificent Seven* at the local fleapit, his territory, the Old West, was somehow exotic. And peculiar. A place where Mexicans were played by Germans. Hearing orange gas hiss in the fire at night, he burnt for home.

Mr Prynne stopped once when he was driving home through Hackney, and I returned a couple of times, on book-delivering expeditions, to Cambridge. The fungal abundance of late Olson was being cleaned and shaped under Prynne's direction, prepared for publication. He understood the rhythms of the work better than anybody else. 'The poem is simple,' Prynne stressed, 'but the life it came out of, and the preoccupations that surround it, immeasurably dense and confused and packed with a kind of fertile obscurity.' We look for the point of stress where story crystallizes into legend.

The young Chicago-born postgraduate Tom Clark moved from Prynne's college to Essex. He was friend, editor, amanuensis to Dorn, witness to all the shifts and small secrets of the era. He was onboard when Olson arrived in Colchester, to hibernate like a bear, to deliver all-night, rasping monologues. Clark was a very shrewd and sharp-eyed babysitter. He was one of the first and best to write about Dorn. Years later, Dorn recalled the London taxi in which Olson's wealthy lover came to collect him, gather him up, setting off for London, books and effects piled on the roof like a gypsy caravan, a train in India.

Dorn and Prynne formed a transatlantic alliance, exchanging

letters and texts, collaborating on giveaway newspapers, provocations. Travelling together through wilderness places. Sharing quarters for autumn sabbaticals in shacks and mountain outposts. When Dorn died, from pancreatic cancer, Prynne flew the Atlantic, and crossed the continent, coast to coast, to deliver the eulogy at Boulder's Green Mountain Cemetery. It was not recorded, nor should it have been. In a conversation, after the event, Prynne remarked on how unusual Dorn had been, in that his ear was so finely tuned to the modulations of the English voice. To John Clare, for example. 'I was in correspondence with Charles Olson at this time,' Prynne told his interviewer, 'and I knew him through the post quite well; and Olson was an extremely difficult, powerful, and overriding personality.'

Towards the end of what had been a dazzling and diverse career, as poet, talker, teacher, Dorn, out of favour and under attack from twitching internet fingers all too easily affronted by his cutting and wilfully incorrect humour, gave his attention to European heresies, the Albigensians of Languedoc. He wanted to get to Rome, where he noticed the cats. Now Dorn, once again, was being published through fugitive editions in England. The poet Nicholas Johnson, through his Etruscan Books imprint, delivered *Westward Haut* and *High West Rendezvous*, in which Dorn remarked: 'It's a lot easier to be a heretic than it used to be. There are more religions willing to kill you.'

The particular rendezvous that brought me into contact with Dorn occurred in Bath. He was stepping westward again, to witness the solar eclipse, which he described as a 'big event'. Jeremy Prynne was with him. They had read together, a scene brokered by Johnson, at the Arnolfini Gallery in Bristol. The unusual, probably unique, aspect of this was that Prynne *never* gave public readings of his poetry in England. He explained once that there might be a confusion of identity, as he had a professional role as a lecturer. The other business was conducted on his own terms. He might perform in Canada or Paris, not here. So this was something very special. And given, without any prior publicity, out of respect and friendship. Prynne spoke of his admiration for 'Thesis', from *The North Atlantic Turbine*. A poem of the far north written in Colchester. 'Only the illegitimate are beautiful.' Dorn arrived, Prynne recalled in his obituary interview, at a small remote settlement in Newfoundland, so impoverished that the people there had no desire to know anything of the casual visitors. They turn their backs on them, pushing Dorn not towards resentment or shame but pride: the rare achievement of getting the scene down in measured, careful description. Mapping it just as it stood.

We filmed and recorded the Dorn part of the evening, none too effectively, keeping our distance. Prynne of course banished the cameras and ripped out the microphone. He explained, quite slowly, what he was going to read. And then he read it, without Dorn's anecdotal asides and the obvious, chemically enhanced emotion.

When we met next day, by arrangement, in Bath, in the abundant garden of a cheese-stone Georgian house, it wasn't easy to set aside the knowledge that this would, in all probability, be one of the last interviews.

Dorn had always been lean and cool in appearance, hard times known and survived. But there was no surviving the pregnancy of the tumour, or the news from Baghdad, the ruined 'Cradle of Civilization'. 'My tumour is interested in what interests me . . . My tumour is not interested in love.'

'Before Languedoc,' Dorn told me, 'I always had a thing about the Apaches, because their rejection of European values and European existence actually was total. Total. And their hostility was total. And the Apaches were absolutely unapologetic about their primitiveness and their ruthless measures to survive and to exist alongside the juggernaut of what they could see. They saw this juggernaut as unresistible. They saw that. They probably didn't see the use of the telephone.'

And what about that big shadow on the gallery wall, the missing presence in Bristol, Charles Olson? What were the memories of the era when they all travelled so recklessly and to such purpose?

'Oh yes,' Dorn replied, 'those were amazing times. There were notable evenings in Colchester. Jeremy came over from Cambridge and Tom Clark came around. Olson turned our house into a kind of salon. Those were beautiful active times. I mean not literary active, but more expanded. It was never literary with Charles. He liked the literary. But that was a small role for him.'

And London back then?

'A lot more traffic and a lot less clutter. The traffic, as random as it sometimes seemed, seemed also purposeful. People actually did have things on their minds, no matter how strange those things were. They were actually going to a place, no matter if they arrived there or not, or if it was the wrong place. For a poet the world is always static in the sense that you're a mass observer and you can't afford to care whether people are busy or not. You're a witness.'

And the Arnolfini – did it matter that there was no proper documentary record?

'I think last night's reading was historically interesting and significant. But things of that nature have to be borne away by the witnesses. Sometimes I think that it's a shame it's not captured. But, in a way, it's such a moment that capturing it is defeating it.'

Lowell

An old man, made slow and gracile by the years on him, wakes in a strange house in an industrial town. His own, his home. And they are in the flux of transition, both of them, man and town. He moves now with such stiff, mimicked precision, feeling for parts that creak and resist, reaching towards fresh morning pains, paddling his way to heavy velveteen curtains he will not open. Or so another man, myself, in an unfamiliar place, a Massachusetts fishing port also in transition, in steady rain, tries to imagine. Coming back, careful with door handles, table edges, from the cold narrow bathroom, in blue Texas T-shirt and no pants.

The man in Lowell I hope to meet, later this day, is John Sampas, Jack Kerouac's brother-in-law, last survivor of a family of ten: keeper of the archive. How does it feel to sleep in a house pillowed and bolstered with all that *stuff*? The early novellas, the work journals, typewriters, raincoats, rucksacks. The meticulously kept files, the photographs from the road. The letters, postcards. The maps, football helmets. The Catholic-Buddhist scrolls and relics from which no life can ever be reassembled. Kerouac was the dark angel, freeing himself from the wheel of karma, the corporeal shroud. But he was also, and it was the source of the tension that fired his art, 'Memory Babe', an inspired celebrator of the ordinary: passing seasons, winter streets, floods, bars, factories (from the outside), woodsmoke, night, touch, family, friends, restlessness, kitchens, insanity, murder. John Sampas, my conduit to all this, if he appeared at the restaurant, if he approved my conversation, was going to challenge, or completely abort, the managed schizophrenia of my two worlds: fictional projections (myths, myths, myths) and the evidence of the eyes (never to be trusted). Trying to keep it together, the Lowell of my reading, with the Lowell revealed through the rain-streaked car window, brought everything to a grinding halt. There is a special kind of writer's block when there is just *too much* material; all those journeys to the end of the night become, like the Kerouac archive, chains and anchors. How does Sampas sleep among the terrors of so many unborn or abandoned projects, Kerouac seizures that never became living books? *Does he sleep?* Does he stand erect, trembling, licking the cold sweat of the moon from his frozen window?

It wasn't easy in the Gloucester Writers Center, in my generously stocked roadside hut, to reinvent myself as a single man in a narrow bed, denied the warm curve of companionship, that earthing of dreams Anna provided for so many years. She experienced the worst of my imaginings, while I snored contentedly. She saw the things that were there, the elements in the room, the others. I was always too dumb to put much faith in visible spectres. But this hut pulsed with the man who had just stepped out, the late Vincent Ferrini, his books, belts, blankets. He worked here, framing pictures. He ate here, slept here. He conducted his affairs. He scribbled compulsively at this table. He listened to cars on the wet road, rain beating against the flat roof, moans from the harbour. Olson was more of an invoked presence: a collection of books by and about him, without the thumbprint of ownership. Photographs as proof of absence. Texts reduced to artworks. A blackboard, close to the door, flagged up future events. Strange to see my own name among that scatter of local activities and open evenings, beneath POET LAUREATE and above THE DEVIL AWAKENS and POTTY TRAINING. 'Man in America was late,' Olson said. And now I believed it.

Henry Ferrini was a used man in a used car, in the most honourable sense of that term. Preoccupied, life-enhanced. Troubled. He sported an Afro-American jazzman carpet-cap, a brown leather jacket, black waistcoat, warm pink shirt. Contacts made, when he shot his film *Lowell Blues* in Kerouac's town (of childhood, adolescence, late return), smoothed our venture. Henry could be persuasive or persistent, obviously. I was here, on the wrong side of the Atlantic, to prove it; watching windscreen wipers scratch and smear. A wooded highway in low visibility, the road between Gloucester and Lowell, a short American drive.

When the two men, Henry and his friend Greg Gibson, author and antiquarian bookseller, met me in Boston, that first night, they were reassuringly non-corporate, unshaven. They referenced a fondly remembered past as house painters, getting by on ten good days a year, if they were lucky. The Gloucester road, siphoning heavy commuter traffic towards the new bridge, was a river of culinary temptations for Greg. He talked about chomping his way south down Route 1, all the way to the Florida Keys, investigating off-highway eateries. Red-and-yellow lights, emphatic signage. Pancakes, bacon. Weak-coffee refills. Big wet windows. Book-hunting as an excuse, but really the release of being away from home, out, on the move. A tree had fallen on his shop, freeing him from that duty, being there, dealing with customers. Greg was a man who liked to take his solitary evening cigar a short distance from the motel, into the trees at the end of the field; intimations of pioneer America in animal noises, rustlings, sweeping headlights on the Interstate. Before whisky in a hot room, the long night.

They spoke, taking turns, about oil companies, the fishermen of Gloucester screwed by Obama and the banking interests who tug his strings. But the Portuguese are adaptable. Look outside, every few miles another branch of Dunkin' Donuts. Sugar-dough treats launched with pay-off fish money, juice of cod. Boston is a winking panorama of immigrants still orientating themselves after a few hundred years, conversing in dim sports bars: Robert Mitchum in *The Friends of Eddie Coyle*. They read crime, Henry and Greg. They quote Elmore Leonard. Greg calls him 'Dutch'. He hopes to get a quote for his new hardboiled novel. It's probably too late. Leonard's old. He's generous but fading. He's not going to get through 200 pages.

South Boston sprawls in managed decay. How did crime boss Whitey Bulger, killer and patron of killers, stay free for so long? As an informant, a conduit, that's how. My twin Gloucester guides run the conspiracies you'd expect. After the close of business, Whitey goes west. The FBI pick him up in San Diego. He wasn't ready for Mexico. All Americans dream of better elsewheres under the protective shade of the same flag.

What I brought into the car was a cold shudder of the Thames, a journey from Hastings on the Sussex coast, by sea and river, to the Olympic Park in the Lower Lea Valley. I told Henry and Greg about the Andrew Kötting film with which I'd been involved; a mock-Homeric swan pedalo odyssey through the miraculous late warmth of St Luke's Little Summer. We had pedalled our unnervingly dignified and stable creature through Kerouac's favourite month: 'October in the Railroad Earth'. It was my intention, unrealized, to counter the hubris and mass hallucination of the Olympic moment with a marathon of our own through the secret waterways of Kent, the Medway and the Thames Estuary. I failed of course. Having to step ashore at Trinity Buoy Wharf and rush across town to make my flight. Deserting Kötting and the project.

They were amused, I think, Boston possessing a lake with the mother of all swan boats. Greg had identified his own measure of difficulty, on an altogether more impressive scale, by deciding to walk down the Connecticut River. He would keep a record of his adventures and publish his journal in annual instalments. No Thoreau raft on the Concord for him; no paddle and drift. 'A man who finds himself getting old, but not too old to walk,' he said. Greg dresses his venture in respectable trappings. 'A deconstruction of the legend of John Ledyard, who made a similar journey in 1773.' The reality is a noble but futile attempt to outdistance age; to trudge, grind, suffer, because Ledyard, sensibly, travelled in a canoe. Latecomers to an old land, we blend absurdity with hobbled heroism, in marching after legends of the frontier, wonders of geography, aboriginals, monsters of the forest. 'He finds Ledyard strange, and he finds the American people strange.' Without doubt, Greg finds me strange too, tramping London's motorway verges, gasping through tunnels under the Thames, pedalling a plastic swan like a

Saga-holiday veteran on a treadmill. The refinements of elective masochism are subtle and sublime.

The Connecticut River is a watershed sister to Lowell's Merrimack, wellspring of Kerouac's mythology in *Dr Sax* and *Maggie Cassidy*. The helicopter shots of Henry Ferrini's lyrical film, the swoops over bridges and bends, factories, falls and eddies, the tumble of Kerouac's evocative prose, are complemented by readings from Johnny Depp, Gregory Corso, Carolyn Cassady, Robert Creeley.

'How did you land those names – on such a tight budget?'

'Find the number and ask.'

The film, Henry tells me, is on a loop. It plays as a perpetual Kerouac memorial in a town that never had much use for him when he was around. The great Blakean mills of Lowell, copied from Lancashire, have been rebranded as universities, intellectual hubs. Serious investment follows. Kerouac festivals. Everybody needs a measure of exploitable content. A handsome face with a brave smile for the poster.

Henry started me at the grave. Rain was still coming down, more mood music than nuisance. At first we drove through the gates of the wrong cemetery, St Patrick's; then on, directly, to Edson. We made a few slow passes down broad avenues before Henry got his alignment right. A rush of remembered photographs: Bob Dylan, hands in pockets, accompanied by Ginsberg and the gang. The Rolling Thunder Revue. *Renaldo & Clara*.

Kerouac wasn't in the ground with his father and brother in Nashua, New Hampshire. Capitalized on a grey granite envelope, he was inducted into the sprawling Sampas clan, the Lowell Greeks. HE HONORED LIFE. And reverted, in eternity, to John Kerouac: the name on the cover of his first realist novel, *The Town and the City*. Ti Jean. A French-Canadian incomer who spoke in patois and understood no English until he was six years old. Dead Jack is with Stella, his last wife. And alongside his childhood buddy, and early literary conscience, Sebastian 'Sammy' Sampas. The brother who died of his wounds, after Anzio, in 1944. Around the rim of the memorial panel is a neatly arranged crown of red-gold maple leaves, a fiery wreath.

'Most days you'll find messages, joints, prayers,' Henry said. But this October morning, it's a flag; the right size to float in a Florida cocktail. The Stars and Stripes skewered through a tribute to the dead man composed in very large letters on lined white paper. WE BELIEVE IN YOUR BELIEF.

Driving over the bridge was my first sight of the Merrimack, with Henry providing necessary guidebook information, the verbal footnotes he left out of his film. Infiltrating the set of a Massachusetts mill town was in so many ways a raid on my own past, a return to memory movies conjured by my adolescent reading of the Kerouac saga. I'd been given *Maggie Cassidy* at just the right moment; the narrative structure, I recognized, was much cannier than I appreciated at the time. I took a deep breath and submerged myself in the breathless physicality of competitive sprints (Kerouac the failed sports reporter). Kitchen conferences of a suffocatingly close family. Snow outside. Distances recorded of meandering walks across town. And that lovely dark-haired girl, down on the straw, in an off-the-shoulder print dress and black stockings. She was nothing like Maggie or her real-life inspiration, the Irish girl Mary Carney. As she sprawled invitingly on the cover of the slim 1960 Panther paperback original. 'I won't even know where your grave is,' Mary says.

Invaders sniff around cold post-mortem traces, measuring ripples in the tar, photographing funeral homes, referencing the now-silent mills, as Charles Dickens once did, and making pointless reports. They cough out books and papers in sorry imitations of spontaneous composition, their antics anticipated by Kerouac in the figure of Count Condu from *Dr Sax.* Condu is a vampire, newly arrived from Europe, hot for innocent American blood, ticking over on a pint and a half decanted from a young girl, 'just below the ear lobe', after stepping ashore in slushy, fish-smelling Boston. The coming energy thieves, fact-checkers from the academies of Budapest, Berlin, Rome, London, must be countered by the native Dr Sax (an avatar of W. C. Fields and William Burroughs), who takes the form, this time round, in a perfect Kerouacian shift of gears, of the poet Carl Sandburg: 'thin as a shadow on the wall', walking at night through a black area of Long Island, having just come off a Montana freight train.

9 Lupine Street in Centralville, the birth house – remembered, in shimmering golden hurt of light, 12 March 1922 – is a quotation. Fresh-painted, balconied, red-shingled, with drooping flag and satellite dish on the roof. On the street are two deep-red recycling bins. This is now a well-kept, security-fenced neighbourhood of shiny black cars and broad puddles reflecting and inverting the quiet scene. A green memorial plaque confirms absence, end of story.

'I have a recurrent dream,' Kerouac said, 'of simply walking around the deserted twilight streets of Lowell, in the mist, eager to turn every known and fabled corner.'

From the moment of reading *Maggie Cassidy*, in Wales, at the period when I was researching the life and mythology of Dylan Thomas by interviewing his friend the poet Vernon Watkins in his Gower bungalow, and BBC producers in Cardiff, and publicans and fishermen and fellow drinkers in Laugharne, a process of twinning and twisting and overlaying began to evolve. I wouldn't have presumed on identification with Kerouac's achievement, only with some of the biographical incidents that went into the mix. There was the attraction of the footballer held back by the compulsion to write, accepting poetry as a filter between experience and the invention of a self fit for the world that contains it. Kerouac grew up hearing that French-Canadian patois, as I was attuned to Welsh as the first language of my mother, maternal grandparents and great-aunt, and of the small mining town as I moved around it, an appendage of the old folk, kicking my heels, waiting for elaborate exchanges of courtesy, in words I experience but do not properly understand, to play themselves out.

So there was place: working, failing, romanced. I went with my father to visit a hermit who lived under a corrugated-iron roof in an excavated warren, in the tolerated corner of a farmer's field. The image stayed with me, that there were such invisibles, grizzled solitaries who performed a role like the disreputable vagrant figures out of the western states, coming to lodge in riverside Lowell huts, before fading into their fictional roles as spooks or freaks in the apocalyptic vision of a provincial town splitting open to reveal the maw of hell, the day of judgement, at the climax of *Dr Sax*. When hills and lakes are revealed as manifestations of a life-swallowing serpent: the labyrinthine cellars of tortures, heresies, imprisonments. The murders Kerouac would witness directly or share with friends like William Burroughs.

South Wales/Massachusetts: if there was a secret in America worth extracting, it was known to Dylan Thomas and to Kerouac, both of them drawing on the Joyce of *Finnegans Wake*. But without that Homeric reach, the confidence to go all the way back to the roots of language. They traded, these drinkers, small-town boys on show in cities, in the hot, wet secretions of their hyper-magnified childhoods. Funerals of siblings, aunts, parents. Do not go gentle. Unresolved arguments with dead fathers who won't go away. *Dr Sax* composed in Mexico City, 'Ancient Capital of Azteca', in 1952, as Dylan Thomas is tinkering with *Under Milk Wood* in claustrophobic New York, on his fatal fourth reading tour. And just after Charles Olson returned from Yucatán: a barefoot sabbatical playing the archaeologist of morning, picking up broken shards and composing fevered letters to Robert Creeley. 'And I waste time reading, murders.'

Robert Frank, the great Swiss-American photographer who collaborated with Kerouac on the film *Pull My Daisy*, and the record of transcontinental drives published as *The Americans*, comes to London: for Bethnal Green hearses, tight-rolled City bankers, coalmen heaving sacks. In 1953 he undertakes a documentary record of mining life in the Welsh town where I grew up, Maesteg. Now he has me studying prints to see if I can find my ten-year-old self among the children venturing on a thinly grassed mound at the head of the valley. I track Frank to the graveyard he passes on his way to the railway station. His return to London. 'My absent memory rests within these photographs,' he says.

Like Kerouac, I heard about the early death of a sibling, in my case a sister. It happened too soon in her short life to have the haunting impact of Kerouac's brother Gerard, who was gone at the age of nine. With all the curdling pieties and rituals of immigrant Catholic loss. Like Kerouac I was slow to draw breath, a blue baby. Provoked to shout only when hope was fading, after my visiting father dropped a book, a detective story, on my head. *Crackerjack.* Lupine Road absorbed the tragedy of new life. The writer's fated entry to the wheel of existence. Safe in heaven dead, Kerouac said. It is all emptiness. 'I could walk right through you.'

Would John Sampas come to the restaurant? The place was his choice, not Henry's. Henry knew better spots, but Sampas was the keeper of the archive. If he liked us, if I performed, we would be invited to the house. There had been so many bitter battles over the Kerouac estate, which was now worth millions of dollars; juvenilia, false starts and fragments appearing in nicely produced hardback editions. No longer Panther and Avon and WDL. The friable paper, the gaudy covers, the sensational copy. *Tristessa*: 'The real tragedy of narcotics and prostitution. A young American writer staggering between the forces of desire for her and horror for what she has become.' *Maggie Cassidy* of Lowell: 'The vibrant, demanding, woman-bodied girl who fascinated and confused the man she yearned for.' 1960. The covered market by the bus station, Maesteg. Two shillings and sixpence.

When the bloated body of Jack Kerouac was flown from Florida to the Archambault Funeral Parlor, the doorway Henry points out as we drive alongside, Gregory Corso wanted to find a way to assert the revulsion he felt, the evident fact of the thing: *Doctor Death*. His poet friends and members of the Sampas clan had to restrain him before he tipped the corpse from the open coffin and dragged it across the floor, screaming: 'Nobody at home. Nothing left. Jack's *gone*.'

Already the politics of possession are established; work, published and unpublished, has become an estate. Before too many years have passed, Hollywood will take notice of a property they spurned when Kerouac was doing the pitching, and offering Marlon Brando the historic, career-defining role of Neal Cassady in the movie of *On the Road*. With Jack impersonating his mythologized self, Sal Paradise.

Down these Lowell steps they come, the pall-bearing Greek cousins in tight coats, the bar owners, the Kerouac chauffeurs and drinking buddies of the last desperate years, along with the frowning, bearded Ginsberg in his shiny anorak, chairman of Beats Inc., the underground corporation. A glittering-eyed Jewish intellectual among mill-town working men. The old alliance, damaged and set aside, between the booze-addled Kerouac (in flight from the noise of Vietnam) and the ever-available, public Ginsberg, was mended in death. There was a twilight rebirth coming for both of them, of millennial reissues, new introductions, archives made over to wealthy academic institutions. Agents and percentage deals and personal assistants in white trainers. Corso, the canny street kid, was right. This was a clown-as-Hamlet afternoon, a chance to ventriloquize the bleached skull. To finesse whispers of forgotten Montreal TV into approved legacy promos. Celebrity seances and horribly bad journeys will be remade in heaven on gold cards.

The last phone calls were ugly. Kerouac told his editor that he was going to Germany: 'to see the concentration camps and dance on Jews' graves'. And the worst of it was, this man reported, that Jack didn't even sound drunk.

The *Dr Sax* grotto was our final call before the restaurant. You could hear, close at hand, the rush and surge of the Merrimack. 'This is New England,' Kerouac wrote, 'half like rainy Welsh mining towns.' Rainwater was running in thick beads like glycerine tears down the square chin of the saint with the upturned eyes. These sideshow stations of the cross would be blasphemy among the slate chapels of the primitive Methodism of Maesteg; whitewashed temples like

Libanus, where, at six or seven years of age, I recited a few verses of the Old Testament, learnt phonetically, in Welsh. To a chorus of approval from the nodding elders.

Kerouac positions his grotto between orphanage and roaring river. 'Fireflies in the night flickering to the waxy stare of statues.' Some of the display cases for buttermilk figures representing the passion of Christ are empty. Stolen? Removed for renovation? There is a rocky Lourdes shrine with a Cecil B. DeMille crucifix and a near-naked martyred man. Nailed, agonized, unrisen. In the cave of the grotto, thick votive candles splutter in medicine jars dressed with novelty illustrations of Mexican vitality. The supplicants, this day, are Cambodians. Henry is a little distracted. He's waiting for a call from his wife – at home in Gloucester, facing hospital tests – and trying to negotiate the sale of their car.

Kerouac was always looking for new borders. When situations of his own making – publishers, wives, mother – became difficult or impossible, he ran to Mexico City; the adobe hut on the roof, the company of Bill Garver, wise old junky, a connection who asked nothing of him. He liked the economics of 'fellaheen' streets, the cheap prostitutes and stimulants. He liked the solitude, the opportunity to uncoil narratives at his own pace, to improvise. *Mexico City Blues.*

Ellis Amburn, a sympathetic but undeceived witness of the end of Kerouac's writing career, his editor on *Visions of Cody*, has the troubled author, in the grip of hallucination, spooked by intimations of future fame, striking out, in July 1950, to walk from Mexico City to New York, carrying two and a half pounds of marijuana wrapped in silk and lashed to his waist. Jack seems, already, to be trespassing on arrows of predetermined energy, directions of travel, undertaken by Malcolm Lowry or fictionalized by Roberto Bolaño. His fate as a rootless wanderer is confirmed after he crosses the border at Laredo and encounters an old man with long white hair. 'Go moan for man,' he is told. 'After that,' Amburn reports, 'Jack seemed to accept that it was his destiny to walk across America on foot, often in total darkness.' The manifest of the essential bad journey, the suicide tarantella attempted and endured by Lowry, Neal Cassady, the poet John Hoffman, and Cabeza de Vaca in the sixteenth century, was in place. Magnetic attraction in the shape and shadow of a smouldering volcano. A land breast. The dark god Vulcan of the Lowell Mills made actual in sparks of iron-fire.

There is an 'immense triangle', Kerouac said, between New York, Mexico City and San Francisco. Self-defined as a 'religious wanderer', he would trudge, in hobo mask and threadbare disguise, from city to city, never settling, endlessly perching, recording, remembering, suffering: to gain his 'foothold in heaven'.

John Sampas

Remember the scene in *The Godfather*? The neighbourhood trattoria, the garlic-and-tomato ooze of the kitchen, the tightness of the tables? The gun hidden in the toilet cistern? Large men with heavy elbows. Big white plates. Wine bottles. Cones of laundered napkin flicked open, bibbed around bullish necks. All that screwed-down testosterone rage, liable at any moment to send bread rolls, forks, spoons, water jug, cigarettes flying into the air in a Futurist explosion. Marinetti meets Mario Puzo. Which would, Hollywood style, cut into a montage of spinning newspaper headlines (a vortex), final editions soaking up lung blood. *This was not like that.* The restaurant, chosen by John Sampas, was deserted. Even by Sampas. Maybe it was too wet for him to come out. A long, low room with tables in regimented lines lit like the interior of a satin-padded, diamond-pattern coffin. A soundproof immersion-chamber for a wealthy narcoleptic who wants just enough light, should he wake up, to read *The Premature Burial*. It is rumoured, as I'm sure John Sampas, a cultivated man, would know, that Edgar Allan Poe visited the Lowell tavern known as the Worthen House, where he composed part of 'The Raven'. This town was also the birthplace of Bette Davis and James McNeill Whistler, both of whom got as far away as possible as soon as they could.

The spaghetti joint where little, broken-mouthed Al Pacino proves himself by blowing away Sterling Hayden (in life, a disgraced leftist namer of names) is square on to a working street in a part of the Bronx unvisited by restaurant critics. (Relocated for convenience to the Luna Restaurant on White Plains Road, off Gun Hill Road.) From a midway table, keeping your back to the washroom, you face a wet window, slithery with neon, passing traffic. *Nothing passes in Lowell.* We're downtown, close to the civic centre, and it's reasonable to expect a knot of black suits with expense accounts, relaxing dealmakers, worldly priests and patrons. *Nobody*. Efficient staff come straight at us for our drinks order, then vanish. Grape-bulb lights depending. Icy-white cloth. Pink napkins. Tall menus like Orders of Service at the crematorium. Red-rimmed chairs with curved backs. No windows, no street. Reproduction French posters advertising drinks they don't serve. Empty mirrors innocent of breath.

Knowing something of the period when Kerouac, having mar-ried Stella, John's sister (as a surrogate for his soulmate, Sammy), was sheltered, indulged, adopted by the Greek clan, I formed the impression of a group of local fixers who worked hard and got lucky. They always had a stool for Jack in Nicky's, the Sampas-owned bar managed by Manuel 'Chiefy' Nobriga. John's father, George, back in 1941, got into some bother with a man called Peter Aposta-lakos. 'That guy is *stalking* me.' He responded to this annoyance by shooting him dead. The argument between the two men had been running since 1920. John Sampas explained that the Lowell commu-nity turned against his father because he had once led strikes in the local mills.

The first physical attribute that struck me about John, when he was led to our table, and after he had removed his cap, was the per-manently raised eyebrows: lightly pencilled accents. Punctuation marks signalling a certain fastidiousness of discourse. This man had endured many such conversations, clearly; biographers, thesis bro-kers, bounty hunters circling around the Kerouac archive. He demonstrated immaculate, almost military, grooming: clipped white moustache, low-slung attentive ears, and high, thin neck. Careful, wounded eyes. A dark corduroy jacket with blue-check, button-down shirt. The spectacles on a string were brought into play to interrogate a menu with few surprises. He ordered, with an imperceptible sigh, what is always ordered. He ate slowly; cutting, laying the knife aside, employing his fork for tuning unheard mel-odies, not spearing and lifting. A practised ritual of public dining around which a dialogue will, eventually, take shape: with Henry as silent referee, mediator, witness. And timekeeper too, because issues back home in Gloucester are preying on him.

'I did lunch with Olson, oh yes, at the Ritz Carlton in Boston. Along with Mr Jonathan Williams and his ex-lover, Ronald Johnson. The poet.'

What we never appreciated, as students back in Dublin, was how tribal and interconnected the American countercultural scene actually was: everybody met everybody, everybody fucked everybody (as with any museum-quality art movement). They feuded, fought, formed intense friendships, sulked for generations. And they all kept records (pension plans). Gunslinger poets, jealous of reputation, were forced to become air-miles performers on Midwest campuses, checking out student audiences for potential lovers and patrons. The first-generation Beats of the 1940s all slept together at some point, in a writhing pod of favours and exchanges, permutations now being catalogued and exhibited like sacred relics with unholy price tags.

'Jack admired Olson, which was why he made that trip to Gloucester. He was fascinated by the *idea* of the poet.'

As we ate, in swift raids, trying not to make a hungry mess of the beautiful still-life arrangements on our large plates, the rich red sauces and drowned vegetables, I learnt from John Sampas something about how solitary these writers were in the working New England world. Alienated, in the end, by the view of the harbour from the seven windows at Fort Square, Charles Olson turned inland to the ancient rocks of Dogtown, the glacial moraines. 'Distance is closing in,' said the poet Tom Clark, who crafted an Olson biography that succeeded in enraging most of those who knew him in Gloucester, or who had a heavy investment in contriving legends acceptable to the paymasters of charitable foundations and universities. Once the most public and engaged of the makers of lives of the poets, in the classical tradition, Clark had retired, somewhat bruised but still active, into his own forms of silence. Or to presenting himself, as he was at the start, as a pure poet. Behind him, or alongside him, producing invisible versions of the same stories, was the Black Mountain survivor I wanted to track down, the unrecorded and unphotographed Cal Shutter. I thought of Shutter, rumoured to have crossed into Mexico, as the last man standing in a very long line. If Shutter had been too young to live up to his boast of taking classes with Olson at Black Mountain, he had certainly been in England for a few years, studying (and editing small magazines with Andrew Crozier and Roy Fisher) at Keele. When all that went wrong, he lived in a Peak District cave. Some say that, fuelled on pills and whisky, supplied with a portable typewriter and a torch strapped to his head, he died there.

The trade, today, is gossip. We settled to it, we established some measure of common ground. I offered just enough, by way of names and dates, to engage John Sampas. There was the night when a dealer we both knew, call him Jeff Klippenberg, came to the door to ask if he could introduce a potential customer, a very good customer, to the Kerouac archive. A person called Johnny Depp. Had John fixed a price yet for Jack's old raincoat?

I was grateful, decades ago, to have shifted all the remaining copies of my long, thin book on Allen Ginsberg's 1967 visit to London, *The Kodak Mantra Diaries*, to Klippenberg's address in Massachusetts. For a pittance. But making room in our tight terraced house for plenty more stock, the books I trawled from the streets of Hackney and Whitechapel. John Sampas didn't have these problems, the items in his care were valuable. They were relics. They could be edited, dusted down, released on to the market.

Depp dropped around. With his chequebook. A deal was struck. He was a pleasant, modest young man. Not bad looking. Polite. The quantity of noughts made the eyes water, but what I never managed to learn as a dealer is that *you can't charge too much* for the unique item. Price confers value. The customer expects it. The least you can do is to offer your client the status of having paid a spectacular premium, thereby demonstrating seriousness. Vendor and Hollywood vendee did their best, in this case, to cut out the middleman. They went to dinner. They sat in this restaurant. They had a decent bottle. They enjoyed themselves.

A little of the Sampas history emerged. An office career, account-ancy or some such, the Boston money markets, and then American antiques. Henry characterized it as 'bits and pieces, smart junk'. A good eye, probably, a fondness for scavenging: collector and trader. John tells us how he acquired, sight unseen, a case of inscribed Ish-erwood first editions. But that was then; now he's like a senior Beat Generation diplomat, an ambassador with polished skull, silver half-moon moustache, dangling spectacles, freshly ironed shirt. A man for whom there will always be lunches.

With Olson it was more about drinking, that day at the Ritz Carl-ton, than poetry. Olson liked to smoke and talk, to build up a head of steam for an audience that included his publisher, Jonathan Wil-liams. Sampas met other poets too, Philip Whalen and Lew Welch, as they passed through town on reading tours. Hubert Selby, John said, was a civilized man dealing with a savage hinterland. And then there was the night cruiser John Rechy who reported on adventures in leather bars and bus stations.

Sampas is a little hard of hearing. There is that brief delay of a news report from a dirt road in Afghanistan, when the questioner in the studio has to fix an interested expression while he waits. The most recent visitors are connections of Walter Salles and the team making the movie translation of *On the Road*. (A film that turned out to be more about research than delivery.) John's sister Stella invaded the office of Kerouac's agent, Sterling Lord, to demand the original, pasted-together teletype roll on which Kerouac typed his most famous novel. John was caught up in complicated dealings with Ferlinghetti at City Lights, out in San Francisco. The veteran poet and publisher was hanging on to his cache of Kerouac manu-scripts with studied tardiness in correspondence. Henry travelled out there to shoot an interview, but got nothing. He tried his *Lowell Blues* script on a barker outside a North Beach strip club. Depp was gracious enough to do his readings for this film as a favour, an act of respect for a writer he admired.

I told John how heart-stopping it had been to be confronted with the brown, stiff-covered Kerouac exercise book with his progress report, the word count of the composition of *On the Road*, in that temperature-controlled vault at the Harry Ransom Center in Austin, Texas. The work journals Kerouac kept so meticulously were dated year by year. A life in paper. I wondered how this one had escaped the archive in Lowell.

'No mystery,' John said. 'Gregory Corso. He stole it.'

Corso lifted what he could from his friends, to run to the New York bookdealers who looked after him, giving him a place in which to live, and collecting his heroin. Ginsberg left instructions with this benevolent couple, to call him so that he could come down to the shop and buy back his own presentation copies and manuscripts, after Gregory had been paid. In the end, many of the failing Beat veterans passed into the hands of youthful carers in pressed white jeans; male nurses, business managers, curators of the legend, granters of access. John Sampas adopted a young Chinese boy and was putting him through law school.

I picked up the bill, modest by Charlotte Street standards, and we drifted out to the street. We were invited back to the Sampas property for coffee and a leisurely tour of the holdings. But it was not to be; Henry needed to get back on the road, time was pressing, he had a car to sell in Gloucester.

Safe Haven

For Olson, the big man, there were no true friends, no listeners left in Gloucester. Apart from Vincent Ferrini, that striding presence in the leather cowboy hat voicing his wise-guy poems, working through domestic estrangements in the roadside cabin, the picture-framer's hut where I was now lodged in my own dank October. You could smell the moves Ferrini made, from bed to kitchen, to backyard, to the shed where materials were kept and bottles left over from poetry readings. Betty Olson, the one who brought Charles to Fort Square, and who resisted this financially necessary move, to take up the distinguished professorship at the State University of New York at Buffalo, was dead. A late driver, resenting the enforced country solitude of their new base at Wyoming, New York, Betty undertook a number of hazardous and unplanned trips, botched returns to Gloucester, escapes from this frozen nowhere. The black Volkswagen bug, bought on impulse, was navigated without a valid licence through snowstorms on unfamiliar roads.

I don't know what movie was playing in the small town of Batavia on the afternoon of 28 March 1964, but Betty went to the show after buying an Easter basket for her son, Charles Peter. Her husband was much taken with *A Hard Day's Night* and the Beatles. He responded to the presence of the Liverpool quartet, the news of them, as to something strikingly fresh, but not original; a self-confident street shamanism attracting and holding an audience poets could only dream about. Olson was a convinced Jungian, an advocate of 'The Secret of the Golden Flower', the alchemy of the black chrysanthemum. Liverpool had a peculiar significance for Jung: it contained the magnolia tree at the heart of the mandala, the Pool of Life. Olson insisted on sitting through a screening of the Dick Lester film for a second time. A new kind of disposable wit and populist energy was emerging, and he felt, again, his own time was done. The beached whale, the schlump of Gloucester.

Before making her return to the empty house, Betty might have lost a few hours with *My Fair Lady*, *Goldfinger*, *Viva Las Vegas*, *The Night of the Iguana*, or Billy Wilder's *Kiss Me, Stupid*. Olson, in a previous life, in the heat of his pioneering first book, the supercharged but compacted Melville scholarship of *Call me Ishmael*, went out to Hollywood to meet John Huston, *Iguana*'s director, and to discuss *Moby-Dick*. Jey Leyda sent a copy of *Call me Ishmael* to Sergei Eisenstein, who fired off a congratulatory telegram. Eisenstein, ahead of the Beats and Malcolm Lowry, went south, over the border: *¡Que viva México!* Another lost or aborted project, the Maya in Yucatán (before Olson), revolution, Day of the Dead: all funded by bemused Sinclairs (the novelist Upton and his wife, Mary).

Olson dropped in on Huston at the Warner Brothers studios. Jack Warner was away, until October, on the French Riviera. No hiring or firing could be undertaken. Or so the tactful Huston intimated. They talked books and existentialist philosophy (bluffing, both of them). The mechanical version of the White Whale wouldn't float in the studio tank. 'Kill that fucking fish,' Jack said on his return. The property died, until Huston managed to resurrect it, with a Ray Bradbury script, nine years later. (By way of the film, Melville's novel became J. G. Ballard's favourite book.) The only other director in town to receive Olson was Jean Renoir: to whom he proposed a movie based on the shipwreck of the *Essex*. The Frenchman was polite but perplexed. He passed.

Olson, as was his way, persisted; he dug deep into material on John Sutter and the Californian Gold Rush, an episode of cannibalism on an ill-fated crossing of the Sierra Nevada in 1846. He inspected ravished, strip-mined terrain. He dragged himself through the tedium of grant applications, contemplating bad journeys to Arizona, New Mexico and across the border. Nobody was listening. John Huston, in the same year, 1947, went south to shoot *The Treasure of the Sierra Madre*: gold fever, gold dust blowing across barren ground. Huston, the man in a white suit, puffing a good cigar, takes a cameo, beating off a desperate Humphrey Bogart, as he would dozens of other Los Angeles panhandlers peddling scripts and sure-fire literary properties. It would be a while before he suffered the ultimate Mexican nightmare with his 1984 version of Lowry's *Under the Volcano*. Bad journey, bad juju: Albert Finney failing to ham his way out of the wrong hangover. Rich flesh on the skull. Dead dogs in ditches.

Betty skids on black ice. Her Volkswagen swerves into the head-lights of an oncoming truck. Her chest is crushed. An ambulance returns her to Batavia, where she dies.

When Olson was dying in New York, losing bulk, receiving friends and disciples like a shrunken pope, he asked Ferrini to drive over from Gloucester after visiting the apartment on Fort Square to gather up a number of objects, in order to create what Tom Clark called: 'a force field of magical aura-action against eternity'. Olson specified a map of the Atlantic sea floor, taken down from the wall and now faded to the point of erasure. Rusty pin holes in each corner. Then a portrait of the man himself, the one snatched by Gerard Malanga on the occasion of that awkward and grating interview for the *Paris Review*. Olson is frowning into a low sun, tweed coat draped over shoulders, playing with something that might be a feather. He's rapping. Workman's boots, unlaced, on feet that have retired from walking. Vincent successfully locates the Indian blanket, the Russian spoon, the crystal ball (shades of Dr Dee). And two oranges. (Shades of Ballard, who kept a lemon on his Shepperton mantel-piece for years.) Poets know that such power as they have is soon absorbed by the fetishized objects that surround them. Relics are the true autobiography.

Which was part of my difficulty in Ferrini's hut. The objects, on shelves, table, walls, floor, pulsed at such a high sonic pitch, and there were so many of them. Who could have imagined a song, found among a stack of random CDs, called 'Like the Swan was a Boulevard'? I played it, several times. The voyage by swan pedalo was so fresh in my mind. The white plastic vessel, once it was launched, and named, came to life. Our water roads, hugging the coast to Rye, then the rivers of Sussex and Kent, were indeed a shining boulevard.

Slumping in an old chair shaped to the warp of Ferrini's spine, I sliced through a mound of likely books. Olson's correspondence with the local paper, philippics launched against the despoilers of his polis, the written city of Gloucester. Memoirs. Histories of the fishing industry. Albums of photographs. And the paperback with which I finally settled down for the night, *Hubert's Freaks* by Gregory Gibson. Greg was coming early next morning to pick me up for a ride to Northampton, where he was going to stall out at a book fair. This was the right preparation, a tale of dealers, scouts, madmen, and the melancholy underworld of Times Square freaks. The hook was a cache of 'lost' Diane Arbus photographs. Greg knew this territory well: the shabby motel rooms, the heavy breakfasts, the dry-mouthed phone calls, interminable sessions with unreliable middlemen. And the remote possibility – teasing, almost within reach – of that big score. Fate games on endless roads. The narrative played, in skilled hands, like a crime novel.

Greg wrote, published, stopped back, published again. Until he arrived at the point when what he wanted most was to trudge along the flank of the Connecticut River, releasing his reports, a chapter at a time, under his own imprint. John Ledyard, Greg's inspiration, set out in 1786 to walk the world: from London, around the Baltic to Germany, through Russia and Siberia to the Arctic Sea. A ship would be found to carry him to the Pacific Northwest. Then on across unmapped and unimagined America. Ledyard, who laid down the model for future pilgrims of derangement, achieved 10,000 miles, on foot and alone. He fired up Ed Dorn who wrote a poem called 'Ledyard: The Exhaustion of Sheer Distance'. Dorn noticed that the great man's journals said nothing about the condition of his shoes, but much about how he tramped towards the Pacific coast of Russia, as the best way of reaching the other side of America. The Ledyard quote Dorn selects for an epigraph is: 'I give up. I give up.'

*

The Northampton book fair had the same institutional claustrophobia, cooked up from postponed suicides and pharmaceutical jollity, that you find everywhere, Bloomsbury to Berkeley. Grieving books, accidents of purchase, were displayed like shrink-wrapped evidence in a show trial. I made a couple of circuits, for old times' sake, and then I hiked through leafy suburbs into the quiet, Sunday-morning town. Of course a couple of discounted purchases had somehow stuck to my hands. My reading, outside immediate research, came down to a select group of authors: Louis-Ferdinand Céline (worked through in chronological order), Don DeLillo (backwards), Malcolm Lowry, Roberto Bolaño, Walter Abish. On my second lap of the fair, I found a promising route to Mexico in Abish's *Eclipse Fever*. 'I have never been to the United States,' he wrote. 'I avoid it out of fear that it will not approximate the United States of my imagination.'

Greg gave me the keys, pressing me to take his car, drive into the country. I thought of Amherst and Emily Dickinson, and then I started walking. Northampton does not have much in common with its English namesake, but the well-kept acres of Smith, the Ivy League women's college, do invoke St Andrew's Hospital, the manicured grounds of the asylum where John Clare endured his final exile.

Disturbingly healthy young ladies on bicycles, lustrous in their privilege, passed from hall to sports field to church. 'It's a dyke town,' I heard a beatnik juvenile say to his heavy-metal nest-mate at a folding table where they were trying to flog the accumulated junk of a disestablished community house. Junk that included a tattered pamphlet by Cal Shutter, *Night and More Night*, with supporting quotes from Joanne Kyger and Robert Creeley. There were more joggers than dogs. And you can take jogging, as I knew from the parks and canal paths of Hackney, as an accurate indicator of a vertiginous upward sweep of the socio-economic curve. Along with branded T-shirts mixing conspicuous charity with international merchant banks.

My ramble took me through the centre of town and out the other side. All roads led to a low building with a blue-and-white sign: SLEEP DISORDERS LABORATORY. Stencilled graffiti featured spliff-toking cartoon heads on redbrick walls. A silver-bearded guru with prominent ears and a third eye had a poster announcing the occupation of Northampton. MEET FIRST WITH YOUR FRIENDS IN PRIVATE, THEN CONVENE AT BANK OF AMERICA.

I couldn't get inside any of this. I could flip the images like a carousel and inscribe found texts in my notebook. I could visit the museum and appreciate river-culture figures brought back from the Congo and the usual Euro plunder (Cézanne, Munch, Monet, Seurat). There is a Winslow Homer painting of shipbuilding in Gloucester and a Marsden Hartley mackerel. The museum shop has the smartest scarves in New England. There is good coffee for the laptop scholars.

Obliged to acknowledge the generosity of Greg's gesture in giving me the keys to his car, I head back to the book fair. The event is taking place in a building on the far side of the hospital. BABY SAFE HAVEN. PLEASE LEAVE NEWBORN BABY AT HOSPITAL EMERGENCY ROOM OR A (STAFFED) FIRE STATION. NO QUESTIONS ASKED.

Greg told me to follow the Indian trail. In a book-bearing, automatic car I have never previously driven? Down roads I didn't know? My first rule in America is: *walk*. Use public transport. Don't trail Indians. They are much better at it. The surrounding woods were not to be taken lightly. I looped around a few junctions, trying to identify some piece of quiet ground on which to eat a gas-station sandwich. I settled for a cemetery field, alongside the military section. The landscape made more sense once it was framed in the thick rectangle of the nearside mirror. Blank stone slabs leaning against a grey hut, waiting for names and dates.

When a long black limo, sleek as Valentino's hair, cruised slowly down the cemetery avenue, looking for a particular grave, I thought about Jack Kerouac's October 1968 excursion: to visit Charles Olson in Fort Square, Gloucester. Widowed, ursine, hibernating, Olson was Shakespearean (*Timon of Athens*) in his solitude. He spoke, early, of Kerouac as 'the greatest writer in America'. And he feared this new power coming from the poets of the Beat Generation: that it would challenge or somehow undo his hard-won stance as the major poet of place on the Atlantic rim, successor to William Carlos Williams. The push he made over all those years to forge a republic of letters. With himself, alongside Robert Duncan, as twin consuls: East Coast and West.

When young men arrived at the door on which he left hand-written notices telling them to *go away* (he was sick, under the blankets), Olson riffed on Bob Dylan. 'He is just beautiful. He is just an absolute delicate thing.' Kerouac had the authentic voice too, native register. Sturdier than Dylan. Iroquois stock, French-Canadian. This Lowell football player, in a way Olson couldn't figure, had written the new America into being. The cadences, the rhythms, the runs. *The peripheral vision, the detail.* Jack Kerouac was the embodiment of Olson's theory of poetics, his dogma nailed to the church door: *Projective Verse.* 'Keep moving, keep in, speed, the nerves, their speed, the perceptions, theirs, the acts, the split second acts, the whole business.'

All those books composed on the run in the late 1940s, early 1950s. The sieving and sifting of memory. Now Jack, sick with success, had to argue his way around the bulk of the intellectually intimidating Charles Olson. It was just that, size. 'If I was six foot six I could write anything, couldn't I?' he said, selling the Gloucester poet short by three or four inches. Jack envied Olson's dominance over his peers, the academic distinction. How this other man from a working New England town moved to the centre of public life: tutoring the Kennedy boys at Harvard (rich kids who swam a bit and paid others to compose their term papers), then working for the Democrats in Washington and visiting Ezra Pound in the bughouse, to argue out contrary visions of history.

As a direct challenge to Olson and the Black Mountaineers, Kerouac published his *Essentials of Spontaneous Prose.* 'Swimming in sea of English with no discipline other than rhythms of rhetorical exhalation and expostulated statement, like a fist coming down on a table with each complete utterance, bang!'

Sea! Water flooded the Sampas bar. The power and reach of the Atlantic Ocean as witnessed daily from those seven windows in Fort Square could not be countered by the flood of sound from Lowell's Merrimack. Jack's heavy, befuddled head hit the table, his thickening body slumped, and he told the boys to fetch the limo. They would thread a little landscape through the window. Drive, day into night, to visit those New England phoneys, the challengers: Charles Olson in Gloucester and then John Updike.

Nick and Tony were with him. Or, some say, Joe Chaput. It's not a long run, Lowell to Gloucester. The Sampas boys, humouring Jack, stretched it out. Drinks in the car and a few stops along the way.

'I was the one formulated the theory of breath as measure, back in '53, for Burroughs and Ginzy,' Kerouac slurred.

'Sure you did, Jackie.'

They glugged Michelob with Teacher's Scotch chasers. Jack did Céline again, extemporizing brilliantly, in a single-breath, forty-mile sentence, on *Journey to the End of the Night* and *Death on the Instalment Plan*, his favourite novels. 'He *knew*, that crazy Frenchman nailed it, human existence is rotten and mad.'

Nobody did specifics like Jack, the great noticer. So that became his grudge with Olson, all those dates and names worked into the texture, the chart of the Gloucester man's epic voyage, *The Maximus Poems*. A hound dog on a beach. The worst of Kerouac's worst delirium was when Ferlinghetti lent him the cabin in Bixby Canyon and he tried to transcribe the sound of the sea. 'Someone jacking off on a beach? What does Olson call it, Shit-town? Dogtown? I would never insult the place I lived that way.'

Olson was avid for conversation, the audience that Kerouac could never be. They held the door open and Jack crawled from the car. There were newspapers spread up the slippery steps, a welcome mat for a literary cardinal. The Lowell writer was trampling over one of those sneering Boston reviews and he took it as an intended insult. The night never picked up. Olson had been known to keep young poets, across from England, probably Cambridge, trapped for forty-eight hours while he pounded them with metaphors, poetry and truth. He whaled his Camels in two drags, as Ed Dorn said. He finished the bottle. He dry-swallowed psilocybin buttons from the cache Leary gave him, a container the size of one of those old-fashioned confectioner's jars. Pink pills: peanuts. Sweaty excitement fed by the evident intelligence and attentive respect of the willing victim, now groggy, green-white, punchdrunk. He sucked them dry, husked them, striding to the window, then back across the steamy room, temperature cranked to tropical hothouse by the blue flare of the gas stove. Shirt soaked. Gripping the rim of the table. That mesmerizing voice seemed to come now from all corners of the room at once as the formerly young man crawls towards the distant exit, the dangerous steps. 'The world has moved,' he reported, 'in another context, on.'

One of the people I questioned about the Olson/Kerouac confrontation thought he recalled the presence of a woman, a researcher offering secretarial assistance, tucked away in the next room, exhausted, taking this opportunity to catch up on her sleep. She overheard some of what happened. And she was the only one. Name mislaid, present whereabouts unknown. Another teasing mystery. Cal Shutter's first wife?

Peter Anastas, who came out on the boat with me, around the harbour, saw Olson, earlier that day. Peter, back then, had the appearance of a bearded anchorite. Olson asked the young poet to help him with his Greek. Now Peter was helping me too. I read his books in my hut. I appreciated the tact and warmth of his introductions, the editorial jobs on the Olson archive. I also appreciated the fish soup Anastas and his partner brought in a saucepan to my door. There was a deep reservoir of affection for the man, Charles Olson, and for the way he lived, as night wanderer and chronicler, in this town. The biography by Tom Clark, making a complex allegory from available materials, was much resented. But beyond the fact of the arrival of Kerouac in the black limousine, and the staggering entry to 28 Fort Square over a carpet of newspapers, the slumping into sleep, Olson's sadness at a lost opportunity, the bringing together of two compelling and contradictory visions of America, nothing was established. Jack never made it to Updike.

Driving back with Greg after the Northampton book fair, we stalled into a slow-motion jam. 'It always happens around this point,' he said. 'It'll clear.' There was more hair in the dealer's recent past than my own. The dust-jacket photograph from 1998 was pure frontier: Wild Bill Hickok, Colonel Cody, General Custer. Shoulder-length locks spreading over a nice tweed jacket. Greg was less of a dandy, in his hardcore beard, than any of those fabled publicity hounds with their gravity-celebrating moustaches. He looked like a log-cabin survivalist. With big spectacles. Or like the fated man who comes back from the whaleboat disaster to ghost a tale of marine cannibalism. The eyes were haunted and dark-ringed. Which, as I knew very well, is how they get from years on the road, reading too many small-print catalogues and badly typed lists of food substitutes in dim off-highway restaurants.

'I don't care for dogs,' Greg said. 'There is a common gene with the stupidity of the owners.' The road would remain snarled, around here, for a month or so. Folk drive out on Sunday afternoons to witness the red-leaf spectacle along the blacktop rim of the forest. We spotted deer. Geese have taken to the inaccessible ground between freeways, cropping grass until they are too fat to fly. Sad ponds choked with goose shit.

'What do you think about the occupation of Wall Street?'

Greg says that he turns over $650,000 a year for an $80,000 profit. Which makes it a tight operation. There was some insurance dividend from the Ten Pound Island shop after the tree smashed through the roof. But still it nagged at me, as a former dealer, wondering how he kept two places in play, and managed regular buying trips to London. The Gibsons had a house near Cork, bought at the peak of the Celtic Tiger boom, a better place for their daughter's schooling. 'In Ireland the kids don't all climb straight into cars,' Greg said.

One of the things Greg did, for the hundredth anniversary of

Olson's birth, was to assemble a catalogue of his publications. He put the books on show at the Sawyer Free Library in Gloucester. A number of gaps in the collection were filled by Peter Howard in Berkeley. There were items I coveted, of course, but prices started at around $500 and climbed into thousands. *Apollonius of Tyana*, set in print at Black Mountain College by Ed Dorn, and carrying a presentation inscription, was priced at $6,500. A little beyond my reach, fortunately. Greg reminded me that Olson's rent at Fort Square, when he could find it, was $28 a month.

The big payout came with the death of Greg's son. I read *Gone Boy: A Walkabout* when I got back to the Writers Center. Galen Gibson, an eighteen-year-old student at Simon's Rock College in Great Barrington, Massachusetts, was shot and killed at the library door by Wayne Lo, a disturbed youth who mail-ordered a semi-automatic weapon. Here was a brave book, clinical and remorseless. It was well received by the critics, but short of readers. *They couldn't bear for this thing to happen.* The story had all the hardboiled elements, including pace, drive, construction, but it was not fiction. There was no consolation to be found when the book was returned to the shelf. It offered an unvarnished register of a reality we might avoid by choosing not to open the first page.

The old life stopped for Greg at the split second of this event, and writing the book was one step towards whatever was coming next. What was required in the enveloping darkness, he felt, was a journey, a walkabout (a concept Greg admitted he barely understood). He developed a technique for 'revisiting those power spots that are part of your geography'. The terrible pain does not disappear, or take new forms, but very slowly, day after day, the world shifts to accommodate it. 'It's a comedy in the classical sense,' Greg said, 'in that it begins in disorder and moves to order.'

It was dark now and the traffic had eased. We were back on the road in the stream of red-gold light, heading home.

The Party

Then there was the other New England of witch trials, the abiding darkness of reflux Calvinism, legends of hunting parties making necessary sacrifices to the older gods. Out at the ragged edge of Gloucester was an area I would have to explore before I returned to London: Dogtown.

Greg Gibson delivered a gracious introduction to my talk on Olson at the Cape Ann Museum, making allusion to my role as 'co-commander' of the swan pedalo voyage through the backwaters of Kent. And then he stepped aside, ducked out, before other friends of the Writers Center, with a straggle of accidental attendees at the event, made their way to a redbrick bar called Alchemy.

After the formality of the lecture, a nervous interlude for sponsor and performer, the Gloucester art community found tables, or spots at the bar, and let out their belts a couple of notches as they settled to beer and pizzas. The overspill of emotion around the idea of Olson, in his absence, was touching. An elderly lady, limping slowly down the stairs towards the room where the talk was supposed to happen, not lifting her eyes to that painting of the bathers, was pleased to have it confirmed that, yes indeed, this was the right place and I was the person. She was a veteran of Black Mountain College, having come there, she didn't quite know how, in flight from Vienna. An artist, dancer, writer: as they all were.

There were hard-breathing enthusiasts of the poet John Wieners, across from Lowell, with newly published collections and magazines. *A Book of Prophecies*: Wieners writes about Olson and his own mother. He makes lists of poets he has met and celebrities observed or encountered on the streets of Boston. 'Jean Seberg in a blue coat on Stuart Street, Steve McQueen in hot pursuit.' Liberal academics from the same city made it to the dimly lit bar. A ponytailed man with a red notebook took the bus from New York City. The casual chatter, over the fizz of sports screens, the sliding and slopping of big jugs, warm pizza wheels, was a revival meeting for whatever Olson and Black Mountain once represented; a seance at which the tapping of shot glasses on circular tables spelled out legends of the departed poet, his incantatory letters, the songs made from the raw materials of a working community. The amiable drinkers of Alchemy were honouring a sempiternal Olson wake. Against pad-locked fish sheds and failing businesses. The Inner and the Outer Harbor.

'I was interested in the connection with Lovecraft. What was all that about?'

Lovecraft? Did I really throw him into the mix? The spiked youth in the Bolaño T-shirt was sucking water from a plastic bottle like a petrol thief. He was twitchy to get outside for a smoke. His choice of chest adornment? *Nazi Literature in the Americas*. A print made from the New Directions cover. The image, as the goth's protuberant belly rose and fell, was distinctly Lovecraftian: a grey man, his apparently naked back lurid with obscenely white vegetative matter, staggering head first towards a door that might be a shrouded mirror, or the portal to some unspeakable soul-shredding dimension of eldritch horror. He's not naked. It's worse than that. The spine is unhoused, breaking through the fleshy membrane in reptilian metamorphosis. And what appears to be the skin of this man's back *is not his own*. There is a visible cuff-line. The nightmare figure, like the blood-cupped emanation in Blake's *The Ghost of a Flea*, can't lift the weight of his burdened skull. Bone spurs are clearly visible, an external pigtail making an awkward ridge in the skin-shirt the stumbler has borrowed from some peeled and reluctant donor.

I remember that Bolaño, in his fictive directory of American fascist authors (from all the Americas, north and south), mentions the fact that the father of Rory Long (Pittsburgh, 1952–Laguna Beach, 2017) was 'a friend and disciple of Charles Olson'. I wondered quite how fictive that encyclopaedia actually was. If I said something to the goth about his T-shirt he was sure to reveal the fact that Bolaño had presented him with it at a science-fiction convention in Albuquerque, after assuring him that *Nazi Literature in the Americas* was reportage, a quick-fire literary gloss on evidence gathered over ten years by an indigent Mexican journalist against a share of future royalties.

Olson, according to Bolaño's briskly sketched account, visits the poet Marcus Long, father of Rory, at his house in Aserradero, near Phoenix. 'Hiding under the porch, Rory listened to them talking, while the Arizona dust settled into eternal fixity.' This was a moment of inspiration, a confirmation of destiny, comparable to Olson's own initiation, when he eavesdropped on the old men who were smoking, and facing the sunset sea, on their bench in Stage Fort Park.

Schooled in the theory of projective verse, the illusory freedom of open-field poetics, Rory comes to believe that it is his destiny to be 'a hunter (the poet) tracking down the memory of his tribe for the recipient and constituent of the memory (the reader).' He embarks on a whirlwind counter-clockwise tour through New Mexico, Arizona, Texas, Oklahoma, Kansas, Colorado, Utah, and back to his starting point, a desert hut. Disillusioned, husked to essence, he decides that the time has come to actually read *The Maximus Poems*. Afterwards, he vomits for three hours, before striking out to lose himself among the pensioned hippies, decommissioned whores, and cold-turkey poetry junkies of the 1970s (the ones who later become traders in used books). Rory contemplates suicide, but is sidetracked into authorship: a neurotic but ultimately successful blend of available genres in the form of speculative screenplays, aborted novels, top-heavy comic strips, pamphlets and polemics. He arrives, in tribute to the grandstanding eloquence of Olson, at the oral. Voice as form. Rory Long preaches, many hours at a stretch, channelling the hunger of his audience and playing it right back at them, for the Texan Church of the Last Days. Biography is a road map that only makes sense with the death of the subject, the writer.

In Bolaño's absurdist comedy there is just enough of a kernel of truth to hold it together. And to make us wonder if he has cracked the code. One of Olson's retreats was the ranch of Drummond and Diana Hadley in the mountains near Tucson. After an exhausting assault on the Californian poetry scene, 'his mobility limited to the insides of cars' (as Tom Clark has it), he headed for Arizona.

When the Gloucester giant first encountered Drummond Hadley in Vancouver, he was attracted to the aura of energy and confidence surrounding the westerner. Clark, drawing on the witness of Ed Dorn, and interviews with Hadley himself, reports that Olson demanded a private jet, or at least a helicopter, to carry him to the remote estate for an intended elopement with a young (and reluctant) woman he met at the conference. 'The best Drummond could do on such short notice was the promise of a pickup ride.' But it was during this brief Arizona stopover that Olson experienced, within his body and being, a vision of the heart of American reality: earth, not smoke. A purification of the gates of perception engineered in the spirit of Carlos Castaneda. Hadley drove the Gloucester poet, perched like a huge crow, on the storage rack of a four-wheel-drive International Travelall, south towards the border, Mexico. The Baboquivari Peak, away to the west, Clark tells us, was sacred to the Papago Indians. They knew it as the centre of the world. 'I come from the last walking period of man,' Olson said. He fingered three terms and laid them out like counters: *Mother, Earth, Alone.*

The invented poet, Rory Long, a fusion of many themes and geographies, his biography completed, all there is to be known of him, in six pages of Bolaño's translated prose, folds back into Europe. He composes a text around the lovemaking of the ancient Ernst Jünger and Leni Riefenstahl, up in the heavens, bone on bone, vampiric lusts never to be salved. 'Why are so many Nazis still alive?' he asks, remarking that Rudolf Hess, the last prisoner of Spandau, would have made it to a hundred if he hadn't committed suicide.

'And Lovecraft?' the goth said, returning me to the moment, the bar on Duncan Street.

'It wasn't anything special. He visited Gloucester in 1927 on one of his strange tours. It just popped into my head, mid-delivery, how

Olson in Gloucester, and Lovecraft in Providence, Rhode Island, were both walkers, doing most of their work at night, living about the same distance from Boston. Lovecraft has his nutty Cthulhu Mythos, stitched together from arcane researches, almost like a parody of the excesses of some of Olson's disciples. Myself included. And then, many years ago, when he was still a student – he's now an established performance artist, writer and Oxford academic – Brian Catling tried to get me interested in Lovecraft, while I was pushing him towards *Call me Ishmael* and *Human Universe*. It didn't really take, in either direction.'

The senior poet resident in Gloucester, a classmate of John Ashbery at Harvard and a friend of Olson, was Gerrit Lansing. Lansing had been there at the party with the clam chowder, crisp white bread, wine and talk, after my boat trip around the harbour. He stayed off the water. Now he was generous enough to host a gathering at his home for the crowd from the lecture, when they had done at the Alchemy bar.

The headlights of Henry Ferrini's car swept the driveway as we bumped over the kerb and up the slope towards the bright windows of the detached house. Most of the guests were gathered in the kitchen. The Lansing property was on the west side of town, a quiet avenue a little inland from the house where the Olson family boarded for those fondly remembered summer vacations.

After refilling my glass, our host, patron of the whole scene, led me away to the sofa in another, more private, room.

'Do you pronounce it May-chin or Mack-en?' he said. Not like the Rugby League malcontent of David Storey's *This Sporting Life*, as impersonated by Richard Harris, I told him. 'Oh, Mack-en, Mack-en,' he tasted, now satisfied.

Arthur Machen, fantasist of the Welsh borders, wanderer of the London byways, was a mutual enthusiasm, a safe topic over which to initiate a conversation between strangers. Many British poets, some of them friends of mine, had stayed in this house. 'Lee Harwood was here last year.'

Like Olson, Lansing was fascinated by Jung, and by the notion of poetry as magic. He had a photocopy of *Lud Heat*, a self-published oddity of mine from 1975, from the days when I was lucky enough to be paid to cut grass on the Isle of Dogs, to collect broken sherry bottles from the grounds of Hawksmoor churches. Books, Lansing implied, and I was happy to agree, do rather more than furnish a room.

A William Burroughs collector called Jed Birmingham, trawling through three boxes of little magazines, finds a 'worn out' copy of an anthology called *A Controversy of Poets*. Excited by a cigarette burn 'the size of a dime' on one of the yellowed pages, he convinces himself that this scar was inflicted by Charles Olson during an all-night, table-thumping monologue. He recalls, perhaps, the 'sad party' in Ferrini's hut, when Vincent, in company with Olson and Lansing, drank and debated their reception of the groundbreaking Don Allen book, *The New American Poetry*. Olson, writing to Allen, marvels at how 'the little man – Ferrini – held his broken heart in his throat'.

The clincher, for the connection of the cigarette burn to Olson, arrives when Birmingham discovers the ownership signature in his battered book: *Gerrit Lansing*. He looks again at Lansing's introduction to Olson's *Letters to the Gloucester Times*, published by Greg Gibson's Ten Pound Island Books. 'It was the eyes I noticed and was noticed by when I first came on the man sitting behind the table at 28 Fort Square.'

Gerard Malanga, who featured in Warhol's *Chelsea Girls*, *Vinyl* and *Kiss*, was the houseguest of Lansing when he conducted that interview for the *Paris Review*. Birmingham decides that Malanga borrowed Lansing's copy of the anthology, and brought it along to Fort Square, where an increasingly irritated Olson, whaling his Camels with rasping gulps, burnt a hole in the offending page. 'Never in my life in court or in secret,' the poet fumes, 'have I known such questions. I think you're an agent of a foreign power. Signor Malanga, I will expose you to your nation.'

Gerrit Lansing is establishment, old family, hospitable to our floating court of strangers. We talk, but in the shifting modes of the party, the demands on his attention, we are not going to advance beyond the niceties of the social. Lansing is one of those figures, affectionately referenced in all the memoirs, that never quite come into focus. A Henry James extra in a Hunter S. Thompson report. He's alert, youthful in style and sweater, but outside time: like a Marsden Hartley portrait, in an upstairs room at Cape Ann Museum, growing a little younger, a little smoother, with each passing year.

Jonathan Williams, publisher from Stuttgart, during his military service overseas, of *The Maximus Poems 1–10*, credits Lansing for the introduction to his long-term partner, Tom Meyer. 'We were talking, just the usual stuff. I said to Gerrit at one point, God, I said, I get really tired of these third-rate straight poets. Aren't there any good gay poets? And Gerrit happened to have met Tom and suggested I write to him.'

As a youth, Williams haunted the Argus Bookshop in New York; he started on poetry when he had finished with Lovecraft. Only when there was absolutely nothing else by Lovecraft to secure, not a contribution or a fugitive letter, did he broach Olson.

Richard Owens, writing about Williams, soon after he died, called him 'a living library'. The man had touched, handled, absorbed so much; making it his profession to seek out the reforgotten, the retired, the convalescent gods of heroic modernism. He photographed them in their lairs in New Mexico, Colorado, Brooklyn, or the Welsh borders: shocked, proud, exposed. But he was also a walker, covering 1,500 miles of the Appalachian Trail, and roaming over much of northern England, France and Spain, before returning to his base near the Quaker Meeting House at Brigflatts in Cumbria. The home he shared with Tom Meyer.

A covert American geometry was starting to reveal itself through the contrary figures of Charles Olson and H. P. Lovecraft: walks as fugues, a delight in magic (without initiation). Gerrit Lansing, remembered and referenced, infrequently photographed, was guide or witness or conduit. He hovered, a shifting fan of elegant self-superimpositions, where Olson remained a loud absence. 'I really miss having Charles around,' Jonathan Williams said. 'He doesn't go away. He stays with you.'

How deep into the practice of ritual magic did Lansing go? He was billed to give a private reading to the Knights Templar Order at their Thelemic Symposium. The promoters of this event glossed their distinguished guest as belonging to the tradition of Aleister Crowley, a poet capable of subjugating the whole universe to individual will. 'Everything that he perceives is in a certain sense a part of his being.' The alchemy is not the social transmutation of the Gloucester bar, pizza and beer into gossip and speculation, through the alembic of strong digestive juices and whisky chasers. Lansing is a seeker whose mission is to dissolve experience in order to 'climb the ladder of the visionary spinal chord to issue in the thousand-petalled sun'.

All of which brought us, after circling around Arthur Machen and Algernon Blackwood, to that other topic beloved of poets: money. Patronage. The funding of impossible projects. The situation for Olson in the early months of 1960, locked into his *Maximus* researches, put him beyond the reach of ordinary employment. He *was* employed. The nights were long. Wealthy art fanciers from the New York scene, collectors of fashionable poets, took houses for the summer in Gloucester. Olson paid his respects to Panna Grady, a young woman who was keeping much of the counterculture on both sides of the Atlantic afloat. She was sharing a property for the season with John Wieners, out on the fringe of the city, near Dogtown. Wieners was a Black Mountaineer, colleague and friend. He was the one who managed, with risk-taking address, a jazzy articulation of the state of coming apart at the seams, bursting the stitches: discontinued telegrams from cold-turkey hotel rooms in Boston or San Francisco.

The big shot at megabucks was John Hays Hammond, Jr, a retired eccentric who built himself a 'Medieval Castle' on the headland, a few miles down the coast, high above a wreckers' reef, in a protected enclave called Magnolia Shore. Hammond invented underwater guidance systems for the navy and was known as the 'Father of

Remote Control'. He used his fortune to have Finnish masons run up a Disneyland folly made from stones shipped over from the Gothic ruins of Europe. Olson described these vaults as manifest claustrophobia out of *The Masque of the Red Death*. There were ill-directed quotations from every occulted era known to architecture. Sixty-nine 'Aztec steps' led down to an inverted-pyramid crypt at the water's edge; a site prepared in advance, under his own supervision, for the inventor's tomb. When a potential patron starts drawing up grandiose funerary plans and calling his preposterous seaside villa a 'museum', it's time to look elsewhere.

Gerrit Lansing made the introductions. And Olson, using Ferrini as go-between, put forward an application for a bursary of $10,000 a year, for five years, to carry forward the necessary scaffolding of *The Maximus Poems*. This, in a better world, was a modest proposal. For Hammond, a man of means, capable of anticipating the requirement for a handheld electrical device to save humanity from the tedious labour of crossing the floor to the TV set to change channels, it was beggary. Olson gave readings in the castle, but he also found himself coerced into an Addams Family scenario, acting as outsize greeter at the gate, offering leaflets and canapés before some magical-cultural soirée. Vincent Price meets Vincent Ferrini.

After exploring Stage Fort Park, registering Olson's bench, the rock with the plaque boasting of the site where, in 1623, 'a company of fishermen and farmers from Dorchester, England, under the direction of Rev. John White, founded THE MASSACHUSETTS BAY COLONY', I struck off down the road in search of the Hammond Museum.

It was a warm day and the blacktop reflected the heat, the rising carriageway shimmered and wobbled. Managed woodland provided limited shade and screened the life, if any, within spectacular sea-facing properties. On high posts, as I closed on Magnolia Shore, were other white houses, small enough for squirrels, but immaculately crafted. The miniature retreats had shingled roofs and detailing as precise as an architect's model.

Arched windows of the expensively ruined part of Hammond Castle picked up dancing light from the sea below. The parking area was deserted and the museum closed. Two workmen pulled in to eat their lunch. Venturing a yard from a family car, a woman tried to make a tricky shot, through lush yellow-gold foliage. Her husband, wedged at the wheel, was nervous. He knew his Stephen King. He'd seen movies about weird places in the New England woods.

The plaque I photographed in Stage Fort Park drew Olson's thoughts across the Atlantic. 'I want to go to England very soon,' he said to Ferrini, 'to get the information to show how this city was in the mind of John White without his knowing what she was, as a place to go fishing from.' Which meant: Dorchester. Another museum. More research. Hardy country. Powys country. The reasons for the founding of a settlement were easy to understand on such a gilded October day. Half Moon Beach drew lovers and picnickers on to the mammal rocks. In tender groups that formed and re-formed, unconsciously recreating the painting of bathers I studied as preparation for my lecture.

After Olson's death, aged fifty-nine, on 10 January 1970, a manuscript was found in the Fort Square apartment. A fragment that was the whole.

> Now I begin to
> go – hear me I
> have sent you the
> message – I am
> gone

Dogtown

Navigating a route out of town, through Halloween decorations against neat weatherboard houses, in their greys and pinks and whites, brought back the uneasy impressions of my first walk: here was a new place on old ground. Little more than 400 years from Samuel de Champlain, in 1606, making landfall in what is now Gloucester Harbor, to draw up an accurate chart of the place he called 'Le Beauport', to the commercial venturing of the Dorchester Company, under the direction of Revd John White, in 1623: the founding of a colony. To the setting of an oxidized plaque into a rock on Stage Fort Park by the citizens of Gloucester in 1907.

The dark shades of colonization, the burnings, drownings, broken treaties with indigenous peoples, coloured my local expeditions. It took me a few days to be sure that I was *really* here and that I had caught up with the person freighted so recklessly over the Atlantic. Granite boulders were in evidence at the back of my roadside hut, behind the bar, shouldering through the glacial debris that overhung the convenience store. Human habitation could very easily be swept away. October was the season of storms.

On another beach, in Catalonia, his final port of exile, Roberto Bolaño watched a trio of Russian girls with cellphones. He took them for hookers. There was an old man, near death, a skull on a tight bronzed body – Bolaño wrote about him several times – whose departure, the voyeuristic author convinces himself, will unleash a tsunami to destroy the innocent resort with a giant wave. 'The earth would begin to shake and a massive earthquake would swallow up the whole town in a wave of dust.' Would this happen in Gloucester as a consequence of the death of Charles Olson?

CAPE ANN PARANORMAL SOCIETY: GOT GHOSTS? Candlelit pumpkin heads, American flags. Dancing skeletons. They are in

sympathy with the red-white-and-blue election notices. ELECT JOE
CIOLINI: ABILITY, VISION & EXPERIENCE. ELECT BOB WHYNOTT:
COUNCILLOR-AT-LARGE. A painting on the side of the pizza parlour
stays within the same register. An outsize child in dungarees presents
an old fisherman with a mastless craft, a version of the ship held by
the blue-robed Virgin, Our Lady of Good Voyage. Acid rains have
melted the fisherman's eyes, a spill of black treacle down his cheeks,
so that he is indeed Gloucester: vile jellies gouged out, the Gloucester of *Lear*.

I cleared the fixed settlement, through subdued trick-or-treat suburbs of devil-masked children on red bicycles. Dogtown was the far
side of the Babson Reservoir. I didn't know exactly where the house
Panna Grady rented for the summer season was to be found. It was
close to here, certainly, in Riverdale. Olson came often to see Wieners. He wrote of striking deep into the Dogtown woods, to refine
the art of getting creatively lost. Without panic.

Dogtown Common is such a solid metaphor. It enfolds the
unwary walker so suddenly; a step away from tarmac and contemporary Gloucester vanishes. There is ambiguity in the written
records of this place, it wants to be older than it is. Even the name
Dogtown is etymologically suspect: spurned, sour, clag-footed. A
huddle of the expelled and ill-favoured. Old women threatened by
pirates or witchfinders and protected by slavering hounds. An abandoned camp, on high ground, on the track between Rockport and
Gloucester, occupied by feral dogs or the spirits of dogs. A forest of
unexplained noises and whispers.

Dogtown, as a habitation for Christians, came into being in 1641.
It failed and failed better, faster, more visibly, than the rest. Cellar
holes beneath ruined houses, stones spilled over stones, became
natural forms among the boulders of the terminal glacial moraine.
Woodland, cut back by farmers, returned. The metaphor was the
reality, the lumber of fearful minds: swamps, bondage tangles,
whipped branches, botched sacrifices. The new town with the
new churches, clinging to the shoreline, needed the gravitas of the

granite mass behind it; an impossible thicket of interknitted paths opening on a hulk of split rock known as 'Whale's Jaw'. *Dogtown*. The very sound of the word was an onomatopoeic moan of undead animals calling to the moon.

There were sounds, gunshots. And signs of a work camp: a tractor, a trailer. One man encountered, early on, loped out from the interior: red cap, red tabard over grey waistcoat, mid-thigh boots, shotgun over left shoulder, hound on a leash.

Dogtown has been worked and worked hard, quarried. The town of Gloucester is made from the bones of the former settlement. In 1967 Briar Swamp was surveyed as a suitable site for a radar emplacement for the Sentinel anti-ballistic missile system. By the 1970s, exploiters and promoters had moved with the fashion: now they proposed a heritage village with windmill and attendant wind farm. As yet, mercifully, there are no legends by Lovecraft carved into glacial erratics, no Innsmouth theme-park caverns with rubber effigies of octopus gods and limited editions of *The Necronomicon*.

Dogtown is the physical manifestation of Lovecraft's adjectival overlay, ruts into rivulets, sheep into stones. The ancient rocks counter the sexual hysteria the Provincetown tourist experienced when he was pitched against the sea: the slippery, sucking, reeking, rotting mulch of fish docks. The wild women of the fishermen's bars. The sickly luminescence of marine decay, when suppurating clouds rub against a lurid sunset waterline.

'I have hated fish and feared the sea and everything connected with it since I was two years old,' Lovecraft said. In his tale 'The Shadow over Innsmouth', an ill-advised visitor, arriving on a clapped-out bus, is drawn towards the inherited traces that repel him most, a corrupted bloodline. Noticing 'dead stumps and crumbling foundation-walls', he remembers passages from his antiquarian researches. 'This was once a fertile and thickly-settled countryside.'

The trail known as 'Dogtown Road' leads to Granny Day Swamp. The temptation to follow obliterated Indian paths through meadows of juniper and thorn is hard to resist. Low rims of brick and rubble encircle unreadable pits, dwellings that seem as much unstarted as collapsed. The ground is soft. Recent plantings are spindly-thin, black strings of wood like beads of rain smearing ink sketches.

When you can no longer hear the rifle range, you don't hear anything, even your own footfall. The walk absorbs the walker. You must put aside any hope of navigation. The baffle of the trees, the electromagnetic pulse of the rocks, a rising vortex between claustrophobia and agoraphobia, makes for a clammy hour. Hour? Day. Time has no meaning here. It is not the ghosts, but the knowledge that *there are no ghosts.* Beyond yourself, the solitary hiker with the book in his pocket. The overreacher. Trespasser. Scribbler of lies.

To have a destination, I settled on the clearing where the handsome sailor James Merry fought a young bull, and was gored, tossed, trampled. Self-sacrificed to his own vanity. And drunkenness. An episode of great fascination for Charles Olson, who addresses it in the Dogtown poems of *Maximus*. 'The bios/of nature in this/park of eternal/events.'

Now, with trails branching off, left and right, I found myself in the place I needed to be. Green-white lichen on a stone beside the path. Letters cut, shallow declivities repainted in red: JAS. MERRY DIED SEPTEMBER 1892. The confirmation of the poem, first read so many years ago, so far away; as myth or fable, like the *Mabinogion*, now fact. I stood in the clearing with its alien grass, like hair or mattress stuffing, summoning the sound of the bull. Or the memory of young bullocks charging me on an Iron Age fort in Dorset, with no obvious way off the track; in spring, away from my pregnant wife, my daughter, trying to assemble the conflicted elements of another book, London. Turf blackened with traces of recent fire.

Olson brought visitors out to Dogtown. Ed Sanders, having driven from New York with Ken Weaver, drummer to the Fugs, made 'Maximus from Dogtown' into a song, a chant, a performance. 'The sea was born of the earth without sweet union of love Hesiod says.' What Olson wanted to demonstrate was the hinterland of his poem. Dogtown was where the great project cooked;

where pages could be drawn down from above and upwards from the earth.

When Olson came to Dogtown with Sanders, he was wrecked, afloat on bourbon and the leftovers of the Leary experiment in his medicine cupboard, a fistful of psilocybin 'peanuts' and a bottle of LSD. 'Twenty *million* micrograms,' Sanders said. 'Enough for Manhattan.' Olson creeps along in a battered station wagon, ferrying the boys to the Panna Grady house. Sanders (a classicist) envisions him as Poseidon. That greasy sailor's mane held in place with a rubber band. Ed is downloading, through involuntary chemical rushes, the Lovecraft nightmare of Gloucester's inhabitants as part-fish; mutating in front of his bulging red-rimmed eyes. Cold-blooded Puritan creatures with gills-in-the-throat. Ocean returnees, reverse evolutionists. The future recorder, through *The Family*, of the Charles Manson dune-buggy madness, wanders off into the serpentine trails of Dogtown; where he is found and rescued by the police in the early hours of the morning. He is wearing his stage outfit, an all-red suit.

The man who comes closest to my own experience of the rock-encrusted kame is the painter Marsden Hartley. Hartley, a seasonal visitor, not a Gloucester native, discovered what he needed in this abandoned landscape, the reservation of holes and stones. Tired, after years of restless travel – Berlin, Taos, Italy, Mexico – he arrived, one summer, expecting not much more than a few weeks of uncomplicated sunbathing on Niles Beach. Then he discovered Dogtown and started work, dividing his day between writing and painting.

Olson was struck by Hartley's hands; the worn-down ends of the fingers like those of a frostbitten Arctic voyager. He made comparisons with Jake, a native fisherman, nails gone, peeled from years in brine, the wounds of baiting hooks. The painter's fingers have that sense of being soaked too long. They are, as Olson chooses to interpret it (in the spirit of Wilhelm Reich), blunted from neurotic tension: 'refusing woman's flesh'. Away from the sunbathers' beach,

Hartley's obscene paws are fins or paint-smeared paddles. The town of Gloucester is a fractured cubist vision of 'immense houses', within which are concealed, as Lovecraft wrote, 'certain kinfolk whose personal aspect forbade public view'.

Hartley's sexuality, declared or undeclared, troubled Olson, who required a physical signature for what he read as a biological defect. The prejudice warped his critique of Hartley's Dogtown paintings. The painter would 'stay too long getting that rock in paint'. And presenting *Whale's Jaw* (1934), a 'bald jaw of stone', as a malignant soft thing, a skin puppet. Olson challenged the eros of Hartley's transformations, stone into cloth. And his processing of Hart Crane, a reckless poet (avatar of Wieners), into 'a Marseilles matelot'. The way to confront geology was head-on, in play; as Olson's father did it: putting himself between the hinges of split rock for a holiday photograph.

In the second movement of *Maximus*, Olson pulls back from harbour to Dogtown – which he associates, in its elevation, with Stage Fort Park. His dad, the mail-carrier, emerges from his tent, a bread-knife between his teeth, to threaten the man who is alleged to have made a mild pass at the laughing, round-faced Mrs Olson. He dies, Karl Joseph, of a heart attack following a second stroke. He was fifty-three. His oversize son, wrists poking from his sleeves, refused him, before Mr Olson set off for the last time, the loan of a suitcase with steamship labels.

Marsden Hartley paid a visit to Olson in Greenwich Village, New York, in the winter of 1940/41. There is a process whereby sons become their own fathers, become their own sons. They raise each other up, push each other aside, find new fathers, accept new disciples, new sons: challenging, loving, stalling in guilt and awkwardness. Olson's cold-water flat on Christopher Street was another cabin, sanctified by poverty, awash with papers and projects. Hartley, in his elegant sea-green suit, knocked at the door. And was served a cup of hot water. In the shock of it, the excitement, Olson failed to add the tea. He offered instead a poem on Hart Crane. Hartley read it and left, without comment.

Undecided 'between monastery and crematorium', Hartley took lodgings at 1 Eastern Point Road in Gloucester, where he made five Dogtown paintings. At the end of the summer he didn't return to New York, he took up residence in a white house with green blinds in Rocky Neck Avenue. The home of a postman. Dogtown was more than a metaphor. In *Rock Doxology* (1931), Hartley's pods of stone, under a thin strip of sky, 'deliver sermons of integrity' (as he wrote to the photographer Alfred Stieglitz). Olson's gods were older, more elemental: the scrape and scour of ice. Finding a passage out of the rock labyrinth offered him a glimpse at the vault of heaven. 'I have eaten my father/piece by piece.'

The summer visitors in the art colony at Rocky Neck did not interest Hartley. He conversed with city lawyers and the husbands of women who painted. He spent as much time as he could in solitude among the boulders and scrub. But there were others in the bohemian community, in and out of their swimming costumes, searching for deserted coves, risking new friendships, enjoying picnic parties and sketching sessions, in groups and arrangements echoing the painting that attracted me so much in Cape Ann Museum. The man in his trunks, heaving himself up on a rock, to confront the reclining girl. And the other woman, making up the erotic equation, off to the side; bare-legged in white wrap, hugging the stump of a tree. The only artists Hartley mentions in his letters are Ernest Thurn and his close companion, Helen Stein. 'She has the touch.' Stein made portraits of Hartley. While the three of them, going out together most evenings, looked for a movie.

After the Merry memorial and the hidden meadow, Dogtown became oppressive. I decided to divert through the woods in the direction of the Babson Reservoir and the railway. Tracks came and went; much of the way was blind instinct. Hartley had been disturbed in his private meditations out here by the noise of chisel on stone. Scandinavian masons employed by Roger Babson, founder of Babson College, landowner, politician, had been employed to cut uplifting slogans into the boulders: 'a final and permanent book'.

NEVER TRY NEVER WIN was the mocking codicil to James Merry's assault on the bull.

Above the reservoir, I found a flat ledge on which to take my lunch. Then I crossed the high-speed tracks, scrambled through bush and thorn, dodged traffic on Route 128, and returned to Gloucester by way of retail parks, hypermarkets and more suburban housing dressed for Halloween.

On my last morning before flying back to London, I booked a whale-watch cruise. I liked the idea of putting out to sea, even for a few miles, but the excursion was being made for my wife, who spoke so often of her desire to witness the transit of these mysterious creatures. It was late in the season. Rain set in before first light, wind rattled the roof tiles. The voyage was cancelled. I bought a blue T-shirt saying IN COD WE TRUST and made for the Sawyer Free Library. I had heard that some of Olson's own books had been lodged, after his death, on the open shelves. There were unrecorded annotations.

I started with *Paintings of D. H. Lawrence*, New York, 1964. Notes and prompts in Olson's hand – future poems? – sprayed across the endpapers. 'Monday evening – Dec 13, XLV.' The script was not easy to decode. But the librarian was prepared to make photocopies. A remark of Lawrence's was flagged up: 'Things happen, and we have no choice.' I came on a painting from 1928, *North Sea*. Two naked women, one man. It had been bought by Aldous Huxley and destroyed by fire in California, 'some years ago'. I did my best to transcribe the Olson poem. With so many cancellations and revisions, this was a harder task than the hours I spent with a magnifying glass reworking John Clare's *Journey Out of Essex* in the Northampton Public Library. 'New Wld bullshit,' I read. 'Universalism'.

The only way to properly experience Olson was to watch one of the extra features on Henry Ferrini's DVD. The poet, caught sweatily close, mammal head lolling and rocking, reads 'The Cow of Dogtown' from *Maximus Poems IV, V, VI*. I could have attempted this without leaving Hackney. But having absorbed a little of the weather of place, the poet's performance hit with new force. In his Fort Square apartment, up against a wall of maps and photographs, Olson is, absolutely, in flow of inspiration. The balletic precision in the waving and signalling of arms as he conducts this torrent of words, at varying pace, cigarette stub pinched flat between finger and thumb. I never witnessed such a thing, such naked delivery. The gathering together of geological particulars, and the processing of technical terms into the energy field of the poem, was what I wanted from Gloucester.

Nothing more than that, he taught us how to read. The gossip of slack biography is impertinence. The man lives in language. He knows just how to end a passage, arms flung wide, as he brings 'Maximus from Dogtown – II' into harbour. What is broken and fragmentary on the page coheres. A secret formula. 'Heart to be turned to Black/Stone/is the throne of Creation.' The other side of heaven, for Charles Olson, after Dogtown, is the ocean. I play Ferrini's film again. And again. And again. I love the way Olson says *carbon*.

Fire

In the movie one of the actors said 'we're being chased by a volcano'.

– Roberto Bolaño

There's No Home

I've never forgotten the day Alexander Baron, the once-celebrated author, returned to Hare Marsh, the home of his grandparents, and to his original identity as Alec Bernstein. Hands deep in pockets, feet fixed to the earth, as if set in concrete, Baron twisted his head to avoid the interrogation of the camera. The deep past of Whitechapel's tenter grounds, behind Brick Lane and Truman's Brewery, and alongside the corrugated-iron fence, the cropping ponies, the bridge over the railway, visibly tested the tough old soldier. In his white raincoat, landed with this abrupt challenge, to recall the gestation of those early novels, he resembled the Italian-born actor and former prizefighter Lino Ventura, who made a career playing serious men, on both sides of the law, in films by Jean-Pierre Melville and Jacques Becker. Baron, a Hackney boy, and in his younger days a committed Marxist, had something of the wounded commissar about him, a history lived and not regretted. He was still writing because that was what he did, but there was no expectation now of his books finding an audience. 'I don't know who the publishers are.' He split himself into the two brothers of his 1963 novel, *The Lowlife*. He enjoyed the respectability and silence of the North London Jewish suburbs and the remembered topography of a difficult past. Baron spoke, and his speech seemed to be pre-written like the text of a set-aside autobiography, about his return from the war. He came back to his parents' house to rest and recover. 'You've stirred up memories there,' he said, spectacles glinting.

It was hard now to imagine the scale of success of Baron's first book, *From the City, From the Plough*, published by Jonathan Cape. An account of war from the ranks. In paperback, Baron's gritty fiction ran through countless editions. 'It brought me a healthy income,' he said. 'I can't complain.' His second novel, *There's No Home*, dealt with the invasion of Sicily, the interval between battles, the bored military and the abandoned wives. Later he drifted into serial adaptations of heritage classics for television; bit by bit the novels thinned out and finally disappeared.

'The writer's job,' Baron said, 'is to be a spectator, to step back, to see more of the game. And to make sense of it.'

He laid out, very succinctly, my own statement of intent. One which I had lived with for more than forty years, but which I was now determined to subvert, by travelling to places where I would be a stranger, without language or backstory. Roberto Bolaño caught it in a sentence. 'For him *exile* was the secret word for *journey*.'

On the ridge of a park on the wrong side of the river, everything is skewed and ripe with novelty. The view, over the trees, across regiments of uniform houses, sets out a different London. The suburban villas at the crown of the hill are private, recessive. Nobody walks the morning streets.

Muriel Walker is waiting for me. I can't estimate her age, but she was involved with the radical Unity Theatre, in the 1940s. Which was where she met and became friendly, a comrade and a colleague, with Alec Bernstein. Muriel wrote me a letter.

*I recently bought the new edition of Alexander Baron's 'Lowlife', with
your introduction. I first met Alec Bernstein, as he then was, at the Unity
Theatre, soon after the war. Having read your introduction, I thought you
might be interested to see a copy of a letter Alec wrote to me in August
1949, when I had left to go to Italy, where I worked as production
secretary to the director William Dieterle on the film 'VULCANO', and
subsequently back to Rome with Anna Magnani as her private secretary.
Alec describes the work involved in writing a new novel. I hope this proves
of interest.*

As of course it did. The film *Vulcano*, about which I knew nothing, had a title that sat squarely with material I was gathering up for a new book. The accident of being held in San Francisco, in May 2011, by the eruption in Iceland, converted a bureaucratic nuisance into a gift, the smokescreen for a new adventure: the tracing of bad journeys aimed in the direction of smoking volcanoes in Mexico or the Aeolian Islands. I was inspired by films shot by Francis Alÿs, the Belgian artist, now living in Mexico City, who ran into the vortex of dust storms and whirlwinds, often at the expense of his recording equipment. The sound was like death talking.

At a certain point in the journey of any life, a home is curated; it becomes an occupied memorial to dispersed family and friends; a museum of loneliness decorated with photographs of dissolved beings, paintings keeping rectangles of sunlight away from fading wallpaper. Votive objects achieve status only through our long engagement with them.

Muriel is trim, alert, dark-haired. Her hands tremble slightly as she slides the evidence, the letters, magazines, theatre programmes, spectral photocopies, across the dining table in her front room. Again I have that sense of a scripted narrative that an actor – in this case Muriel Walker, shorthand wizard, lightning typist – delivers, by reading aloud from the autobiography of an intimate stranger. Before we come to the colour footage of Rome in 1949, the dust and sulphur of the volcanic island, and the young woman of twenty-two who hoped to stay away from London for six months, we must understand the founding fables of a life as it might have been contrived in an Alexander Baron novel.

Muriel Walker was born on Commercial Road to an immigrant Jewish family. Her grandparents wrote to the brothers and sisters left behind in Russia, sending prepaid postcards in hope of a return. Muriel has seen the letters. Her son, who lives in Paris, arranged for their translation by an old man who had been in the camps.

The phoney war is a vivid memory. Muriel watches while her cousin 'clatters away' at a sewing machine. She is transported by tram on a cruel diagonal across London, Hackney to West Norwood.

'The matron asked my mother to wait while I was taken up the central staircase. I was taken to a bathroom and made to bathe. There were two or three other new arrivals, but they spoke no English. I learnt subsequently that they were German Jewish refugees.'

The regime at the Jewish Orphanage in West Norwood is benign, the food nutritious. The cooks are Irish. The education efficient. Attendance at synagogue is not optional. With the outbreak of war in September 1939, the orphans decamp for the south coast. At fourteen Muriel wins a scholarship to Wandsworth Technical College, which has now relocated to Guildford. She acquires the secretarial skills that will carry her to the Unity Theatre and, later, to Rome.

Muriel said that she had no objection to my making a recording of our conversation.

When I was at the Unity Theatre, I got to know various people, and we became great friends. Warren Mitchell was part of our particular group. Lionel Bart, Bill Owen, Julian Glover, Alfie Bass. Beryl, who Alec refers to in his letter, came to Italy with me. We went off, just on spec, one February. We bought one-way tickets for £8. With no return date.

When we got to Rome, we found a bedsitter. Then I got an introduction to somebody who was doing pre-production work on a film called Quo Vadis. *It didn't actually get made. Another version did. Then somebody introduced me to a woman who ran a newspaper. She said, 'Would you be free to go down to Sicily tomorrow?' 'Sure.' I left Beryl in Rome. I travelled down with the assistant director and the writer Piero Tellini who had worked with Rossellini on* Rome, Open City. *We stayed, the three of us together, in Ravello. For about three weeks. Writing the script. We used to take the Italian version, which Piero wrote every day, drive down to Naples, and give it to Erskine Caldwell. He would do the English version.*

You know the history of Vulcano? *Rossellini went off with Ingrid Bergman to make a film on Stromboli. So, at very short notice, Anna Magnani got the company together: the director William Dieterle, Rossano Brazzi, Anna herself, and the American girl, Geraldine Brooks. Even with all those talents, the films failed. Both of them. When we finished filming, Anna asked me to go back to Rome and work with her, in her apartment. She just fancied the cachet of an English secretary. She wasn't filming at that stage. We'd go off in her car, everyone knew her. She was a great personality. People would stop and shout, 'Ciao, Anna. Ciao, Anna.' And she waved. It was good fun. At the end of the year, I'd met somebody. I decided, OK I've done it. I came back to London with an Italian husband.*

In some unexpected way, through Muriel Walker and Alexander Baron, who both belonged at various times to Jewish Hackney, those tributaries off the great north-flowing stream of Kingsland High Street and Stoke Newington Road, I was being nudged towards Sicily and the Aeolian Islands. 'A very strong smell of sulphur.' A smouldering volcano as the mouth of hell. Scandalous women in billowing skirts running barefoot over hot ashes. A sea as blue as murder.

Sicily was very much part of Baron's own bad journey to the end of the light, the experiences that left him, at the end of the war, wandering like a sleepwalker through the nocturnal streets of Hackney. Traumatic events in remote, sun-bleached places made him a writer, his politics tactfully subsumed in the crafting of those early triumphant fictions. I read Baron's London books first, because they revealed to me layers of social history, alive with wit and spunk; and the territory from which my own fictions were being dredged. Much later, as an older man, I went back to the beginning, to the Italian novel, the book of invasion, *There's No Home*.

'With the black wall of lava rising behind them in a menacing silhouette,' Baron wrote, 'the men looked up from the floor of an infinite cavern of sky into whose shadowed and mysterious depths the black shapes fell away beneath them.'

I wondered about the photograph of the young woman in the striped knee-length dress and the high sandals on the inside cover of the paperback reprint. Who was she? The model for the woman with whom the sergeant in the occupying army has an affair? Any potential autobiographical overlay is further emphasized by the photograph, inside the rear cover, of a bespectacled Alexander Baron, cigarette in mouth, cleaning his rifle.

Muriel couldn't confirm or deny the affair. Baron, many years later, said: 'The women of Sicily were to be the subject of my second novel. They were more natural and knowing than English women. The girls wore short print dresses faded by much washing. They walked clack-clack down the street on wooden sandals.' He recalled an incident when, during one of his solitary walks, he found himself 'squeezed on a bench among an audience of women who were all weeping loudly'. They had gathered, like starlings, in an open-air cinema, in a hidden square. They were watching William Wyler's version of *Wuthering Heights* and keening at the fate of Merle Oberon's Cathy Earnshaw. 'Ah, la poverina, la poverina!'

When the young Muriel was in Italy she received a letter from Baron, back in Hackney.

I wandered out to the letterbox at the end of a horrible day's work, feeling very tired, and behold! – there was a sunlit little picture of Rome staring up at me from the mat. After a first sensation of pleasure that bore a remarkable resemblance to a four thousand volt electric shock, I sat down and drifted off into a daydream about all the things that (in order to get on with my job) I had forced into the background of my mind; the white glare of the sunshine, the incredible shrill chatter and babble in the streets, the white villas on the hillsides and the cypresses guarding them like black spears, the trams swooping past with that screaming whine and as much clashing and clanging as a brigade of tanks.

Have the colours faded off those lovely picture-postcard visions? Is it just like London to you, only hotter and noisier? Do you get fed up with the people, their bewildering volatility, the shameless and quite childlike greediness and cowardice that so many of them readily display? Are you ever homesick?

You probably know more about what's going on at Unity than I do, for I only wander out of the house (in a daze!) once every couple of weeks and spend a half-hour or so in the theatre bar drinking those vile Coca-Colas and trying to find out what's going on there.

As for me, I have never worked so hard in all my life. I had hardly finished one novel and put it into the press when – while I was resting

*and wondering which part of the Continent to grace with my presence – I
went mad about yet another, and started on it. It will take me at least till
November, and as it is a very long, complex and delicately-woven story the
labour is quite heartbreaking. I write and write, round the clock, tear up,
revise, polish passages again and again, go to bed at one in the morning
and – after lying awake for an hour – return to the typewriter at two
o'clock and work till daylight. It is all quite insane. I haven't gone out,
even for the simplest form of relaxation or human company, for months,
and am in fact merely a sort of human (if human is the right word)
extension of my typewriter. I suppose the gruesome end of it will be that
the book will turn out to be no good.*

*I dream – though heaven knows what will happen! – of finishing this
latest before Christmas, then going out to Italy (Rome, Florence, Venice)
for the three worst (in England) months of the New Year.*

On the beaches of Sicily, Baron cleared mines under constant
enemy fire. *There's No Home* is a dreamlike lull, an interlude; infan-
trymen who are waiting for the next push form liaisons with the
deserted wives of Catania. White light scalds. He works through
the night, in Foulden Road, Stoke Newington, tapping his portable
typewriter like a man drumming on a hollow skull, driving it to talk.
At dawn, once again, he takes to the wet streets. Heading south,
without taking any conscious decision, towards the Whitechapel
labyrinth. Hare Marsh and the tenter grounds.

The table in the house that overlooks the park has been set out with
archival boxes and grey photographs held with paperclips. Muriel's
hands flutter as she shuffles the pages, searching for confirming evidence. 'At Norwood there was a girl I didn't know, she was there
sometime before me. Lily Sheil. She went on to become the muse
of F. Scott Fitzgerald. And a Hollywood gossip columnist. Sheilah
Graham. The orphanage was supported by the Rothschilds, people
like that. It was pulled down, twenty or thirty years ago. An empty
site. Now they are turning it into a leisure centre.'

Showgirl, Fleet Street freelance, syndicated columnist, Sheilah

Graham was an author by other means, siphoning (and supporting) the Fitzgerald of *The Last Tycoon*, the broken Hollywood drunk of *The Pat Hobby Stories*. At the West Norwood orphanage, Lily Sheil was head girl and captain of cricket. The children of her marriage to Trevor Westbrook, whose company manufactured Spitfire fighter planes, were fathered, so it was rumoured, by the philosopher A. J. Ayer and the actor Robert Taylor. In 1969 Graham revised the name of her column: *Hollywood Everywhere*.

The elements of autobiography that Muriel Walker presented, by way of the items in her collection, gathered in this drowsy Denmark Hill suburb, were as fascinating to me as those of her fellow Norwood orphan. She spoke of the crazy celebrity carousel of looking after Lionel Bart as he raced through drugs, booze and short-circuit inspiration, towards the latest musical disaster, whatever big show he was backing with all his previous smash-hit dividends.

'Before I went to work for Lionel, he introduced me to Larry Parnes. I worked for him for a number of years, taking care of all those boys: Tommy Steele, Marty Wilde, Billy Fury. They came into the office every day. I had to chase them up for everything, deal with their mums. It was quite fun.'

Coffee-bar rock and roll. Movie-star divas between assignments. Former party members morphing into generators of West End musical fiascos: honky-tonk Brecht, a Marxist interpretation of the Robin Hood legend written and rewritten until it was sure to lose every last penny of investment. Capitalism screwed by other means.

'And then *Twang!!* An unholy disaster,' Muriel said. 'Joan Littlewood, who was the first director, was very subversive. She'd turn everything upside down. Although it was a comedy, she took it very seriously indeed. We had Oliver Messel doing the sets. They came on with these beautiful costumes and velvet-lined trees and Joan would say, "Put them on back to front or inside out." Catastrophe!'

Muriel stuck with Bart, even after this. She found herself reconnecting with William Dieterle when Lionel screened Charles Laughton's *The Hunchback of Notre Dame*; before composing his own, never-produced *Quasimodo*. 'It was brilliant,' Muriel said. 'I've got the script here. Lionel didn't have time to read the book. So I condensed the whole of the Victor Hugo for him. Then I hired a projectionist and a projection room. It was only when I saw the credits that I realized it was Dieterle who directed it.'

There was another meeting with Joan Littlewood. 'She gave me the names of half a dozen people and said, "Could you come tomorrow morning, to the flat, at seven o'clock?" Seven in the morning! In November! Barbara Windsor, James Booth, a few other people. She had an apartment over in Maida Vale. I arrived in a taxi. Barbara was getting out of another. She said, "What's she want us for at this time in the morning?" We went upstairs. And it was Joan's birthday party! Cold grouse and champagne. Tom Driberg was there, for some unknown reason. Bizarre. Joan was very close to the Rothschilds.'

Muriel's generosity was alarming. She let me carry away the journal of the *Vulcano* shoot, the diary of her young life in Italy. And the photographs that went with it. Soon afterwards, Muriel, who was a prolific correspondent, a writer of proper letters (typed for clarity), added a postscript to our conversation. 'When we bought this house in 1966 we had been proceeding with the purchase when the agent told us it had gone off the market.' Another offer – one that couldn't be refused – had been put in. By a Richardson brother. The Richardsons, contemporaries of the Krays on the other side of the river, were scrap-metal dealers from Camberwell with interests in South Africa, mining, property. They were also enthusiastic torture buffs and amateur (*sans* anaesthetic) dentists. Denmark Hill was an area favoured by urban villains who wanted to rise, literally, above the Elephant and Castle and the Old Kent Road. The neighbouring hospital was another convenience. Freddie Mills, the club-owning boxer with Soho connections, lived around the corner.

Fortunately for Muriel, the Richardsons went down, long sentences handed out in a flurry of moral indignation from the same tabloid journalists who had bigged them up in the first place, while boozing at their expense in dives like the one operated by

Mills. Underworld faces inflate suburban property values in direct competition with bent Vice Squad detectives. The first era of gangster-businessmen as the patrons of fading TV stars and cabaret singers, sexual predators who liked to rub shoulders with boxers and gay politicians like Tom Driberg and Lord Boothby, drew to a close. Giving way to teenage scream shows compèred by middle-aged eccentrics hiding behind the shield of conspicuous charity. The toxic jukebox of Jimmy Savile, marathon man, hospital stalker, and marriage counsellor, by appointment, to Charles and Diana.

There was a final word of advice from Muriel about the diaries. 'You will have seen that the making of the film was a very laid-back affair. We were such a small unit, quite a family, first names all round. There was no hierarchy. I can't imagine any of it happening like that now. My engagement was casual to say the least, no applications, no interviews, CVs, references, no commitment to diversity.'

I marvelled at how a little, faded, olive-green book, packed with fresh-minted diary entries, could transport me, so immediately, to the Rome of 1949. I admired the photographs of the young Muriel on those unforgiving islands, sitting on hot stones, typewriter on her lap. Anna called her Ingrid. Because of her supposed resemblance to Magnani's deadly rival, Rossellini's new mistress: Ingrid Bergman. The Bergman of Hitchcock and of *Casablanca*.

Oscar

Certain figures, in transit between Buenos Aires, Bogotá, Havana, Mexico City, Rome, Athens, Johannesburg, fetch up on the fringes of Hampstead Heath: in Highgate, West Hampstead, even Kentish Town. And they stick, they nest. They like the cafés, the sad bookshops. The indifference of London suits them. Our nicely managed corruption. The potential for disappearance. In a city of exiles only wealth allows you to feel at home. Some of these stalled drifters, in the old days, were patronized by the multimillionaire Marxist publisher Giangiacomo Feltrinelli. There were letters of authentication for commissions that would never be fulfilled, or passed down the line to local ghostwriters willing to work for a pittance. I had, from time to time, been one of these. Paperbacks with unlikely covers surfaced in Milan and Paris, then vanished. Crime novels with a political agenda. A temporary sideline for risk-assessment technicians, on a retainer from some Swiss bank, working out of Istanbul or Seville. Occasionally police procedurals were picked up as the excuse for a quickie by Chabrol or Jean-Luc Godard.

Feltrinelli, who later blew himself to pieces in an incident alongside an electricity substation, published translations of Malcolm Lowry. He would make regular trips to see Castro, then on to Mexico City to visit an overnight marriage bureau with his latest mistress (in gold lamé toreador pants and Lolita sunglasses); before hitting the sharp end of the New York literary scene, where he gave a recklessly frank radio interview to Barney Rosset (of Grove Press and *Evergreen Review*), before meeting the respected publisher Roger Straus for drinks and dinner.

Like myself, so many years later, Feltrinelli chased the rank and elusive essence of Beat writing. He said that he was on the trail of Jack Kerouac. (He caught him and became the Milanese outlet for

The Subterraneans.) In a diary entry, Feltrinelli marked the day when he released a paperback edition of the writings of Ho Chi Minh. His partner, Inge, took herself to the cinema to view a subtitled version of Antonioni's *Blow-Up*. Feltrinelli reminded her to send fraternal greetings to the Berlin Congress, as coming from himself, Alberto Moravia and Monica Vitti.

The family villa at Gargano on Lake Garda was commandeered in October 1941 to serve as the private residence of Benito Mussolini, who detested the Italian lakes, calling them 'a hybrid of rivers and the sea'. When the fascist dictator left the villa, it really was the end: the Götterdämmerung for his Republic of Salò, the inspiration for Pasolini's supremely perverse final film, *Salò, or the 120 Days of Sodom*. (Pasolini was, of course, published by Feltrinelli. Charles Olson revered him as a poet, calling him the best thing to come out of the Spoleto Festival.)

The parties at Gargano, endless, enervated, featuring guest appearances by Saul Bellow, Robert Maxwell, James Baldwin, Tennessee Williams, Max Frisch, Ingeborg Bachmann, Cal and Veronica Shutter, were the inspiration for the dissolute and melancholy affair in Antonioni's Milanese masterpiece, *La notte*. The scene in the wealthy industrialist's house in which Monica Vitti is pretending to read Hermann Broch's *The Sleepwalkers* is a tribute to Feltrinelli's famed hospitality. (He was often out of town when the parties took place; contracts, page proofs, propaganda in his elegant black luggage.) Muriel Walker, as was inevitable, went to Lake Garda. She lent me a copy of Feltrinelli's astonishing diaries (which were no more astonishing than her own).

'I made friends, when I came back to London,' Muriel said, 'with Bianca Feltrinelli. And her sister Lily. Bianca was married to Giangiacomo Feltrinelli, who was the head of the publishing house. He was an aristocrat, a *marchese*, a Communist. A very good Communist. And eventually he blew himself up with his own bomb. I stayed with the family for a weekend at the villa.'

I switched, the two books laid out, side by side, between Feltrinelli's diaries, published in translation by Granta in 2001, and Muriel's private pasted-up typescript. Whenever, as a young woman, she qualified an Italian friend as belonging to the Communist Party, Muriel inked over the potentially damaging association. Feltrinelli had no such inhibitions; he catalogued, without embellishment, random trajectories across Europe, flights to Cuba, Mexico, East Berlin. The woman on the Brussels train. The policeman from Bolivia, hiding out in the 6th arrondissement of Paris, who is revealed as a 'pitiless' torturer. Feltrinelli deals in lost libraries, archives of revolution. He loves Citroën cars. 'The triangle can never be closed,' he wrote. 'Milan, Moscow, Amsterdam.' A breakfast meeting is arranged with the man he calls 'Jaguar': '28, glasses, moustache, tall and robust, thick as pigshit, with interests in lumber, the construction business, refrigerators, a Coca-Cola franchise'. A CIA contact gives him a photocopied MI6 dossier at an airport in Malta. A girl says that she has photographed Hemingway, Picasso, Gary Cooper, Anna Magnani. She looks like Audrey Hepburn with a big black eye, after a night on the town. She tells Bellow that he got it all wrong, in his story set at Feltrinelli's villa: the pool was covered with pine needles, not algae. Grisha von Rezzori turns up at a party with Anita Pallenberg. Gregory Corso arrives, unannounced, in Milan. The police have every second of Feltrinelli's trip to Bologna covered. Mounting a surveillance camera on the Asinelli Tower, they have a clean shot of the entrance to Montroni's bookshop.

The housekeeper, out of breath, calls Inge to the telephone: Mr Huffzky is reported dead in Berlin, three bullets. Thirteen sticks of dynamite were found at the base of the pylon. Feltrinelli's sand-coloured Volkswagen minibus had yellow drapes over the rear window.

Muriel's diary, when I examine it closely, is constructed from thin, typed sheets pasted over the original handwritten pages. Occasionally she misses a day, or a couple of days. She is caught up in the excitement of a new city; drinks with friends, theatre visits, dances, debates, flirtations.

Tuesday 7th April, 1949. Luchino Visconti, he explained, was something of a madman. He is apparently very eccentric, with flaming tempers one minute, and best of friends the next. He is a very wealthy man, and Felice says it doesn't matter to him whether he has a financial return, as long as he can indulge in his art. We very much want to meet him, and will endeavour to do so.

When she arrives in Sicily, Muriel receives another letter from Alexander Baron. There are a number of contacts in left-wing and journalistic circles. 'After I left you,' Baron writes, 'I remembered who Robert Lowry is. He's a novelist, and Jonathan Cape published one of his books, *Under the Volcano*, last year. So now you can look intelligent when you see him.'

And even get his name right: Malcolm. Their paths do not cross, but Muriel makes it her business to read *Under the Volcano*. She is young, attractive, in demand. Working. Rising early. Waiting for letters. Years later, towards the end of his journey, Lowry comes there too: Vulcano. An Aeolian stopover on the way to the English Lake District. Paying his respects to another dormant volcano. A rock that stands in for the tempestuous Anna Magnani. Her wild Medea hair, her heaving bosom. A great cinema poster. *Mamma Roma.*

The rings on the table in the café overlooking Waterlow Park are like imprints of the Olympic manacles. They'd better get the Dettol Surface Cleanser out, fast, before the branding police get to hear of this. The rings map the position of Oscar's coffee mug over the last few months. Sprays have not been applied. This is Highgate. The politics are laissez-faire, green tinged. Oscar X is not, like Alexander Baron, an internal exile, out of key with the system, but a respected editor and artist who functions within an established alternative, socialism. Oscar flies across oceans, uncomfortably, between crises, professional and personal – and otherwise sticks to his chair, as if it had been built around him. None of the other Highgate regulars, who cluster close to the counter, would dream of encroaching on his territory. They all look as if they are trying to get up the courage to face the Whittington Hospital. Woodpeckers grind like hand-cranked drills performing prefrontal lobotomies. Smog-coloured squirrels chase their unnecessary tails.

'And you are going *where*?'

'America,' I said. 'Gloucester, Massachusetts.'

'You do not say this, *America*. United States, ahh! America is a continent. You are not flying to America. I should make you swim. Santiago is America, Cancún, the Aleutian Islands.'

Oscar grooms his beard as a mime of contemplation. He translates his monologue, in advance, out of Spanish, so that the minor time delay allows the hanging clauses to hover between gravitas and humour. He loves London, it is evident. A good city in which to take meetings. He has summoned me to the old place, where, in the past, I put on time between dental appointments and raids on a basement of used books. Oscar is more of a facilitator, a cut-out man, than a commissar. After letting it lie dormant for a dozen years, he has re-jacketed a book of comic strips called *It's Darker in London*. He wants me to provide a little padding, firewalls of text between tightly scripted storylines for unmade films. Oscar has rounded up a strategic mix of retired comedians, unemployed TV directors, female slasher novelists, names generous with their favours (Alan Moore, Neil Gaiman, Dave McKean), and disgruntled artists eager to break free of success, the dismal ghetto of paid commissions. The Evil Empire of multimillion-dollar CGI movies and spin-off toys.

What strikes me, as I watch Oscar replace his brown mug, precisely, in last Friday's ring, is how prophetic the comic strips now look. London *is* darker, while the public faces of politicians and boosters are ever pinker and brighter; the meat more tightly packed, injected with collagens and vitamin boosts. Jack Kennedy the model: sunlamp sickness, smooth bloat as a newscast of moneyed health. Pleasure-beach cancers. Spinal injections, steel corsets. Perfect smiles. Everything exposed and enquired: nothing done.

Combing stray hairs from his mouth, Oscar is as gloomy as a wet owl. He is talking about a day trip to Barcelona, some Mexican anarchists he met in a bar. I ask him if he ever came across Roberto Bolaño.

'That last page of yours. I can't, can't . . .' He shrugs, he shakes his dark feathers. Hesitation implies sincerity.

I check my strip. Nothing makes more sense. Thefts from Burroughs. 'Paranoia is knowing more than you can use. Intelligent machines make prophetic guesses from our mistakes. All stories end in death.'

Nothing surprised Oscar like the posthumous fame of Bolaño. He met him several times in Barcelona. And failed to commission a comic strip, a genre adventure, which the Chilean author would have been happy to provide. Money was tight. Roberto hung around the bars, unwashed, gone in the teeth. He devoured graphic novels and science fiction. Or that was the impression Oscar formed, a mirror of his own interests.

'This man was so . . . *dirty*.'

I pressed for specifics. I fetched Oscar another coffee. He told me to read a Flemish author he had just discovered, Georges Rodenbach. *Bruges-La-Morte*. 'The saddest story. It is how he writes the city into being: the walls, the water in the canal, they talk to you. Bolaño? He bummed a cigarette, kept the packet. A drinker. We were a loose group, friends, acquaintances. On the move. Barcelona, Las Ramblas. Before the Games. Around Bolaño it always seemed to be raining.'

Now there is regret. Those extraordinary books, folding one into another. Oscar gave me his contacts, people who knew the dead author. Email addresses. I decided to postpone America, all of it, and to book a flight. In past times, as a student and a documentary film-maker, I drove, camped, or came south by train and bus. There was a decent interval in which to get used to the idea of travel.

Marcelo Cohen lived in Barcelona for decades, before he returned to Buenos Aires. Oscar said that he was 'the first person to write a review of one of those early Bolaño novels'. The two men never met, but Bolaño made a number of 'strange and funny' telephone calls in response to this positive notice. Marcelo could tell me all about them, if I could wangle a ticket to Argentina. Couldn't I find a suitable film festival or a new author to sell to the broadsheets? Oscar lived with a European sense of the status and commercial potential of writers. I'd been invited, once, to walk across Mexico City, side to side, to patch together a lively account for a travel supplement. I accepted immediately. The commission was withdrawn. Anyone crazy enough to take that one on, without discussing a fee, or the need for an armed minder, was too crazy for a sensible English readership.

After a long weekend poking around stadiums on hills, drinking coffee with friends of Bolaño, watching other tourists and subdued premarital celebrants in drooping reindeer horns, I took the train, off-peak, to Blanes. Everything I had in my notebook was contradictory. A poet. And a compulsive quoter of poets. A night person. And a family man. A mature geek collecting PlayStation war games on credit. A discriminating and an indiscriminating reader. A fastidious book thief, silent among exiles in red Formica fast-food joints. A phone pest whose calls were always welcome. A private man who made speeches to large crowds. A carsick passenger crossing Spain to judge literary competitions. Bolaño had glasses, dark glasses, no glasses. Bad teeth, no teeth, fixed teeth. He looked good in a crumpled black T-shirt, in a weak-eyed, unshaven, cigarette-suckling way. Like a minor cop in a French movie, doing bad things to Algerians, then reading Louis Aragon, over brandy, in hidden bars.

From the train window, white buildings and unfarmed farmland gave way to industry, retail-park outskirts (like Taunton, like Liège), seafront hotels and apartment blocks. I could have stayed at home and run this fruitless expedition on Google Earth. As long as you don't leave the road, it's all there. There are barriers on the station, indifferently policed. Returning students, beach sleepers and economic migrants stream through a large gap in the mesh fence.

The Paseo Marítimo is exactly as Bolaño describes it, a place to saunter, watch, kill time. It's early evening, the waiters in black trousers and white shirts are changing shift. Some of them stop to play football. One crosses the road to a beach bar where he meets a Nordic woman, bronzed and draped, if such a thing is possible, with ropes of discreet bling. Gold on gold: lizard neck offset by investment glitter. A trophy wife approaching her trade-in date. I can take photographs of the ten addresses I'm given for the apartment of Bolaño's widow, the seven statues in anonymous squares that mark the supposed studio where he worked, so feverishly, in the final years. I can walk through elements of *Antwerp* and *The Third Reich*. But I can't find the beach barricade, the off-duty pedalos. Blanes, I recognize, is a good place in which to write. It has something of the spirit of our English Hastings: discounted, mythologized, less than itself.

The following day, in the pinewoods, close to the campsite where Bolaño operated as a security guard, an off-season caretaker, I accept the futility of my expedition. Did I expect to find the hunchback from *Antwerp*? Or that mysterious foreigner? 'The English writer talks to the hunchback in the woods.' But there is no hunchback. There are a few Englishmen, in tight shorts, on the cycle trail. But the voices are German, Russian, cross-border French.

Under a blue-striped awning in a breeze-block bar, where sand gets in everything, I zoom in on my prime suspect, the only man in a black jacket. He is scribbling. He has a pile of cards arranged beside his cigarettes and the cheap plastic lighter, his beer. It feels as if a single, lengthy letter is being composed, at speed, on a number of picture postcards. 'He writes postcards because breathing prevents him from writing the poems he'd like to write.' Bolaño's invented English hack struggles to keep his tenses consistent. I sympathize. I jumped, after my second cup of perfectly bitter coffee, to the melancholy owl, Oscar X, in Highgate, his boneless back to the rain and the green park.

What if I were the rapidly sketched Englishman who talks to the hunchback in the woods? What if – and this is the biggest fiction of them all – *Bolaño was not actually dead*. That made sense. The books kept rolling out: *Between Parentheses*, *The Secret of Evil*, *Woes of the True Policeman*. The posthumous bibliography would put an

Ackroyd or a Moorcock to shame; two, three, four titles a year. The horrible illness and reported end had been so bravely organized around huge works, to be divided into serial segments for the benefit of his family. Extinction would affirm the legend and underwrite claims of wayward genius, by laying down a large black period. Susan Sontag. Patti Smith. Colm Tóibín (who knew Spain). They lined up to pay their respects. To eulogize the oeuvre. In this beachside shack, it didn't fit. The Patricia Highsmith version was more convincing. The Chilean author, who is working the market like a disciple of Ripley, disappears. Perhaps he stayed where he was in Blanes, like Flann O'Brien's James Joyce in Dalkey. I don't think he went back to managing a bar. He liked movement: Mexico City, Paris, Barcelona, Blanes. Why not Vulcano? He often spoke about eruptions.

One postcard was left on the floor, under the table, when the man in black walked out. I picked it up. It was a quote from Georges Perec, *Species of Spaces and Other Pieces*. 'Rule 36: Get drunk with Malcolm Lowry.'

Vulcano

The film of our swan pedalo voyage, from Hastings to Hackney and the Olympic site, opened at the Curzon Soho to the usual mob of well-wishers and peer-group friends hoping for the worst. And meanwhile slopping down overpriced drinks. Kissing and shouting and waving. But the Homeric voyage, mesmerizingly slow and absurdist, came at the right moment, playing against the noise of grand events, and coinciding with the summer's super-hyped blockbuster, *The Dark Knight Rises*. The *Financial Times* led with *Swandown*. A headline, jumped on by the PR people, said: GIANT SWAN ATTACKS GIANT BAT – AND WINS!

English pastoral unravelled as riverbank dwellers crept from the woods to show off their tattoos. The refuseniks of the urban fringe, hiding out on a ghost fleet at the mouth of the Medway, welcomed us aboard their rusting hulks, to gesture at onboard swimming pools, refurbished bars, snooker tables and giant plasma-screen TV sets driven by generators.

Trying to make my way to daylight from the warm dark of the cinema basement, I was caught up in a series of those exchanges where random faces with no names attached move in to reignite aborted conversations from previous gatherings in Bristol, Middlesbrough, Milton Keynes. One woman, advancing with intent on a sure-footed diagonal, had, in her own stylishly bohemian fashion, the eye. Black leather jacket, dark hair and a bright, challenging look. She began to talk about an English painter in Rome. It threw me. I didn't expect to see her on the north side of the river: Muriel Walker of Denmark Hill. In her eighties, brisk enough, interested enough, to be turning out, with all the verve and momentum I found in her diaries, Muriel was prepared to view another film, another doomed project.

Up and out by 8.30 and off to Fregene for the day. Spent a very pleasant morning on the beach. It seemed that everybody in the film industry was here. Rossano Brazzi and his wife, Orson Welles.

September 1949.

And now, still worrying at the past, still trying to get the faces fixed, the story straight, Muriel has bought a ticket to the Curzon. July 2012. Shaftesbury Avenue.

Off to eat in pizzeria, then to station. Transported Joyce back home and we sat chattering till 2.00 a.m.

The entry in the diary that she wanted to check was for 27 August 1949.

Projection all morning. Saw all the underwater stuff that had just arrived. On my way back was stopped by a car – a boy I used to work with (an artist), name of Lucian, and his friend, Flavio, film architect. So spent a pleasant evening. Drove to the quarter Savoia. Stopped at a little open-air café for a while, then drove to Pincio and various other points in Rome. Back home about midnight.

Could this have been Lucian Freud? Unlikely. Muriel remembered the Italian adventure as a flight, an escape from greyness and ration cards. Her friend Beryl had lost her job with the Civil Service. They had no money, few contacts. They were so young. Now it was a question of cataloguing the archive, pencilling in the surnames. Shaping the story.

To come at Muriel's journal from another direction, and to acclimatize myself through geographic immersion in available DVDs, I started with that classic bad journey (for all concerned), Antonioni's *Il grido*. Here was a bleak romance fitted to a muddy track between highway and swollen river. The original script, pared down but as complex as a philosophical novel, a displaced *nouveau roman*, was undone by weather, the icy mists of winter in the Po Valley.

Steve Cochran, a black-Irish Hollywood B-feature import, sump-oil hair flat-handed into place, trudges the wilderness of the world, tugging his pigtailed and fabulously self-contained daughter, Rosina. (Early models, I thought, for my *Swandown* colleague Andrew Kötting and his round-Britain *Gallivant* companion, the bird-voiced Eden. Cochran's trousers, like those of Kötting after a month in and out of the river, are stiff with discriminations of mud and splash.) It is Cochran's jacket, collar turned up, that carries the burden of narrative, a peculiar untailored morality. The camera shifts, without hesitation, between road and river. The drama is road-bound: if anything happens elsewhere, beyond hoardings, refineries, petrol stations, it doesn't signify. *It doesn't really happen.* What we see is what there is: Cochran. Who is not large, but solid in the shoulder. Rescued from westerns and black-hosed studio streets, brassy blondes and fake whisky. Searching for cigarettes in musty drawers. He doesn't relish, any more than Richard Harris in *Il deserto rosso*, being directed as an attribute of architecture, a moving object in the landscape. He wants words, justification. Post-Freudian permission to frown or ball a fist in his jacket pocket. He strikes disobedient women. He fucks in ditches. He broods in empty bars. He walks to the open door of a hall in which two silent boxers are clubbing each other before a howling audience. Then, after rousing his sleeping daughter, he marches away into the night, beyond electricity.

Antonioni later charged Cochran with stupidity. The American detested his director, having European ambitions of his own, beyond the range of studio-tolerated psychological realism. Hollywood's recipe for action was based on gestures as formalized as kabuki. The stupidity denounced by the Italian aesthete was the stupidity of difference, disobedience, an infantile need to have every twitch explained and approved. 'Slap her.' Mist thickened into sleet. Steve tramped alongside a plantation of dwarf willows, a line of Lombardy poplars. The production stills were breathtaking. It is not Cochran's voice coming out of his tight mouth. Women smell smoke and sediment in his wet tweed. They smell California, Cadillacs. The trigger reek of a dumb male in transit.

'Cochran came to Italy expecting a job as a director, which was absurd,' Antonioni said. But that is what he achieved. Sullen, bottled up, hurting, betrayed, dragging his daughter by the hand down a bad road, Cochran directs himself. Against instruction. While standing where he is supposed to stand, refusing food, refusing attachment.

Muriel Walker came to Italy with few expectations, and it was all there, waiting for her: companionship, employment, love. A significant footnote in the history of cinema.

Muriel is in Rome. It is not, for her, the city of monuments. Nor a newsreel city of ruins: Rossellini's *Roma, città aperta*, featuring his mistress, spirit of place, Anna Magnani. There are orphans, plenty of them, orphans of war; but they are not the boarding-school Jewish girls of West Norwood. Solemn black crocodiles of pinched starvelings, shepherded by nuns, chant their status as abandoned waifs, as they process to church. The same ones who made such an impression on my child self, a couple of years later, in Rapallo. I didn't know then, or for years to come, that Rapallo was the resort of Ezra Pound, who made wartime broadcasts comparing Mussolini with Thomas Jefferson. Rapallo is where Pound, and his helper Basil Bunting, along with Yeats and Eliot, contributed to a detective novel being written by the modernist composer George Antheil, under the pseudonym Stacey Bishop. The book was published, in a striking pictorial jacket, by Eliot's firm, Faber, in 1930. I heard the tale from the legendary collector Alan Clodd, who then of course produced a pristine copy for my inspection. *Death in the Dark*. Mystery novels conceal collateral mysteries, darkness within the dark. Diaries are smokescreens.

Muriel falls into the nocturnal life, late meals, cinemas, groups of friends, secretarial gigs there for the taking.

When we had finished our meal we left Bob and Eileen at a cinema, as they wanted to see an Italian film. The three of us were to meet

Felice at the stage door at midnight. It was the premiere of Oreste, and when we arrived we found the courtyard filled with every type of luxurious car. Anna Magnani passed us and went into the restaurant next door to the theatre. I was completely disillusioned, having seen her and acclaimed her in such films as Open City, and now to see her emerging from a luxurious car, draped in rich furs, looking very unlike the Anna Magnani of the screen.

A city of pizzerias, boys, writers pitching scripts. There is always someone whistling at the window.

Thursday 26th May, 1949. Today marks the passing of an epoch; my life undergoes a violent change, and I am forced physically out of my present mode of living. At about 11.30, a phone call from Dorothy Bigliani. She calmly asked whether I would like to pack up and go to some island near Sicily tomorrow as secretary to the company who are making a film there with Anna Magnani. I had to give her the answer in about 10 minutes. I wasn't meeting Felice for another hour. I don't know what the deciding factor was – perhaps intuition – but I agreed to go. Since Beryl and I were down to our last 100 lire I decided there and then that I must take whatever comes along. The film is being directed by Hollywood's William Dieterle.

I met Felice for lunch and told him the news. We were both upset to think that we would be separated for that time, but as I said it was not for long. And more important, when I returned, we would have enough money for an apartment.

I went off to the Bernini. I met the girl whose place I was taking. She had just returned from the island, and she gave me a briefing on what to expect. Apparently we are shooting on the island of Vulcano in the Aeolian Islands. The film stars Anna Magnani and a Holly-wood actress, Geraldine Brooks.

When we arrive in Vulcano, we all stay in one big villa together – artists, directors, executives – with everything provided for; I don't have to spend as much as a lire, and on top of that, to have a salary of 35,000 per week (= £17.10.0d). Victor Stoloff came in during the afternoon with Piero Tellini, who is writing the script. (He wrote Open City, Four Steps in the Clouds.*) I started to work and took over immediately from the other girl.*

Magnani is the mistress of Roberto Rossellini. Ingrid Bergman, fresh from her triumphant studio performance against Cary Grant and Claude Rains in Hitchcock's *Notorious*, and the Freudian shallows with Gregory Peck (the future Ahab) in *Spellbound*, is first spellbound and then notorious, a tabloid witch from the frozen north. In Hollywood she catches up with neo-realism, street shot, snatched from history, subtitled: *Roma, città aperta*. The only flaw in Rossellini's docu-fiction is the wrong diva, Bergman wants to offer up her art to this new master. The film is *magnifico* but is it a fake? A screening of *Paisà* in New York, with the director present, convinces her. Enough of America. The final movement of *Paisà* is set in Antonioni's Po Valley. With cloudless Los Angeles under the eclipse of McCarthy's Communist purges, emotionally immature, infantilized – as Bergman sees it – a mature European director and a return to the older civilization is a requirement.

Roberto leaves Magnani in bed, replete and breakfasting, in the room they share at the Hotel Savoy in Rome. He goes out to walk her dogs and he doesn't come back. The dogs are with the concierge. Rossellini has taken a taxi to the airport. He flies to New York. He has a script stolen from his cousin Renzo Avanza and four Sicilian friends. They are developing new techniques for underwater filming. Roberto has viewed the rushes. Stromboli is a safe distance from Anna.

On glistening, wet-black celluloid, newsreel immortals descend from a heavy-bellied aircraft to mortal ground, fresh from another noisy propeller-driven interlude across oceans and continents. Cameras flash. A cicada-frenzy of shutters. Bergman tosses back girlish (serious) hair, smiles, and wrestles the big cellophane cone of sweating roses into submission, before passing them to a helper (another Muriel). Roberto in beret and dark glasses, open white shirt, is a magician. He's more formal, on show. Welcome. *Benvenuto*. These are the rites of passages we are allowed to witness. After public rituals, indoor privacy; crowded solitude, pills, quacks, breakdown. The business, stepping down from the plane, is a form of theatre as formalized as a tomb scene painted by Poussin.

Bergman secures Rossellini, who is denounced by the Church. He decides to make *Stromboli* into an act of heretical piety. Fallen woman, martyr. Miracles of nature: deep seas, burning shores, volcanoes. Metaphors running wild. Northern sophisticates reinvade barren rocks.

Young, free-spirited Muriel Walker from the Jewish Orphanage in West Norwood is an accidental witness. The Magnani she spurns, for her furs and black motors, is now her champion, her employer. William Dieterle, the imported Hollywood-German director, in his white gloves, calls Anna 'the last of the great shameless emotionalists'. She's a proper size, an Italian woman; she smoulders. She kisses her dogs. Magnani played an overbearing stage mother in Visconti's *Bellissima*. Her flashy attendance at the premiere of his play paid dividends. Visconti, the Marxist aristocrat, had been the first to come south, in 1948, to Aci Trezza in Sicily, for *La terra trema*. No performers required, native fishermen only, speaking in dialect. Magnani determines to have her revenge on Bergman. The dignity of the human face, the cubist geometry of block houses in a barren landscape.

And here is the spoiler: Magnani and Dieterle on Vulcano, a neighbouring Aeolian island, making a version of the Rossellini story at the same time. Dieterle combines Hollywood industrial process (elaborate tracking shots) with the standard neo-realist grammar of non-professional actors, undressed locations and agitprop morality. A form that, in the hands of Visconti, could be dignified, awkward and heroic, becomes, in *Stromboli*, a slightly deranged love letter combining all these elements with sexualized pietistic masochism. And a growling, grumbling volcano.

Muriel drives south to Naples with the scriptwriter Piero Tellini. I think about another film Bergman made with Rossellini; a failing

relationship, the road to Naples. The calcified bodies of lovers exca-
vated from volcanic ash. *Viaggio in Italia*. The Rossellini masterpiece
beloved of the *Cahiers du Cinéma* critics Godard and Truffaut.
Another bad journey with great scenery. The car breaks down.
They sit at the roadside, in the shade, while Tellini dictates and
Muriel transcribes in her rapid shorthand.

*At 2 p.m. the car was still not fixed, so we stopped at a little open-air
trattoria and had lunch. I brought the typewriter on to the table, and
continued working till four.*

What I like about Muriel's diary is the lack of artifice. After a few
days, there is no mention of Felice back in Rome. And Tellini, with
nothing much said, emerges as a volatile presence. When he quits
the shoot, Muriel waits hungrily for the boat bringing letters.

*Piero is separated from his wife. We found a restaurant high up above
the sea in the mountains overlooking Naples, with all the lights in the
bay twinkling, and Vesuvius in the background. We had a man with
a mandolin playing and another man singing Neapolitan songs.
They came to our table, and Piero asked them to play two songs
which I had never heard, but I could have cried.*

After such romance, Vulcano is the end of the world: paradise to
inferno.

*We took the little motor boat, and set off to Vulcano; we left Lipari
behind us, with its grey, gruesome, fortress-like prison, right on the
cliff edge.*

*We arrived at Vulcano. My immediate reaction was to run off
home. The only deterrent was the fact that I couldn't swim. There
was nothing to be seen – just nothing except for the rocks of the volcano and at the top smoke pouring out from the crater. In fact, during
this passing of the island in our boat, I had the strangest sensation: I
was here in the middle of the blue, very deep blue Mediterranean,*

very calm, under a clear sky and very hot sun, on a little ship, that had the gramophone playing modern songs.

We disembarked. There seems to be no habitation. Just one or two tiny hut-like constructions, some with straw roofs. There are the rocks, many-coloured, from deep red to green. There is sulphur over everything, sending a strong smell in the heat of the sun. There are cactus plants and a yellow plant, ginestra, that gives an overpowering sweet perfume. Our little hut is on its own in the middle of this

wilderness, with a strange little straw affair for sanitation; the pigs,
goats and chickens run freely about the place. We have no running
water, and have bowls of water brought from the well. We eat all
together, the whole unit, in a tent. There is the sea, unbelievably blue.
And above all, the crater, smoking day and night.

Photographs from that time, from Muriel's carefully preserved
Denmark Hill archive, confirm and refine these impressions. In her
summer dress, with her dark hair, sitting on the rocky ground, typewriter on her lap, Muriel could be cast as Magnani's younger sister,
or the character played by Geraldine Brooks in the film. Geraldine
and Muriel become good friends. Anna starts to call Muriel 'Ingrid'.
She says that the English production secretary has the look of Bergman. Employing this young woman as companion, secretary, coat
carrier, is an insult aimed at her detested rival.

Dieterle stays aloof, forensic in white cotton gloves. Like a Beverly Hills gynaecologist. There is one extraordinary sequence where
Magnani labours, in the reek of sulphur, alongside women in the
hellish quarry of the pumice mines.

We came alongside Lipari's pumice mines. It is a huge, monstrous
mountain, composed entirely of dazzling, chalk-white pumice dust
and stones. My heart sank when I knew that we had to climb right to
the top to find our location. There is no solid matter, but just this
powdery substance which crumbles as one puts one's foot down. The
place was filled with mineworkers – mostly women – a few men and
little boys. Most of the boys wore scarves wound round their heads
Arab fashion.

The critic Manny Farber, talking about another Rossellini film,
The Miracle, catches the physical impetus of Magnani, how she
becomes a force of nature. He says that her sullen intensity 'para-
lyzes the brain'. 'The chaotic editing of unbalanced images captures
existence in its most unrelated, dishevelled state.'

Muriel's innocent recollections of daily life hint at molecular

changes, London is a dreamscape she can hardly imagine. Her
friends at the Unity Theatre are putting on a production of Robert
Tressell's *The Ragged Trousered Philanthropists*. For a moment, reading the letter, she is envious – and then the magnetism of the
mountain, the blue of the sky-reflecting sea wipes all that away.

Errol Flynn parks his yacht and strolls through her sleeping quarters. With one of her new friends she finds a deserted cove, a break in the rocks. They wallow and bask. They flirt with disappearance. As, years later, another Anna, an Antonioni fiction played by Lea Massari, arrives on a neighbouring island, the volcanic stump of Lisca Bianca, to vanish; to pass the narrative burden on to a new mistress, Monica Vitti: *L'avventura*. Massari suffered a heart attack and was unable to complete a swimming sequence. The assistant director, Franco Indovina, pulled on a petalled cap and bikini to double the passage between pleasure boat and shore.

Worlds are splitting, duplicating; memory movies impose themselves on starlit skies watched, after dinner, from a flat roof. Rough wine. Bells on the goats. Stones burn the feet. Muriel is spending more time with Geraldine Brooks.

> *Called through to Gerry and went up to her apartment. Spent a few hours giggling like schoolgirls, then had dinner in the hotel.*
>
> *Back in Gerry's rooms we decided to play the 'ouija' board. Really spent a couple of crazy hours. It was a very hot evening, so there we were the three of us, in just our undies, earnestly engrossed in the upturned glass. We were nearly hysterical at times, but kept at it till 1 a.m.*

The stage blocking visible beneath the record of the filming of *Vulcano* – and even the framing of the stills (Tellini sitting against a wall with Magnani and Harriet White, her previous companion) – brought me right back to the painting in the Cape Ann Museum: two women, one man (beached swimmer), a rocky ledge. That figure kept repeating. There were the opposed divas, Magnani and Bergman, with their cannibalistic love object, the director in his black beret and dark glasses, open-necked white shirt, lying on the ground: fed, satisfied. And the vanished Anna of Lea Massari, posed at the left of frame, on Lisca Bianca: pouting, dark, broody. Her summer friend Monica Vitti clutches the hand of Michelangelo

Antonioni as they bump across the ruffled Aeolian Sea in an open boat. One woman, many men.

And now, so the diary records, Muriel Walker (née Dobkin) and Geraldine Brooks (née Stroock) discover that they are both Jewish, both leftist: 'She told me wonderful stories about the Hollywood witch-hunt, during the Un-American Activities Committee.' They notice different men, Piero Tellini and the actor Rossano Brazzi, pulling themselves out of the same sea. The equation never changes. One woman: lethargic, summer dress. One woman: older, with a robe or towel. A man intruding. What does the Ouija board foretell?

I asked a friend from Sag Harbor to ask another friend in Gloucester to visit the museum, and to send me the name of the artist. I have it: Leon Kroll.

I researched the stern-visaged Kroll. He comes across in his studio portrait like a transplanted Hollywood accountant ambitious to produce musicals. 'He has the eye of a hawk and the heart of a dove.' Kroll was born in New York City. He travelled in Europe, making the acquaintance of Chagall and the Delaunays, Robert and Sonia. He spent his summers at Folly Cove, Gloucester, Massachusetts. He died in 1974 at the age of eighty-nine.

Smoke

'To write novels you don't need an imagination,' Bolaño said. 'Just a memory. Novels are written by combining recollections.'

– Javier Cercas

Kodak Mantra Diaries

As I walk over the high-sided railway bridge, through the urban village, down Primrose Hill towards the park, in that fabled summer, I am trying to prepare myself for the coming interview; a measured approach to an unapproachable house. Even as we reinvent ourselves, we are mired in what was there before; the changes in unchanging London. I had been given an address in Hanover Terrace, beside Regent's Park, in the parhelion of wealth and privilege. It was impossible, coming from the register of rented rooms, up and down the Northern Line, to imagine the interiors, the lives lived within these neoclassical Nash terraces, miracles of whiteness with brightly painted doors. When, a little later, we moved east, we would hear from an Essex man, a jobbing electrician, how he rewired a Regent's Park villa for his old mate from Hackney Downs, Harold Pinter. The electrician described Pinter's new house in terms of goods and fittings: white sofas, rich curtains, bowls of waxy fruit, tall flowers on glass tables.

The other picture I had to work with, a series of tracking shots, crane moves between floors, lifts and swerves on spiral staircases, following ascending and descending hierarchies of indoor servants – very much the mode of the Losey/Pinter film of Robin Maugham's *The Servant* – came from my wife, from Anna. Having abandoned her job with a multinational detergent-and-toothpaste company near Blackfriars Bridge, a set-up with which she was never comfortable, she was also walking west: from our single room on Haverstock Hill, where we looked down on a magnificent copper beech tree, but had no access to the garden. She carried her uniform, a blue overall, to the wealthy Jewish household in Swiss Cottage, where she was being instructed in the finer points, the high art, of being an upstairs cleaner. Bathrooms: how to dry the deep marble-surround tub, after the scouring, with a towel. Skirting boards to be treated with a damp cloth, before the chemical spray, the dusting, the Hoover. They were pleased with her. 'You can always tell when Anna has done a room,' they said, over hot chocolate and home-made biscuits, at the morning break. But really you couldn't, she told me, those rooms were never anything but immaculate. Dusters were washed every day. In Haverstock Hill, our room was stacked with camera boxes, shoeboxes of wedding presents, and the shoulder bags of assorted, passing-through-London casuals, former students and pub people from Dublin. The plumes of Sumatra cigar smoke came from the Dutch cameraman who would be working alongside me on the Ginsberg film. There was an insistent Proustian blend of patchouli and cauliflower cheese in unscoured pans.

I had scripted, on a couple of pages of thin blue paper, a documentary film, an essay that was a linear diary of events with no countercurrent, no resolution. It was like composing, on a camping table, above the golden-red umbrella of that tree, a list of happenings from a parallel universe. But London – Camden, Primrose Hill, Hyde Park, Chelsea, Kensington, Notting Hill – was entirely parallel in July 1967: plural, overlapping, narrated in so many excited voices, so many variants of the same tale. I pitched a fiction. *We meet Allen Ginsberg. We visit the bare flat where Ronnie Laing lives with his family. We witness William Burroughs stepping, hat tilted over eyes, from a taxi.* Easy to type, difficult to deliver. The Germans in Cologne approved my proposal. Cameras and sound equipment had been hired from Samuelson's. The countercultural fantasy had, within two days, to be translated into a shooting schedule.

Barry Miles at Indica Bookshop in Southampton Row gifted me with the contact address and now it was up to my limited powers of persuasion; my dumb belief that this would happen because it was already written, and would be written again, as a private record or unpublished book, when the madness of the film moment was over. Summer of love. Season of images.

Ed Dorn, friend, pupil, associate of Charles Olson, gave one of his late poems a title that haunts my remaking of that July evening, the pressing of the bell at the gleaming door of Panna Grady's rented Regent's Park mansion. 'The Deceased are the Travellers Among Us'. Dorn finds his epigram in Adorno: 'Normality is death.' There was nothing normal about this exchange. 'Hands cold,' I wrote in 1971, re-remembering, making the ordinary exceptional. Hands cold, throat dry as newspaper. I am ringing the wrong bell at the wrong house. I am redirected. The Grady property was once the Chinese Embassy. It stood in that relation to the park.

'You want to see Allen?'

She is amused, this slim woman with the thing for poets. The young mother who did so much in terms of supporting the scene. And who caused such havoc among her art-scene admirers. Poets came and went, as courtiers, clowns. Panna Grady was a sexier (more real) version of Katharine Hepburn in all those smart-chat, tennis-racket movies.

'Why don't you do something with Bill? He *likes* making films. And he's around. We had a party the other night. We all went out to dinner with Tom Driberg.'

I was already in correspondence with Burroughs. He might be on for it. But the Congress on the Dialectics of Liberation (for the Demystification of Violence) at the Roundhouse in Camden Town was not an event at which he wanted to appear on the platform. He showed up, to make contact with American friends, connections with Trocchi, and then he faded into the shadows.

I perched on the edge of one of those sofas the Essex electrician described. And I tried to take in the way money rubbed against poetry: in paintings with star names, inscribed limited editions, North African rugs, limply decadent funeral lilies. Filtered evening light from the private garden sharp-focused designated flaws in pale wood. Ginsberg is out there in the summerhouse, with his youthful attendants, one male and one female. He calls the girl his guru. She is thin and fiercely self-contained in perpetual dark glasses. When she emerges from the summerhouse, carrying a shirt on a hanger (fresh from the laundry for the next round of TV interviews and

bookshop signings), she is naked. Waking from a trance to stroll among luxuriant Douanier Rousseau bushes.

'Get that! Get that!' Ginsberg shouts. 'You missed it.'

He's in a hallucinated summer city. It is one of those delirious times (they never last beyond two or three weeks). Like the spontaneous ceremonies around the death of Princess Di: mobs forming and reforming, home-made tributes, flowers, silver balloons, candles. Hyde Park. And Hyde Park again for the 2012 Olympics. Agonized athletes swimming the length of that drowning pond, the Serpentine; cycling, running down tight corridors of close-packed, flag-waving crowds, and through avenues of ancient, dignified trees: broad-leafed lime, red oak, silver birch, weeping beech. The Hyde Park of the Rolling Stones concert, the Brian Jones tributes echoing Shelley, mourning Keats. Shelley's first wife, pregnant, in despair, threw herself into the Serpentine. A monster Olympic screen playing headshots of a triumphalist Boris Johnson working the mob, building the rhythms, repeated phrases, hair flopping, volume rising: all derangement, mass hypnosis. It happens in London, as elsewhere, at regular intervals, a swelling tide, a ripple of choked emotion. As if the dark heart of those public buildings could be exposed: the power, the hidden courtyards. Curls of dead smoke in secret basements. Grand offices and marble staircases lined with portraits. The city releases a sexualized hysteria of flags and cheers and glad contact: kissing and touching and incontinent weeping. Choked performers shudder for cameras in enforced intimacy. Cynical media professionals are watery under the pink powder.

It was palpable in July 1967. How, when I drove Ginsberg across town in my battered red Mini, the youthful tribes, having no clear sense of who he was – a bearded face from TV screens in other people's houses, from tabloid Hyde Park dope-rally headlines – rapped on the roof, leant in at the side window, with daffodils and peace signs. Celebrity as a shattered crystal. William Blake our contemporary. London relents, in cycles of mesmerized communality: free concert, royal wedding or royal funeral, riot. Break the glass. Loot, trash. Ding dong! The witch is dead. Burn down shops and warehouses. Episodes of euphoria alternate with long-suppressed rage. Justified grievances. An unearned sense of entitlement. Before the Swiss banks resume normal service.

'You've missed Charles.'

Olson was here, in bed, upstairs. Here in this room, shrouded in layers of rugs and wraps, talking to those who came to visit, to pay their respects. Long afternoons. In the confusion of my twenty-three-year-old mind, the models for a way forward, the established guides with their honed mythologies, were complicating the issue, dissolving, one into another. *The Deceased are the Travellers Among Us*. They take life, as Dorn says, a lot less seriously. When we write of this, as Tom Clark did with his Olson biography, we forge new fictions. The world leaks like a paper-tissue tourniquet.

We came, as a group, to sit by the lake in Regent's Park. When it was my turn to question Ginsberg, with his glittering eye, his gleaming cranium and shamanic red silk shirt (decorated by Paul McCartney), I knew that I had overprepared, done too much reading. Allen was in the amphetamine rush of rhetoric, peddling breathing techniques from India, busking squeezebox chants, mediating between Black Power and San Francisco Digger opportunism: he didn't need what he took for literary nitpicking, laboured demands for questions he had no way of answering. Ginsberg had perfected a repertoire of standard anecdotes, a constantly revised history – with a hot fix of recent, excited, all-night conversations with Olson, Burroughs, Panna Grady. To which he now added the sight and odour and touch of those master manipulators, the millionaire rock stars with their willingly seduced multitudes. He huddles with McCartney; he tries to teach Mick Jagger how to breathe. Celebrity feeds on celebrity in a cannibalizing ring fuck. Morning interviews, squatting on the grass, hold up the party. Ginsberg is a vampire for fame, immortality.

'It got really scary for me. Then it was all right and I could be scared and live with that, because I was more important than the LSD. In a way, I renounced LSD and at the same time I got a flash of my own presence and the presence of everything around. A unitative experience based on the strength of compassion for myself. The LSD was no longer a god or even an authority above my own authority. After which I went to Vancouver and had a big meeting with all the poets: Olson, Creeley, Philip Whalen, Denise Levertov, Robert Duncan. All the seraphs of that particular area.'

Panna Grady doesn't join in the talk. But she is adjudicating Ginsberg's shifting expressions. The men are in summer shirts. Panna wears a herringbone tweed coat. Hair falling across one eye. It's the face, intelligent, distracted, of a model from another studio. Always on the move, packing her cases, booking tickets on ocean liners, fielding calls.

The twin energy streams of contemporary US writing, Beat and Black Mountain, mingled in Donald Allen's *The New American Poetry*, were now engaged in Pacific Rim conferences, at Berkeley, at Vancouver; or in social gatherings, bars, art openings, brawls in New York and Boston. Some of the Black Mountaineers wanted more of the gold ticket, acknowledgement in *Time* and *Life*, top-dollar transatlantic gigs: a drooling audience of submissives, patrons with Savile

Row tailoring, sex partners with apartments on the park, ranches in New Mexico. Some of the Beats hungered for academic sinecures, placement in the accepted lineage of modernism. They sniffed around each other like prowling beasts, jealous eyes on the lion tamer's polished black boots. They listened for the crack of her whip.

Olson praised Kerouac. Ginsberg visited Panna Grady's summer property in Gloucester, which she was sharing with the Boston poet John Wieners. The bearded New Yorker listened to Olson and absorbed his argument as part of the fabric of what he now delivered as we sat in a broken circle on the Regent's Park grass. Panna's young daughter was climbing on and off her lap. The stone-silent girl from the summerhouse, lost in her hijab of hair and dark glasses, was staring at the ground. Hands interlocked in a mudra grip, as if cradling a small, hot bird.

'Olson declared that history was ended – in the sense that what we know of history is only what we know of images left behind. Those images were an abstraction from the actual event, so history was just another poem, as interpreted by those poets, some of them bum poets, who happened to be around. And now there has been a change of consciousness – to include *event* as part of the abstraction of history. And electronic eavesdropping equipment, now in its primitive stage, will ultimately develop so that anybody can tune in on the president, can get into his bathroom through laser beams. Which means that all secrets are out.'

In the tall-windowed room, I could feel the weight of the absence of Olson, who, for so many months, lay, or sat smoking and growling, in a king-size bed somewhere in this house. I had missed the possibility of that connection; the *Maximus* poet had gone to ground. In hotels. In Berlin. In Dorchester. And back again to Gloucester. Plane tickets, pills. Emergencies. Urgent invitations to female friends, with whom he remained in sporadic correspondence, to join him in Crete. More importantly, much more importantly, his papers were being sifted and sorted and prepared for publication.

Panna wore the short skirts of the time, but they were country quality, not Carnaby Street. Her elegant eyebrows were raised. She sat – Tom Clark says 'like a model' – making beautiful shapes with an arm across a bare knee. 'Astonish me. If you can.' Camera crews disfigure the garden. Cleaners in the kitchen. Men, looking after the shrubs and herbaceous borders, don't smoke until they leave the property.

Wieners surprised her. And she astonished him. He was a gay, Olson-approved poet who voiced, with the directness of a man on a communal telephone in the lobby of a cheap hotel, his version of the lower depths. He noticed, and logged, the fragrant divas of the city, visiting movie stars. He could customize action from Hesiod with headlines from the *Hollywood Reporter*: Kenneth Anger plus narcotics plus suicide attempts plus the secret rose.

Panna fell pregnant. She left Gloucester to obtain an abortion. The Olson scholar Ralph Maud drove her to Long Island. He reports her remark: 'Would you want John Wieners's child?' Maud challenges Tom Clark, on points of fact; he privileges his own accidental acts of witness. But Clark is not composing a biography. He's attempting a fiction of history, large poet in small times: an amnesiac culture that has no use for him. 'The image of approach to godhead in his writings now metamorphosed from an ascent to an inward spiral, a furling of being into the sunlike vortex of the soul.'

Shipping out from Montreal to Liverpool on 28 October 1966, on the *Empress of Canada*, Olson and Panna Grady, with the imagined shrieks of the abandoned Wieners fading in their wake, laid down a Hollywood take on that classic equation; two men, one woman. It was *Casablanca* with an ocean liner for a prop-driven aircraft. Real rain on the Atlantic, not hosepipes spraying a slick studio shimmer. This was a propulsive act: scandalous and ordinary. A headlong flight in postponement of larger problems: the work, the poem. Clark has Olson, taking on the momentum of a Malcolm Lowry, rounding up reluctant disciples in Barnet, sticking Hilton breakfasts for all the boys on Panna's tab, entraining for the Dorn household in Colchester; fisting uppers, lying prone on benches in stations, labouring uphill, arms filled with cheeses. All-night sessions disturbing domestic tranquillity. Cold sweats and cartons of duty-free Camels.

There is an epic riff for Tom Raworth's wife, Val, on an early Welsh voyage across the Atlantic, contact with the Mandan Indians. The story of how Prince Madoc reached the Mississippi, leaving behind a Celtic imprint that is felt to this day, came to Olson by way of Ralph Maud, who was in Aberystwyth. I like to think of the *Maximus* poet carrying around a clipping from the Cardiff daily, the *Western Mail*. But the anecdote only points up Olson's concern with detail, etymology, origin, who did what, and when. In all the shuttling between beds and cities, he never let go of the poem and his hunger for information.

I saw and spoke to Olson for the first and only time at the Queen Elizabeth Hall on the South Bank on 12 July 1967. The Gloucester poet was due to read among his peers: Auden, Spender, Ginsberg, Ungaretti. They programmed him to close before the interval. Such events no longer happen. The gathered poets, some of them world-class bedwetters, private patients in sabbatical asylums, tolerated gropers from Midwestern campuses, debonair dudes from Mexican embassies, could never again be assembled in one place. The trade has gone out of favour. The beard and tremble of John Berryman referenced both Lears, Edward and the peevish Shakespearean king. Cheerleaders from McDaids, across the water from Dublin, as for the Cheltenham Gold Cup (with fewer priests), gave loud and liquid vocal support to Patrick Kavanagh. Sanctioned outlaws anguished over status before a well-behaved English crowd.

Olson put himself in with the people. He sprawled across the aisle, wearing a dirty white suit like a character from John Huston waiting for his barbershop walk-on in *The Treasure of the Sierra Madre*, his turn around the harbour in *Beat the Devil*. He was right alongside the place where we were settled. 'Give him your seat,' my companion said. And I made the offer. Olson preferred the space on the floor, not paying any attention to incomers who were forced to negotiate a passage around his notable bulk.

An attendant, after several attempts, and a tug or two at the sleeve, persuaded Charles Olson, author of *The Maximus Poems*, to take his seat on the stage. He read. He struggled to get the phrasing he wanted. It was another of his Christmas poems, 'An Ode to Nativity'. He summoned 'the boat of the moon' and his own seventh year. Seven was a special number.

'It was an excitement, heart in mouth, to listen,' I said, when I wrote an account of the event, while still in the heat of it. Olson beat time with the ball of his fist. With the other hand, he massaged his throat. There was no opportunity for the sort of open-ended, free-associating performance – more talk (his metier) than reading (his penance) – that he delivered to a packed audience of fellow poets, enthused or aggrieved, at Berkeley. No messianic delirium. The world did not tilt on its axis. Applause was muted.

Now England has been squeezed dry. The affair with Panna Grady is played out. His friends have seen him, listened to him talk, and are not altogether sorry to have him re-migrate, back to the ground where the poem of his life is not yet resolved. If it ever can be. The matter of the founding of the settlement at Gloucester, Massachusetts – the motive for this trip to England – was still to be explored: out west in Thomas Hardy's Dorchester. Ed Dorn, who was always smart on trains, riding towards Oxford, Bath or Bristol, spoke of what this trajectory meant in an English context. 'You get on a train in Paddington and there's the thrill of heading west. And the country does have a broad base and it does go all the way to Land's End. Things get a bit louder out here. You can feel it in the people. There's a kind of pride in being further west than whatever is east.'

Dorchester has a fine museum, with rusting iron bolts in segments of spine, broken pots, a facsimile of Hardy's study (lacking the titular ghost in residence) – and a substantial archive of papers concerning John Smith and the mercantile imperatives behind that Atlantic voyage, the failed Cape Ann venture of 1624. And, later, the achieved settlement of 20,000, largely Puritan, colonists in the 1630s.

Olson, according to R. N. R. Peers, the assistant curator at the time, was a diligent and energetic researcher. He knew his way around records. He knew how to find what he required, documentation to be lifted into a private mythology. He was a large man, an alien, in a particular provincial town, that had already been possessed by Hardy and John Cowper Powys. The Antelope Hotel was a sobering hideaway. Olson went to ground, heartsore, incommunicado from friends – until he responded to an advertisement placed in *The Times*, soliciting information on his whereabouts. He played the slot machine and drowsed through long English afternoons in brown-panelled bars. He found the time to scan the small print of our newspaper of record.

Mr Peers drove him out into the country. Picture Charles Olson on the earth ramparts – where we all go, as we pass through – of Maiden Castle. They stood, collars up, pipes in mouths, to catch the teasing song of a lark. Powys saw this landscape as a receptacle for the mysteries of that great underworld sea into which human consciousness must sink, independent of the fretful dreams and demons that oppress it.

New York

We were at the kerb – WALK DON'T WALK – sauntering from a basement restaurant on Broadway, where we had dined early, and not
very well, on BBC expenses, when she came up alongside me.
'Want a blue jay?' A black woman, a little taller than my six feet, in
a heady clout of perfume. Cured leather with fur collar, the ele-
gance of the city. Heels like crampons, allowing her to sway but not
tumble. She wasn't looking at me and was not, perhaps, addressing
the question to myself in particular. I'm used to being challenged
for directions. Which is a problem, coming out of reverie, bringing
ordinary names and street details into focus. I have to remind myself
that not all pedestrians have a special interest in the point where the
torso of some butchered TV soap star was found floating. Every
route, as I pitched it, was an excursion into the past.

She didn't require information. This was her town. She was offering a service. I wasn't used to such courtesy. It came with the
territory. The encounter was an extension of the hotel where we
were staying, just off Times Square. If not myself, she implied, then
another. Another stranger.

'Wanna blow job?'

13 November 1995. New York, after all these years, a reality. A terrain, constructed from film clips, books, reports of fortunate visitors
(including my parents, who brought back, as requested, US editions,
by luck first printings, of *The Dharma Bums* and *The Subterraneans*),
was now a yellow cab ride from Newark, New Jersey. Which was
more like the A13, downwind of Dagenham, than the credit
sequence of *The Sopranos* – until those Moloch towers, on the far
side of the Hudson River, threatened in the window, solid smears of
second-hand smoke. Out of the tunnel, a shudder in the bones, we
are confronted by the certainty that we are worse dressed than the

doormen, those stalking pavement artists of the Paramount Hotel. It is not an option to be unstyled in arbitrary colours with too short a coat. We were shamed by our failure to equip ourselves with ribbed paramilitary black wool caps. The lean young actors are not there to *carry* your bags; they are evaluating them, to see if you are cool enough to be let in. The kiosk in the lobby, along with hip deathsticks and fancy cigars, offers slim confections by William Burroughs. *Ghost of Chance.* The author signed my copy in Lawrence, Kansas, five days later. 'There were taboos,' he wrote, 'against the killing of ghosts.'

The dissolving of the dream, that land to the west, was an obligation placed on me by a radio producer, Pavel Coen. I met Pavel down the line, cans on head, in a solitary Eichmann booth in Broadcasting House, as he interrogated me, from Cardiff, on the subject of Thomas Pynchon, who was just then making one of his sporadic returns from the shadows. Coen identified in my writing an enthusiasm he shared for submerged American literature (even when that submersion was the part of the pitch that guaranteed future attention). I was older and easier now with the knowledge that my tastes were out of fashion and favour. Elective redundancy was, I had to admit, part of the charm. It takes a healthy dose of ego to flirt so consistently with erasure. I was interested in the cunning ways Malcolm Lowry found to lose, burn, scatter his manuscripts, before he had to face the horrors of making a submission, or, worse still, publication.

Our favoured checklists were complementary but distinct. Beyond the prose of Robert Creeley (especially *The Gold Diggers*) and Ed Dorn (*The Rites of Passage*), I held to the conviction that Douglas Woolf was the finest, surest, most sinewy and subtle craftsman on the planet. He was also a magus of the bad journey, yomping through snow, jogging into the desert (as in *John-Juan*), or even re-presenting the road novel, in *The Timing Chain*, as an ironic farewell to an honourable career. When your publisher doesn't know who (or why) you are, it's time for Arizona or the mountains. Woolf recognized the gravitational field that pulled Kerouac back, time and again, to

Mexico City: where unwritten books are waiting. Sleeve notes set the scene: '*John-Juan begins innocently enough when a friendly amnesiac finds himself in a busy Mexican border town with only his pyjamas and watch.*' 'If there were only one reader left in the world,' Woolf said, 'I would write to that one as lovingly as I do now.'

Pavel Coen, who, as I feared, harboured secret ambitions to compose an epic novel of his own, adapting *Meisterwerk* US techniques to the south-west London suburbs, paid his dues to Pynchon, L-A-N-G-U-A-G-E poets, DeLillo, Burroughs, while confessing to a special affinity with William T. Vollmann. He found, in my novel *Radon Daughters*, themes and threads in sympathy with Vollmann's clotted cycle, his overreach. Both projects were doomed and he liked that, it spoke of integrity. I was happy to play along. I travelled back to Cardiff, city of my birth, where Coen was waiting with a hired car and driver. We took to the hills and recorded, on the move and off the cuff, a programme about a book that had not yet been written. Meanwhile, Vollmann travelled with the mujahideen in Afghanistan. He slept in offices and lived on chocolate bars. He wrote about the settlement of North America. His wife – and this was a link Coen made with *Radon Daughters* – worked as a radiation oncologist. My crazed narrator, actually inspired by Céline, found that the only access to the fading narrative of the city was through seances of illegal X-rays from a decommissioned machine in the Royal London Hospital. Vollmann, in my judgement, was closer to Lowry. In his elaborate and hallucinated mythology – the voyage that never ends – Lowry wallows in the guilt for a dead brother or, sometimes, a Cambridge friend: an accident for which he holds himself responsible. The burden of authorship, malfate, is a karmic consequence. While still a young boy, Vollmann witnessed the drowning of his six-year-old sister while she was under his supervision. William Burroughs said that the shooting of his wife, Joan Vollmer, in Mexico City, made him a writer. He was cursed to labour with words, taking the dictation of a hungry Remington portable, almost to the last breath. To a red clapboard house in Kansas. Suburb without urb. Mid-continental inertia. Nowhere.

My interest in the Beats, simmering since my first experience of their work, as a schoolboy in 1960, was put to the test by Pavel Coen. I would accompany him on a journey across the United States, interviewing survivors for a radio documentary, using the 'Beat Culture and the New America 1950–1965' show at the Whitney Museum in New York as our now-or-never pitch. After all these years, I would collide with the actuality of the place, and risk inevitable disillusion: with setting, characters – and, most of all, myself. My failure to take the trip at the right time, before or after Ireland.

Being here, the reality quota dissipated. Rooms in the Paramount, shallow steel basins with taps too high-concept to operate, were pre-traumatic, low lit in preparation for performance-art episodes of self-surgery. The city growled. My bed was far from the street. We worked long days, cabbing from the Whitney to the cinema where Jonas Mekas hung out, a spectre from an earlier time, heroically unlaved, a steady-stare bohemian in his wide-brimmed black hat. The Mekas diary films, in 8mm or 16mm, casually recording the happenings of his life in America, were inspirational. The method could be applied to prose as well as celluloid. It was impossible, under these circumstances, the duty of bringing back a coherent account of the Beats and counterculturalists in their twilight, to break through from the futile attempt to conduct an interview with one of the myths of my own past.

Ed Sanders, down in the East Village, was rehearsing for a performance in St Mark's Church. He had stuck with, and grown into, that leonine aureole of freak hair, the Tombstone sheriff's soup-strainer moustache. But what was once a confident and chaotic badge of subversion was now a silvery afterthought. Spring growth on an old rock. This barely tolerated interview with the man from London was time lost. I had fed on the playful scholarship of Ed's adaptation of the Egyptian *Book of the Dead* to songs of beatnik glory. I burrowed in and out of the Charles Manson dune-buggy saga, *The Family*. Sanders was a fire-source, as I worked as a gardener in Limehouse, or laboured in the ullage cellar of the

Brick Lane brewery. He was a conduit to Olson and he carried that lineage forward. I admired the way he made sapient music of Matthew Arnold and William Blake. You could position, to advantage, *The Family*, Ed's forensic excavation of Manson's desert cult madness, against Tom Wolfe's hitch on the Ken Kesey bus for *The Electric Kool-Aid Acid Test*. Both these voyages were endgames in an established American tradition: the wagon train through badlands, under assault, sustained by weird belief systems and a hunger for novelty or status (notoriety as fame). Sanders locates, at the back of the Satanist-nudist-messianic-assassin cult something called *The Hole*. A negative space, beyond cinema, beyond easy riders and Zabriskie pointmen, in the brutal, eyeball-frying glare of Death Valley. He realizes that his research – and, after training with the Greeks, Egyptians, Black Mountaineers, he is a master at sifting documents – requires a degree of role play. He poses as a New York porn dealer with a tranche of Andy Warhol offcuts to trade against rumoured orgy-snuff underground movies involving Manson and the family with Hollywood notables (and pondlife). 'I posed as a Satanist, drooling maniac and dope-tranced psychopath,' Sanders said.

It would have been better to limit my encounters with the former Fug to the acquisition of books, as they appeared, from Compendium in Camden Town. That way, the client does half of the work and the New York scene is commodified, reduced to a finite number of objects in a private museum. Some of those Hackney shelves were now thick with dust.

Anna's vision of the USA was more extreme, even lunar. She couldn't convince herself that it existed; certainly not as a landscape where she could walk with the same estrangement as a morning shuffle down Kingsland Road. Our older daughter, travelling through the south as part of a crew shooting autopsies for the Discovery Channel, brought back a packet of seeds, Texas Blue Bonnets, which were kept in the kitchen as proof, as for Noah in his Ark, that ground, on which trees and flowers could grow again, must have risen above the formless waters.

The chance finally came – Anna was getting her hair done in

Islington, I was scouring the City for Marmite and Frank Cooper's Oxford English Marmalade to carry as gifts to Austin, Texas – to board a plane at Heathrow, to fly the Atlantic; to tour the States, giving readings, seeing friends. It had taken years to set this itinerary up; bookshops in Los Angeles, Seattle and Portland were taking me on blind trust. But something was out of kilter in London. I noticed bankers swarming into the street. The hairdressers were whispering, weepy, as wild rumours were confirmed. From what I overheard they anticipated an attack on Canary Wharf. What was new about that? But on 11 September 2001, the horror was elsewhere. Before I got home, silent loops of the unthinkable were running on screens in pubs and offices. Anna put her half-packed suitcase aside. It remained in the bedroom for a month or so. The packet of seeds vanished into an underwear drawer.

Six years later, our daughter now in Washington with her three-month-old baby, Anna made it. I stayed at home, pushing to finish a book, a memoir of Hackney, before the old territory vanished for ever in the outwash of Olympic development. And there they are, coming out of Penn Station, after the train ride from the capital, up into the light and noise of Manhattan, in the belly of that stolen island. One of them has to give way: place or pedestrian. Sensory overload is critical. The dream image and the actuality are so close in this moment of superimposition that Anna sets everything on the ground. She freezes, trembles in shock. The episode is *precisely* what she projected and therefore her former self is annulled; entelechy, childhood, marriage, the lot. Manhattan is true, she is not. What's left? Start again.

I was never as sensitive to atmosphere, but I understood, and experienced in advance, that ontological crisis, as Anna described it to me. Because the city never stopped: ambulances, honking cars, collisions, meat and metal. Because of the thermometer shape of overloaded ground between rivers, the heat from bars and subways, the brash democracy of smells – sizzling chicken, candyfloss, whisky, leather – there was never a fixed interlude in which to sleep. And walking, as we did, Pavel with his recorder slung over his shoulder, myself with a bag of books, from Times Square to the Chelsea Hotel on West 23rd Street, required new skills. WALK DON'T WALK. The stop-start stutter of the grid. I don't doubt that it can be done. I read Nik Cohn's *The Heart of the World*, a stroll down the length of Broadway, making discoveries, chatting to natives. But it would take years to pick up those rhythms. And we had so many names to track down in the few days available before we flew to Kansas City.

Herbert Huncke – Huncke the Junky – was settled as the titular spirit of the Chelsea Hotel, a chirpy day-of-the-dead cricket; a sugar-skull hipster in a tropical hutch, with temperature levels cranked to the hothouse mansion of the bloodless General Sternwood in *The Big Sleep*. Windows nailed shut. The last keeper of the Times Square cafeteria culture of the 1940s toked on bottles of lurid glucose drinks, like a vampire tubed to sachets of vintage plasma. The room was so *smoked* that, despite spidery arrangements of dead grasses and rows of little scented bottles, any draw of breath was a slap of recycled nicotine. With cooked-resin chasers. Decades of genteel infamy had left a slack mask of skin over Huncke's formerly delicate and handsome armature of bone. The retreating ring of hair, real but disconnected from the man, a revenger's wig in a Jacobean drama, was inky black. The mouth, lips painted, snarled and pouted, as the old familiar stories were dusted down. For delivery to the cash-only squares.

Bill was Bill. Allen was Allen. Nice university boys introduced to the lower depths. 'I thought Burroughs was *heat*.' Burroughs repaid the compliment. He remembered Huncke in a pay toilet in Times Square, notebook on knees, 'furtively composing the latest tale from underground'.

The myths of place are overwhelming. It's hard not to break out laughing. Adobe-brown corridors. An overheated check-in mortuary for all the boho legends: Brendan Behan, Janis Joplin (who once went on a disastrous date with Charles Olson), Sid and Nancy. And most potent of all, as I flashed, looking at Huncke, to the film clip of that operatically painted, cabaret marionette in the open coffin, packaged for return to Laugharne: my fellow countryman Dylan Thomas. Of all the transatlantic voyages, the four expeditions made by the Welsh poet, and recounted by John Malcolm Brinnin in his 1956 book, *Dylan Thomas in America*, were the ultimate provocation; a warning and a lingering seduction. When, as a schoolboy, I began to interview some of those who had known Dylan – his friend Vernon Watkins, Aneirin Talfan Davies (the man responsible for many of his broadcasts), Laugharne publicans, Morriston theatricals – the prevailing distaste for Brinnin's undeceived account was much like the attitude in Gloucester towards Tom Clark's Olson biography.

Thomas was living in the Chelsea Hotel when he collapsed for the last time: 'insult to the brain'. Brinnin notes, with somewhat mystified indulgence, the enthusiasm the feted lyric poet demonstrated for the disposable products of pure Americana: pulp novels (routinely assigned to the generic term: *Mickey Spillane*), Chaplin, the Marx Brothers, burlesque, pin tables, jukebox bars, Howard Johnson restaurants in the neon twilight. Dollars leaked from his pockets. Jewish physicians were on tap with cortisone shots. There were workmen's blue shirts to take home. A consumerist cornucopia against the pinched meanness of rationing-book Britain. Cheap cigars instead of Woodbines.

Dylan (his name soon to be purloined by a young Jewish folk singer from Minnesota) was at the tipping point between high seriousness, the rhetoric of apocalypse, black on black, and permission to regress to the sweetest of bites: primary colours, monster hoardings, comic books, Hershey bars, cantilevered breasts, three-cow milkshakes. German expressionism converted into rain-slicked Hollywood melodrama. This crumpled, swollen-bellied man with the stained nicotine teeth was the original post-war performance poet, playing to packed crowds, and losing, in the sweats and fears of hypnotic projection, all sense of self. The preacherly mannerisms of his Methodist ancestors, and the seductive rumble and thunder of voice from the abused instrument of his body, mesmerized the uptown poetry mob. Why had he crossed the Atlantic? The questions never stopped. 'To continue my lifelong search for naked women in wet mackintoshes,' he said. And said again. Until Brinnin flinched and flustered, as he tried to head off the interrogators, tried to keep the exhausted poet on the road. A hundred and fifty readings, up and down the country; death flights, claustrophobic trains, cars bear-squeezed with host-institution academics and faculty wives.

Brinnin has Thomas, newly arrived, posed against the window of his high room in the Beekman Tower Hotel, looking out on the East River. Trembling, groaning at the mid-Manhattan panorama: too much light. Too much confirmation of distance from heartland. From estuary and tide and the quiet, resolved hills and neat white farms. Between the splatter patterns of the hypnagogic show of Manhattan electricity there is so much darkness, negative gravity sucking pools of infolding energies as yet unnamed. 'I am an extinct volcano.'

John Berryman sets off for St Vincent's Hospital as soon as word reaches Princeton: for the final deathwatch. Berryman was the nerve-tuned laureate of obituaries, a suicide long rehearsed. He jumped from a bridge in Minneapolis in 1972. But trauma-ward witness was required, the imprinting of the vision of the dying man: 'lest he freeze our blood with terrible returns'. Thomas is not extinguished, he flies through Berryman's *Dream Songs* like a wisecracking owl. Now there is no hurry. All eternity, time and space, is on the head of a nail driven through his tongue.

No terrible returns. But four times to America was one too many. Allen Ginsberg, hanging out at the San Remo, seated alone at the bar, makes a journal entry for April 1952. He has resolved to seize the day. There is a chance encounter, a failed connection, with Dylan Thomas, who is drinking with a 'thin mediocre type', an American with a big bruise on his forehead. Dylan has already brushed against William Faulkner, whose work he admires very much; intimacy was impossible under the circumstances, as they swerve on fated trajectories, with unregistered female companions, through restaurants and celebrity cocktail lounges.

Thomas treats Ginsberg like a pimp. He says that in his last bar a girl asked him if he'd like to watch her turn a trick with a friend. She wanted fifty dollars. Ginsberg knows a pretty girl who might open her door. She keeps a bottle of beer for emergencies. Phone calls are made. The bartender asks Ginsberg to leave. The troubled young poet hangs around outside. Thomas is tired. He climbs into a cab. Ginsberg runs to the other side, sticks his tongue through the open window. 'I meant it as a friendly gesture.'

In terminal wards and drying-out clinics, brain-burning madhouses and Bellevue towers, voyaging poets overlap or make their solitary penances in Manhattan. Malcolm Lowry, who drank with Dylan Thomas in Soho, Fitzrovia, and the Sylvia Hotel, Vancouver, forged a fiction, *Lunar Caustic*, of his breakdown, saying that he had fallen in love with America. He was pursuing the succubus of the city, not a woman. He wanted to see where Melville lived. He wanted to cast himself adrift in Rimbaud's drunken boat.

Among the reported figures, the premature wake of poets, actors, agents and nuns, come to catch Dylan's last breath, was an unknown woman. She was slender, dark, elegantly dressed; a figure, as Brinnin directs her, from Cocteau's *Orphée*. She does not approach the bed, where the poet lies in high fever with tubes from nose and throat. She stands in the doorway, unmoving, for half an hour. There is no connection, beyond the one I'm now making, but my own attempt to trace part of this story ended in Laugharne with a similar, overcontrived theatrical moment.

West Wales, wet and green, with high hedges and twisty lanes, was mapped in my genetic code to a quantum flattered by expeditions to whitewashed chapels and burial grounds with weathered inscriptions. My mother's family, Welsh-speaking, aboriginally established in Cardigan and Carmarthen, spread across the areas Dylan Thomas emerged from and later occupied. We took family holidays in New Quay, where the poet lived for a time, and where he was assaulted, when a battle-traumatized commando, back from Greece, fired a Sten gun into Thomas's rented bungalow. And followed up by producing a hand grenade. My maternal grandparents spent their honeymoon in Ferryside, across the bay from Laugharne. An aunt, hardy and eccentric, was known to swim, in full black, from Ferryside to Llansteffan.

Those questing days, driven out by an Oxford student, a poet and geographer with cultivated contacts, were an attempt not only to pick up authentic traces of Dylan Thomas, to take photographs for a thesis, but also to sniff around my own family connections. And without the dreadful obligation to actually meet any of them and sit through a Welsh tea.

Laugharne came at the end of the journey. Burial ground. Boat House. Brown's Hotel. Damp shed with postcards of Whitman, Hardy, Lawrence. Back to the pub. More beer and then a kitchen with an oak table and oil lamps. As the conversation ebbs and flows, with loops of reminiscence and Celtic invention, and I begin to nod, having abandoned all attempts to make bullet-point reminders of significant facts (there aren't any), I notice the face of the woman standing at the window, staring in at us. It was raining hard. Her collar was turned up, the stiff ridge disappearing into wild, abundant hair. I point her out to my companion, who is about to give a reading from a booklet recently produced by the Fantasy Press in Oxford. The others, deep in their cups, their anecdotage, do not notice the intruder. The poet, annoyed, impatient to begin, goes to the door. The woman in the white coat has vanished.

My prime target, Gregory Corso, was no longer in the Chelsea Hotel. He shared a patron with Huncke, a bookdealer. Corso, more than any of the other major players, stayed true to the essential aspects of the Beat ethos: poet as seeker, the sentient world as sustainer of that grand illusion. Therefore: derangement, criminality, bad behaviour as a lifestyle choice. The oldest of the youngest, the street boy. Who exploits everything and everybody within range, except his basic belief in Shelley and the integrity of inspiration.

By way of the bookshop, that great display of Corso's trophies, a blizzard of signatures and inscriptions, we track the patron down and make an appointment, just before we have to check out, to see the mercurial poet. He'll be at his grace-and-favour apartment mid-afternoon. Perhaps. If all goes well. If the horses are running in favour of today's occult system. Letters of names assigned numbers. Numbers graphed into code in Enochian tables. Coins laid out with mysterious men on street corners, with cigar smokers in newspaper kiosks, with chipped blondes in bars.

It happened. I think it happened. But all my tapes of the Corso recordings, the Burroughs recordings, the fuzzy evening of conversation with Kathy Acker in San Francisco, her days in the New York sex industry, had disappeared. All the photographs. The diaries. The plane tickets, hotel receipts. The big black box marked 'Generating the Beats'. Pavel, who was nothing if not an obsessive archivist, would have duplicates, originals. There was a particular shot I remembered, in the cutting November wind, by the East River, Pavel looking like a shaven-headed Russian mafia hood, in his zipper jacket and black boots, outside a breeze-block sex club. The only piece of ephemera I could lay my hands on from that New York trip fluttered out of a copy of Corso's *Hitting The Big 5-0* that I bought at the Village bookshop. It was an 'out of series' copy, signed and numbered, 'written in long hand as well'. *Imbalances of joy and sorrow.* The loose card said. PRIVATE EYES SPORTS CABARET. 100 TOPLESS DANCERS. PRIVATE ROOM. NOV 13–20 STACEY STAXXX.

The problem was that Pavel had also disappeared. He left the BBC. He wasn't working at any of the usual freelance operations that infested Silicon Roundabout and Old Street. The patron, another former radio producer, who tolerated Pavel beyond the point of reasonable human benevolence, in a tumbledown property in Shepherd's Bush, had finally kicked him out. Rent was unpaid; the room, the bathroom, the hallway were stacked with cardboard boxes. Old recordings, annotated scripts. And the mountain ranges of research documents required for the definitive Croydon novel.

Pavel invested everything in this project, months ran into years. Nobody saw a line. Nobody saw Pavel. He had become the book. I imagined some impossibly complex, infolding structure, autobiographical (deserted mother, council estate, exams), linguistically innovative, psychotropically charged. Unreadable. Unfinished. A London edgeland epic that absorbed and expanded the pioneering works of Michael Moorcock, Will Self (late-modernist slip-streaming), and the deep-topography of Nick Papadimitriou on the north-west fringes, among sewage farms, motorway slip roads, gravel pits, reservoirs.

I would begin my search for Pavel in Croydon. By way of Croydon, I might recapture that afternoon with Corso.

The Trespasser

I STOLE SEX TOY BECAUSE I WAS BROKE: *Croydon Advertiser.* Headline on sandwich board outside the (in)convenience store as I emerge from the Overground terminal: SEWAGE PLANT FIRE BURNT FOR 10 HOURS.

I was chasing flickers from corpse candles down the irrational curve of the new railway linking Dalston Junction and Croydon West; old suburbs devastated by dubiously funded blitz development, twinned in dereliction and statement regeneration. Statement being: take it or fuck off. Post-architectural reefs made from recycled sunglasses, blank walls of cloud quotations, with no obvious point of access beyond scimitar beaches of trampled cigarette butts. Dust siroccos wrapped free newspapers around confused pedestrians and bent lamp posts. I saw a blind man lay down his white stick to piss in gouts and spurts against the sharp V at the prow of a building where roads divided. One wall was brick-windowed, the other multilayered in advertisements for discontinued bands with ridiculous names. The yellow ammoniac stream blew back against dirty white jeans and naked, swollen ankles. 75 FIREFIGHTERS TACKLE BLAZE.

The nightmare for Malcolm Lowry, a misadept at a spread hand of magical systems (Swedenborgian, Haitian voodoo, Canadian cabbala, Mexican tarot, Crowleyite Golden Dawn), was of being sucked into the swamp of a book already written: by way of wild coincidences, echoes of Joyce, Conrad Aiken, Melville, Poe, Nordahl Grieg. The lobster-complexioned, pipe-chewing Englishman, in the baggy flannels unsecured with golf-club tie, convinced himself that he was essentially a plagiarist: of himself and others. It was his fate to make journeys at the back of the bus, on tramp steamers; to wade through volcanic ash, across railway lines; to wobble along the lip of sewage ditches. His novels were pre-written and their author condemned: beaten, castrated, crucified. Mexican buses were filled with messenger spirits, Chinamen from suppressed short stories, witches with dead babies in wicker baskets. He interpreted his life-in-progress as a book of signs: names of bars, booze advertisements, house numbers, terrifying posters for Peter Lorre (exile and addict) in *Las Manos de Orlac*.

To confess his flaws, his blatant thefts from Grieg (which were all of his own imagining), Lowry determined to go to Oslo, to track down the author of *The Ship Sails On* (a parallel project to *Ultramarine*). He invented the technique I was about to employ in the wilderness of Croydon. No maps, no phone calls. Landfall, strike out. Grieg – as might be the case with Pavel Coen – was living under an assumed name. Lowry takes a cab, pays it off. Follows a man. The man leads him to Grieg's door. 'All his life Lowry relied on the long shot, the amazing coincidence, for his most important contacts with the world that existed so improbably outside himself,' wrote the biographer Douglas Day.

I turned right out of the station: wrong move. My compass was shot by the lightning of urban novelty. I detoured down a strip of ribbon development that was Poland. And Asia. And pound-stretching. I was seduced by a pub called the Ship of Fools. The merciless concertina of phone-boosting, money-transferring, price-slashing enterprises had its minor attractions in windows of gilded bling, bright saris, statuettes of the elephant-headed Lord Ganesh. London Road was not Broadway. But I felt the pull of Pavel Coen and his unwritten novel. How could he extract structure from this mess of street life? The cards in the newsagent's shop flipped the messages I used to read, back in 1962, when I trawled Brixton, Streatham, West Norwood, for somewhere to live. I DOUBLE BED-ROOM, NEAR WEST CROYDON STATION (10 MINT WALK). PRIORITY TO PAKISTANI & INDIAN.

D. H. Lawrence lodged here in his schoolmastering days. That might be worth a line to Pavel. But I wearied, my heart wasn't in it. The loud spectre of Gregory Corso was obliterating whispers of the lost radio producer. I appreciated, after taking photographs of lifeless avenues of pollarded trees, distant factory chimneys, pre-demolition walls with fading trade signs for THE SMOKER'S MATCH, that my quest was futile. I retreated to a pub.

The positive-discrimination barman in the roadhouse barn on the Norbury roundabout: *was it Pavel?* In my Lowry trance, I had to believe in the tarot of coincidence. Black T-shirt, blue arms, a refusal to meet my eye – and a total inability to tap the keys to order chicken wings (a gross at a time). The wasted operative managed the business of hosing cider – the least worst possibility – with the same lack of interest he brought to our interrogations of Beat luminaries in their hothouse American retirements.

It was too dark to read a map. The only other customer, a depressed black man, elbows on table, contemplating an empty pot, nodded his approval of the spicy chicken carnage on my plate. It would be staying there. I was heading straight back to the station. A huge TV screen blasted inarticulate hysteria from the visually impaired judo at the ExCeL Centre.

'The Algerian has put his foot in the British boy's stomach and thrown him over. This really has been a contest of two halves. Remarkable. He won't give up.'

As I head for the door, I can hear them promoting doggie dentures. Neither the barman, nor the man who is poking at my chicken wings, will pay any attention to the screen.

What frustrated me in the sprawl of the Croydon diaspora, where everything appeared to be on the way to other destinations, better places, was the absence of sites in which I might hope to make contact with Pavel: modest all-day breakfast cafés, second-hand bookshops, charity pits. London Road offered no points of entrance. Like most of the pedestrians, I was the wrong demographic. High fences around captured ground boasted of a better future and solicited public collaboration for regeneration through upbeat signage. I was clumping uphill towards the Overground station when I found my first Pavel-possible enclave, a Scope shop dedicated to people with cerebral palsy. The only book that had a whiff of him was *Tales, 1812: And Other Selected Poems* by George Crabbe. A decent volume in dustwrapper, it had been officially discarded by Enfield Libraries. 'Had crimes less weighty on the spirit press'd, / This troubled Conscience might have sunk to rest.'

No signature. No bookplate. No annotations. But I was encouraged to sift the small stack of DVDs, and to come away with *BEAT (This is a True Story . . . As True as Any Story Can Be . . .). New York, 1944. Several students gather at the apartment of Joan Vollmer (Courtney Love) to smoke, drink and experiment with drugs. Among them, William S. Burroughs (Kiefer Sutherland), Lucian [sic] Carr (Norman Reedus) and Alan [sic] Ginsberg (Ron Livingstone).*

Promising. Certainly one to take home. And quite possibly a silver disk with Pavel's fingerprints.

Coming to the crossroads, and pushing on down a pedestrianized precinct, flagshipped by the Ann Summers sex shop from which the impoverished citizen had stolen the pink dildo, I began to feel the pulse of the place. There was an identifiable civic centre, beyond the strumming of the goth band, the mid-morning scrunch and rush of on-the-hoof diners. Croydon gusted with diesel whirlwinds from new towers: company headquarters, supercity blocks of fiscal inanition. George Street was carved by retro-trams offering painless amputation, whistling through ranks of confused or decrepit humans who were window-shopping discounted comics and plastic space monsters. A plaque on the Hospital of the Holy Trinity made a political promise: 'Sustenance and relief of certain maymed, poore, needie or impotent people, to have continuance for ever.'

All the ancient twisting ways led to an island cleared by fire. This sunken zone was under the protection of a locked Minster church, a set of almshouses blessed with a magnificent apple tree. Here was another terminal point: for the London riots of 2011. The furniture store and former auction house of the Reeves dynasty was torched by a flashmob tuned to the theatre of flame by BlackBerries and excited messages racing down the line from Dalston. Now the abandoned site has become a memory-show; blind walls dressed with vast images of bearded entrepreneurs, hierarchies of shopworkers. Did Lawrence select a chair for his bedroom? The Davidson Road Elementary School, where he taught, was close at hand. He lodged at 12 Colworth Road from 1908 to 1912. In the summer of 1909, Jessie Chambers sent a number of his poems to Ford Madox Hueffer, who published them in the *English Review*. Lawrence was tapping Helen Corke, a teacher at another school, for details of her affair with a married man, who later killed himself. This sad story becomes fiction. *The Trespasser.*

I am trespassing. This is not my territory. I'm in New York, in Corso's loft, but I don't belong there either. He's pacing, he won't sit down. We conduct the conversation on our feet, circling, freezing. He challenges. He gestures. *Right! You got it.* Most of his late interviews involve arguments about the way the clip-mike spoils the look of a leather waistcoat. He talks, when he does, sitting down; nodding, teeth gone, hair flopping over his eyes, winking at the person you don't see: the lover, dealer, friend. He has his categories of achievement: *Talent, genius, divine.* With Shelley, alone and unchallenged, the shooting star. *Pour secrecy upon the dying page.* Tourism yielded poems: Corso in London fog, in Berlin zoo, in Paris Beat hotel. On trains, in galleries, in borrowed beds. In Mexico.

Michael Moorcock, London's greatest fabulist of recent times, was sent to Pitman's College in Croydon to learn how to type. He failed the entrance to Whitgift Grammar School. But he came upon the legendary bookshop of our dreams, a time-warp enterprise with all the pristine items from Victorian and Edwardian eras still nestling on the shelves. Novels of the 1920s and 1930s, mysteries and speculative romances, in intact wrappers. And for sale, as he whispered, 'at half their original prices'. In the first flush he told a dealer who scooped the lot. Back to the shorthand. But typewriting skills, over the years, have stood him in good stead. He could fill a dozen of these shops from his backlist.

I understood why the blind man micturated with such urgency

against the wall. And why telephone kiosks, stripped of directories in which I might search for the address of Pavel Coen, were sticky-floored and foul-smelling. The new Croydon didn't cater for ageing prostates, fidgeting kids, doubly burdened pregnant shoppers. Before I reversed my journey on the Overground, I needed a comfort break in one of the department stores: four warehouse floors thinly dressed with goods for a closing sale. Twenty minutes of stairs, failed escalators, misdirections, brought me to a remote basement with an out-of-order door: LADIES. Another eternity, walking faster now, swerving around mothers who have ground to a halt, reluctant partners, vagrants with numerous empty bags, led to a unisex cupboard under the roof.

Near the street door – cosmetics, shoes, handbags – there is some hope of a sale. Assistants switch from disdain to lapel-grabbing intimacy. They are saturated in product, feline musk, and painted until they crack; mask faces slashed with serial-killer red. Deeper inside this retail colony, for which no chart has ever been produced, we understand that the weird boxy clothes, outdated electronic gizmos, off-white goods, mouse pads with portraits of Elvis Presley and Marilyn Monroe, are Croydon's mistranslation of the USA. No passport, no oath of allegiance. Available, without prejudice, to every free man, woman and child.

Floorwalkers don't walk. They lurk. They double as security. They mop out the toilets. They wear black shirts and waistcoats. They are pale as death. The man suppressing a silent scream, allocated a position on the top floor (where only the incontinent come), is Pavel Coen. He is the custodian of a library of VHS tapes dressed to look like books. I notice *Niagara*, *Vanishing Point* and *Boxcar Bertha*. I don't say a word. I rush through men's pyjamas to the lift. It isn't working. Rather than coming close for a second time, confirming Pavel's identity, I make a massive detour to the stairs. And then the street. If he deserves anything, my former colleague has earned the right to obscurity. If he retains a Beat archive from our 1995 US trip, Croydon is the perfect place to bury it.

Corso

Three days later the padded bag arrived. A neighbour took it in and gave it to me when I made my return from the flat in St Leonards-on-Sea, where I had been writing up my Croydon field trip. Circumstances had recalibrated my approach. What was becoming clear was that biography was the biggest fiction of all. At every point where I was present, off-stage, significant details were wrong. Those readings didn't happen in the Albert Hall. This woman was never with that man. Memory is like the Old West; the dead are always crossing back and forth from Arizona to Mexico, Tombstone to Nogales. Olson on the Atlantic Seaboard: Gloucester to Washington. Then further south to Florida Keys, to Yucatán. Lowry up and down the Pacific Rim, Los Angeles to Vancouver. Through drink and derangement, poets raid the forbidden zone where animals have no shape, flesh splits into bubbling magma, fountains run with sand: *how to escape?* How to bring logic to the bounty of sleep? And when it is done, as Lowry discovered, his place found, characters identified, reason will cut you down. Through its special agents, the critics and editors. Customs men requiring 'la mordida'.

On to my desk tumbled two Corso tapes, a Burroughs tape, the BBC radio script, and notes from the afternoon when we confronted – not too strong a word – Gregory Corso. Also: photographs of Huncke with spider plant. And Corso, head thrust forward, ski-jump nose, tongue out, like a gargoyle from Notre-Dame. Huncke: so civilized, contained, precise in recall and terminology. But alien too, another species. Corso confined: raw, challenging. A prisoner of authenticity looking for a new angle, a dropped gold coin. Dark arriviste. Street kid on the make. Allen Ginsberg's adopted changeling. With no excuse but poetry.

Had Pavel spotted me? Had one of the other contacts I'd sounded out reached him with my message? There was no card. All I knew was that I wouldn't play the tapes. They belonged to another project. I glanced at the old script. And flinched. It was wedged so precariously in the wrong time.

In New York bookstores with their racks of Irish Romanticism, their elephantine diet primers, a man stands in a corner babbling about Gary Indiana. It's better when we walk, cutting rapidly through the ethnic contour lines as we move down the numbers towards the Lower East Side. That haunting smell that cinema can't deliver: hot-chilli chickens rotorized in peanut-butter kerosene. White smoke from pyramid towers. Shady neighbourhood bars. Honking horns. Suspect limousines with darkened windows.

It wasn't easy to make contact with Gregory Corso. The phone calls went back and forth. Clinic days. Museum days. We walked beside the river in a gusting wind. Surveillance shops, detective agencies. I snapped the producer outside Badlands Adult Video. Meat-market trucks.

Corso lives a couple of flights up from the street with a pair of book-dealers. Gregory is the Joe Pesci of the Beat Generation, a flute of restless energy. He refuses to talk sitting down, he prison-paces the small, single-bed cell.

At sixty-six he's the youngest of the daddies, the founding fathers. He's worried that literary brokers are nudging him out of the picture. He insists: 'I am the poetry I write.'

You like Corso right off. The problems arrive later when you get to know him. He trades on harsh beginnings. The Italians, the mob. A standard heritage construct: Sinatra, spoiled-priest Scorsese. The faces at the bar in *Mean Streets* and *Goodfellas* are where the poet locates himself when he's making his pitch. A sixteen-year-old member of the Walkie-Talkie Gang who ripped off $64,000 from the safe of the moneylending Household Finance operation. On a roll, Gregory rebranded himself in a zoot suit louder than a confession. He squeezed $7,000 into his jacket and took off for Florida. Later he would write about how dollars leaked away, slippery as mercury: 'Money in every pocket, no wallet, no clip/I just bunch it up and stuff it.' A dangerously occult commodity. 'Money,' he says, 'doesn't come with instructions.'

Anecdotes are part of the texture, the literary pension plan. Back in the late 1940s and early 1950s, when he sat in all-night automats and dyke bars, Horn and Hardart, yapping with Burroughs, Ginsberg and Kerouac, hipsters admired the vigour of their discourse. Now, at a period when Beat Generation revivalism threatens to turn the whole circus into another Bloomsbury Group, Corso has succeeded in opting out – while producing a ceiling-threatening mound of cardboard boxes packed, so he says, with unpublished typescripts.

He is identifiable in the Annie Leibovitz line-up for *Vanity Fair* in December 1995, arm in arm with Chairman Ginsberg, but he's the only one of the veterans who looks as if he'll be walking home after he's pocketed cash payment for the shoot. Notice the dirty trainers against the sheen of David Amram's patent-leather hooves. Notice the billowing untucked shirt. The weight of belly. Ferlinghetti, in broad-brim jungle hat, is an audition for the granddad of Indiana Jones. Corso tilts, letting long hair flop. He knows just how to put his foot on the fender of a car.

The Kerouac estate has a six-figure annual turnover (and rising, fast). Ginsberg's papers have gone to Stanford University for more than a million dollars. Burroughs, in retirement, advertises Nike, and is visited by European camera crews and rock royalty. Ginsberg and Burroughs have been elevated into the American Academy of Arts and Letters. The double-page Leibovitz portraits of Burroughs sculpt him as a Roman senator, a death mask. But Corso remains agentless. 'I've no mamma, no papa, no dente, no casa.' Disinvited, by Bill Clinton, to join high-achieving Italian-Americans, such as Nicolas Cage, Scorsese, at the feast held in honour of President Oscar Luigi Scalfaro, Corso is the typecast outcast. His worry was that his father, seeing him on the cover of *Newsweek*, would think he was going straight to the electric chair.

We talked for more than an hour. When Gregory's fired up, he flows. He described himself as a 'graduate in orphancy', abandoned by a youthful mother who fled back to Italy, leaving him to a series of foster parents, who would pass him on like a bad debt: bedwetter, thief. An early epiphany was the memory of bathing with one of the surrogates while a stream of golden light burnished her thick pubic fleece. 'I remember the black hair on her cunt and the water. Now that's a good shot for a two-year-old.'

Corso lived rough, tracing eidetic visions in the clouds, lions stalking the roofs of tenements. He matriculated in petty crime, boosting radios. He was incarcerated briefly in the Tombs and defined as insane. He spent 'three frightening sad months' in Bellevue. And without the middle-class Lowry option of checking out as soon as he had enough material for a book. The early Corso poems are about his mother and the sea. Or gangsters, suicides: 'When you're dead you can't talk. Yet you feel like you could.'

This was the sketchy biographical outline I carried with me, that New York afternoon with Pavel Coen and his recording machine. As research, I viewed Corso, in tweedy sports jacket, performing at the Albert Hall readings on 11 June 1965. I watched the video. American poets, abroad, wore suits and ties. And didn't worry about being sponsored by the CIA. I read freewheeling interviews in fugitive magazines. Corso answered the old inglorious questions as if he were hearing them for the first time.

Now he has moves to make, before we settle to our chat. It is an experience to cover the East Side with someone who belongs. Gregory describes himself as a spy on life, a peeper but never a fink. Before he met him for the first time in the Pony Stable, a West 12th Street lesbian bar, Corso watched the unknown Ginsberg, in a room across the street, making love to a woman the young Gregory masturbated over on his release from prison. Complicated erotic relationships were congeries of nameless arms and legs. Shared mattresses. The street poet carried a manuscript with him as protection. He sat for hours with the lights out.

Begging for postage stamps, then dodging from a fast-food

joint where he tries to get a bet down on credit, the wired poet bumps – as if by arrangement – into a tall, slender man in a dark 'European-cut' suit, a white silk George Raft scarf around his neck. 'Hey, *Gregory*, how's it going? You still spending Christmas with us?'

'Ooooh, man, hot dude, that guy,' he whistles through the missing teeth. 'Mafiosa, hot shit.'

Circuit completed, Gregory's back where we found him: bifocals on the end of nose, reading and scowling, babysitting an empty bookshop, while he waits for the owners who keep a roof over his head to bring back the necessary package.

Corso remains in childhood territory, a couple of blocks from the Hudson River, in an apartment shared with Roger and Irvyne Richards, the dedicatees ('slayers of homelessness') of his most recent volume, *Mindfield*. Huncke and Peter Orlovsky also hang out at the book room as living exhibits, marginals whose work has never quite been accepted into the official canon. Self-imitation is a rough trade. They sign anything put in front of them.

Retired upstairs, Corso paces his borrowed cabin's length, inflating confession into boast. White open-necked shirt, loose black waistcoat. Grey hair to shoulder. He's sockless in scuffed white casuals. Footwear is important. 'Don't take off your shoes.' That's what they told him when, aged seventeen, he arrived at Clinton State Prison in Dannemora. Any session with Gregory opens with a restatement of the three golden rules. 'Hang on to your shoes, you're walking.' 'Don't serve time, let time serve you.' 'When you're outside, and you're talking to two people, make sure you see three.'

Corso loves this notion of the invisible third, the guardian angel. All his sins are forgiven if he's an actor in a pre-scripted drama. 'It's the mirror that changes/not poor Gregory.' The shadowy third is the silent witness at the table. Today that role is performed by the man with the microphone, Pavel Coen, scribe to the Court of Thieves. And the person you can rely on to lose the evidence, to bury this small chapter of Corso's legend. As Burroughs said, 'If you wish to conceal anything, you have only to create a lack of interest in the place where it is hidden.' Croydon. Where else? Put a yellow-eyed Madagascar lemur in the window of *Forbidden Planet*, among the blockbuster merchandise, and nobody will pay the slightest attention.

The meeting with Ginsberg was the crucial one. It would be a lifelong bonding. They were the two acknowledged poet heroes of the Beat Generation. 'The poet and the poetry,' Corso stated, 'are inseparable.' Ginsberg, careful of his career, but working hard to promote his friends, continued to support and nurture Corso – even when he had to be expelled from the Cherry Valley Farm for his refusal to abstain from alcohol. And heroin. Their relationship was not faggot, Gregory assured us. 'He sucked me off, but that was it. I didn't want to put my mouth where men go to the bathroom.' It all began, this wary hug, with rear windows. Ginsberg, the lover Corso watched from his eyrie, invited the younger man to share the woman of his fantasy, Dusty Moreland.

What mattered most to the Beats was the intensity of visionary experience. Corso, who had a thing about doors, was lying on his bed one day when he saw the knob turning, the locked door opening. It happened a second time on Crete: *skinless light*. He was young, clean; he wasn't dreaming. There was a spectral form pointing straight at him. He wrote a letter to Ginsberg. 'I saw it, Burroughs saw it – did *you* see it?' And he received a furious reply. Ginsberg had heard the voice of Blake in Harlem. 'But what did he say?' Corso demanded. 'Niente, no word.'

The New York Beats were peppery, competitive. There were presentational differences with the cooler cats on the West Coast, the Portland Buddhists. Corso could never accept Pacific Rim eco dogma. He didn't want to be lectured on the divinity of forests. 'I pounded my fists on a wooden table and said: "*This* is what man does to trees."' It was hard for the sockless city boy to listen to Gary Snyder 'yakking at Dakota farmers on how to plant potatoes' without laughing.

Corso decided to bide his time in the 1960s, to sit out the 1970s. He didn't join in with the essentially West Coast eruption of

Be-Ins, neo-tribalism, communality. The process of marginalization began – in which he was happy to cooperate. 'Drugs,' Corso said, 'were a filthy nurse.' But they gave structure to a day. If Burroughs used addiction as a way of making contact with alien energies, soliciting viral invasion, then Corso, requiring instant gratification, indulged heroin as part of a long-standing argument with himself. The conversion of a 'good-looking little wop', trading on suspect charm, into a toothless seer. The birthday poems and mirror interrogations grew bleaker and bleaker. 'He's probably the greatest poet in America,' Ginsberg said, 'and he's starving in Europe.'

There were stories of bad behaviour. Kathy Acker remembers being dumped from a car in the middle of the night, in a Panther-controlled area of Oakland, for refusing to take part in a Corso threesome. There were scuffles outside the Lower East Side bunker where Burroughs was lodged. 'It's always like this with Gregory,' he complained. 'Wherever he goes it's always *cops* and everything.' By now Corso was well on the way to becoming the Joe Pesci of *Casino*; a white-lipped, amphetamine nemesis for Ginsberg's Jewish De Niro, who was trying to do business, keep the Beat empire moving and growing as a great American resource. Like Las Vegas.

In company with his old rivals, the Black Mountain poets, whom he regarded as 'mental gangsters, hip squares', Corso was out of favour, ignored by major publishers. But he was still producing the work; he showed us the cardboard boxes in his cluttered room. He *was* the poem, so there was no way out. 'Eight years now and I haven't stole a thing! The world owes me a million dollars.' No longer 'randomly young', how should he live? The language geyser was almost dry. Corso downsized as a sperm bank, a child father for hire. And the bank paid dividends. He accepted the tragedy of bringing life into the world. 'I like human beings, but I don't like life.' He reported Kerouac's sorrow when confronted by Corso's infant son. 'O Gregory, you brought up something to die.'

The trapped poet, chased by the tape machine, breaks from his cougar pacing to explain. 'Four blessed children by four different mothers. And very rich mothers. How blessed I am. I don't have to

go to work, I don't have to do anything. I'm happy, I see them. They see me. Oh boy! Great ladies. They wanted to raise their kids alone. One child is enough, Gregory. Sharp women, blessed. Each one, five years a shot. Dig it? No accident.' But now, he says, things are different. 'I need my drinky poo. The ball game is over. I don't want to make more children. I don't go after women any more.'

We get into an animated discussion on the relative merits of the terms 'whack' or 'dust' for a Mafia hit. Corso finds 'whack' an onomatopoeic vulgarity – the sound is there, but the impact is too crude. He prefers 'dust', with the visual scoring of powder rising from old suits, the blue meat of the wasted man returning to clay. Hearing that we are about to visit Burroughs, he tells us that we'll have good hunting, and terminates the interview to write Bill a letter.

In our rambling stop-start dialogue, Corso uses a number of similes drawn from Native American life, an unconscious reconnection with Snyder's concerns. The Beats, Gregory implies, are the Redskins of America: noble savages doomed in all they attempt. Or

Hollywood B-feature braves played by Jews. In his collection *Elegiac Feelings American*, he wrote of Kerouac and his identification with the land. He offered up a 'Spontaneous Requiem for the American Indian'. He saw the metamorphosis of a 'hard nickel faced' Apache Geronimo into a leather-jacket motorcyclist: 'smoking a cigarette in a fishy corner in the night'.

Too many lives, as Kerouac said, are 'written on mirrors in smoke'. 'Am I dead or alive?' John Wieners wondered. 'A feeling of embalming fluid. This is a cheated poet, a chastised citizen who has gotten hepatitis from Herbert Huncke's spike.'

When we take our leave of Corso, his minders ask after first editions of the authors they'd like to feature in the shop: Larkin, Barbara Pym. The masque of England the veteran Beats enthuse over – P. G. Wodehouse, Agatha Christie, Peter Ackroyd – is as much a surprise to me as my fondness for Wieners, Lew Welch and Ed Dorn is to them. We are both chasing, in our ignorance, compensatory stereotypes of difference.

Risking another humiliation from the baggage handlers in torpedo coats, we take a cab to the Paramount Hotel. From the high window, I can see eels of black smoke, but no stars. This is not a good space in which to prepare for William Burroughs. But now I have Corso's letter in my pocket. There are quilted headboard panels behind the bed, so slippery you don't want to lean against them. The TV is hidden inside a thin cupboard with a cut-out Osiris eye. Light, spilling from a surgical tube, is so feeble that it's almost impossible to see the numbers on the telephone. I can't read my copy of *Ghost of Chance*. But the laminated hardcover book is illustrated by monochrome reproductions of late-Burroughs paintings. In the gloom I imagine lizards staring out of a barbed-wire jungle. I think the elegant black lady from Broadway, the one with the leather coat and fur collar, would feel right at home.

Burroughs over Kansas

'The further west you go, the worse it gets,' Burroughs says. 'I was born in St Louis. So was Eliot. Place is of no importance. I've spent my life looking for a better vintage of boredom. A third of my material comes from dreams, from no place at all.'

Flights are dreams. Anna saw herself levitating over these arid plains and blamed it on my book. 'What are you working on?' She dreams for me, and always has. But she has not woken up screaming for years. Circling over the pulsing lights of Kansas City, 1845 hrs, Sunday 20 November 1995, I have never been further away from her. The middle of a vast unconquered landmass.

Very quickly – processing is swift on internal flights before 9/11 – we are in the Hertz Redi-Car lot and I'm adjusting to a left-hand-drive automatic that is unnervingly clean, plastic-smelling and solid. My task, as freeways ravel into a blizzard of signage, is to locate the Sheraton Country Plaza at 770 West 47th Street. Pavel, I discover, is not map literate. He can't do folds and numbers. He's engrossed in paperwork from Jim McCrary at William Burroughs Communications. Our instructions for arrival at the Burroughs hideaway in Lawrence. The phone number is unlisted.

Nobody told Pavel that there were two Kansas Cities, at the confluence of the Missouri and Kansas rivers. He took us into the wrong one, the jazz one, the lived-in place of working Sunday-night bars. I go into one of these, anticipating frontier saloon-movie treatment – piano stopped, glasses frozen midway to mouth – but they were friendly, amused, and set me on the right road. To another swoop of luggage grabbers, parking jockeys confiscating keys. My room, with its cattle-king bed and cinema-sized TV, is like an exploded Premier Inn or mega-ibis. And I'm comfortable with that. I flick through the channels before we go out for dinner. The only available news is English: extracts of Princess Di's simpering confession and clips of Paul McCartney, with his compulsive wink, peddling a Beatles remix. We couldn't set foot outside the hotel in New York without searchlights sweeping the heavens with news of James Bond and *GoldenEye* at Radio City Music Hall. Impossible to eat a bread roll within a mile of Broadway without one of the waiters bursting into a song from *Cats*. Eliot should never have left St Louis. Burroughs should never have returned.

The constipation of mid-continental wealth is in the spread of beef on our jumbo plates in the restaurant on the Country Club Plaza. Steaks, oozing blood, are relief maps of Missouri, three inches thick, with river systems, historic battle sites, and probably an imprint of the face of Judy Garland in *Wizard of Oz* braids. Single glasses of wine are worth half a bottle elsewhere. To order anything beyond that marks you out as an alcoholic. Patrons are semantically smart in ice-blue suits and fat ties, apart from the ones with Stetsons and gambler's string held in place with a steer's head clasp. The muzak is 'Yesterday' and 'Send in the Clowns'.

I tell Pavel that *Ghost of Chance* is the antidote to everything that surrounds us. Burroughs is beginning to look like the last thin man in America, the magus of lean prose, all gristle and strike. And he floats without visible strain both ways in time: which is one of the principle benefits of paranoia. The Burroughs take on ecology, by way of animal hybrids, human stupidity, is as valid as the practical trail notes of Gary Snyder or the mammal rhapsodies of Michael McClure. Burroughs is talking *extinction*: a Museum of Lost Species, the Four Horsemen riding through ruined cities and neglected, weed-grown farms. Dust Bowl Kansas is where the virus burns itself out, its victims have died by the millions. Homo Sap, Burroughs asserts, is the only species that kills for the sheer beauty of the ugliness of the thing. To protect the malignant spirit within. Language, the ultimate virus, ultimate curse, separates us from other living creatures.

Pavel, with his index-card memory-system for dates and addresses, reminds me that McClure came from Wichita. On the map it seems that Wichita is just down the road to the south-west, a little closer than St Louis to the east. A short haul in US terms down Interstate 335. No more than, what, 200 miles? Three hours? Allen Ginsberg, when we had our conversation in Regent's Park in 1967, talked about driving through here in a camper van on the big American quest, fragments of which he published as *Wichita Vortex Sutra*. I asked him what he was working on.

'Ah, scribbling. That's all. I don't have any schematic thing. I just follow what happens. I have a long poem of which *Wichita Vortex Sutra* is a part. It's travelling around the United States using a tape recorder, in a Volkswagen, a camper, with Peter Orlovsky at the wheel and I'm in the back at a table. And I include all the relevant data that comes to my attention: the car radio, whatever news-papers are lying around, the news broadcasts coming through, the landscape through the window, the stops for coffee, the plains or forests or mountains we are passing through, the thoughts going on inside my head, portions of the conversations in the car. In other words, all the simultaneous data of those instants, with the Uher funnelling them, reducing them to language.'

And in other words again, the soundtrack for a silent film by Stan Brakhage or a flick through a bunch of Robert Frank photographs for *The Americans*. A radio-beam circumnavigation of the territory where Burroughs would come to die. Flash frames from Vietnam. The Pepsi Generation. The Chinese written character for 'truth'. 'Has anyone looked in the eyes of the dead?' Dipping downward through low hills, rising narrow on the far horizon. 'I'm an old man now, and a lonesome man in Kansas.'

Arriving in Wichita, Ginsberg marks it as the site where 'McClure's mind burst into animal beauty'. There are multiple superimpositions as we deprogramme invasion karma; we speak with borrowed tongues in our mouths. The cut-up tape, in its abrupt declamatory phrases, and the prominence it grants to adver-tising slogans and cubist scraps of found headlines, echoes the vortex of Wyndham Lewis and Pound, and the war to end all wars; but it also, and more importantly, zeroes in on the weird space–time anomalies of the landlocked settlement, where the great oceans, Pacific and Atlantic, are a distant rumour. Here is origin: in the sense of a propulsive need to escape.

Brakhage, the film-poet from Kansas City, forges a close collaborative friendship with McClure: in San Francisco. They are blood brothers of the Vortex that is geographically aligned with an area somewhere west of Wichita. The poet Charles Plymell called this place: 'about the centre of the United States'. He said that it had 'much significance' in ancient cultures. He found a map from the late nineteenth century depicting the Cheyenne North Path from Oklahoma to Yellowstone. The sacred site is clearly marked. It's the furthest point north for the Navaho, where east–west trails intersect around Monument Rock. The Wichita Vortex draws them all in: medicine men, ghost dancers in buffalo helmets, prairie drifters, redeye bikers, and the sodality of disenfranchised writers who trust to songlines, coincidences, Tourette's syndrome quotations.

Pavel froze over his untouched bucket of side salad. He could see his neat little BBC radio piece dissolving into psychogeographic madness.

'Plymell drove out there with his son. They heard a voice that was neither human nor animal. He found out, later, that this phenomenon was known as the call of the Tent Shaker, a shamanic entity without form. Rocks, he said, have male and female energies. You can use them to get on the astral grid. There are clusters of iron meteorites and impact craters in amazing patterns. The flow back into the troposphere takes the form of a double-helix vortex spiral. That's what brought Burroughs back to Kansas. That's what he is tapping with his orgone accumulator: immortality, dissolution of molecules. A method of lifting clear of the pinched suit of skin.'

Fancying a turn of the pool, to shake off the residue of planes and cars, I went out early to look for a swimming costume. Futile. The mall close to the hotel featured designer outlets, sharp Armani suits in black, high-concept T-shirts the size of bedspreads. The best that the combined efforts of Abercrombie & Fitch, Benetton, Brooks

Brothers, Ralph Lauren, Saks Fifth Avenue could come up with was a pair of grey wool jogging pants that sagged and threatened to slide around my knees as soon as I broke the rippling blue chemical surface. 'Water is your hinge.' I remembered Carlos Castaneda and how the Yaqui magician, Don Juan, submerged his apprentice in an irrigation ditch: as the pivotal point between worlds. In the Sheraton Country Plaza you could swim – in November nobody else did – out from the basement, under an arch, into the open air.

Before we set off for Lawrence and our rendezvous with William Burroughs, I walked down to the river and followed it until it became a man-made canal or sewage channel. The elasticated stretch of soul, between myself and Anna, America and Hackney, was at its critical point. There is a line in the *Beat* DVD I found in Croydon, probably lifted from Malcolm Lowry and *Under the Volcano*, but given to Keifer Sutherland's Burroughs in Mexico City. 'When you stare into the abyss, be sure that the abyss will stare right back.'

Once you are clear of the city and out on the highway, the film flows. Pavel has a medical condition that forbids him to register anything beyond his personal space, the way he grips a black satchel between clamped thighs. The recording kit and the ring-binder with the names and phone numbers are snug in his lap. He is incapable of telling me when a turn-off is approaching, or which lane I need to position us in. The landscape is flat farm country. I take the unilateral decision to come off-road, to ask for confirmation that we haven't slipped into the pull of the Native American Vortex. (The Kansas whirlwind in *Wizard of Oz* was an obvious precursor of the astral stairway.)

Bumping down a dust track towards a solitary farmhouse, with no sign of human habitation, I think of Truman Capote's *In Cold Blood* and the mindless massacre of the Clutter family. When we get to Lawrence, I ask Burroughs about this. He snorts. 'Humpfff. Other side of the state. West Kansas. Ugly place, ugly people.'

To cover up his navigational deficiencies – and he's otherwise excellent company, mute or muttering – Pavel asks about my history with Burroughs. He knows that this is the big encounter of our transcontinental journey. And that I don't need the great man to say one word. I want the opportunity to see if he exists, in physical form: before he doesn't. Before he switches channels. Like Anna, so I discover from *My Education: A Book of Dreams*, Burroughs has been experiencing levitation. 'A neutral timeless space-less place of shadows. I can levitate because there is no gravity here.' As he comes back to ground, in his dream, he encounters a woman who doesn't see him. Her husband is a Weather Cop.

Dublin, 1962. New people exploring an old town set around the curve of the bay, Howth Head to Sandycove. Inky ghosts in soft rain. Humans outlived by their clothes. Solitary walks become conversation pieces at the shoreline, along the river, into evening suburbs. With the usual consequences. All that innocence. The tide went out for ever, rippling contours of worm casts, sick molluscs, the tall chimneys of Ringsend and Irishtown. We would float a magazine. And its name, glorying in failure, elective obscurity, would be: *Albatross*.

We sent out flyers to everybody: T. S. Eliot, Ezra Pound, Paul Bowles, Djuna Barnes, Jean Genet, Samuel Beckett. Some of these mythic figures were honoured by additional cards or letters. There would be a trial edition to raise funds. Then our 'bi-annual' literary bombshell would be fired at the world from the sleepiest of launch pads: Winton House, 53 Strand Road, Dublin 4, Eire.

One person in the universe responded to our request for a contribution: William S. Burroughs of Tangier, Morocco. He wanted his text read across and down. An accompanying note from the author stated: 'This is an experiment – one of many possible – in altering the conventional page format and drawing lines of narrative off the page.' But we never figured out, with jobbing Dublin printers, the proper technology for this effect. Later, we toured the far west in a loud white sports car, trawling for a provincial firm reckless enough to risk the wrath of the priests. Magazines would be routinely banned within the university and I would have to endure some pompous (and ill-informed) don telling me about how he'd seen all this lower-case nonsense years ago, with Cummings. 'There's nothing as old hat as the avant-garde.'

Calder had not yet published the first English edition of *Naked Lunch*. The Digit paperback of *Junkie*, issued in 1957, had already vanished and would become a legendary rarity. Burroughs was a fiction of the New York subways, rolling drunks, as real/unreal as Richard Widmark in Samuel Fuller's *Pickup on South Street*. Bill was on a cannabis farm in East Texas or Louisiana, watching his wife knock lizards from the trees with a rake. This man was a personage as remote from our experience as Homer. In newsprint and magazine photographs, he looked like a composite, a suspect Xeroxed so far from source he might be a Civil War veteran or a hard-veined Chicago exterminator in the 1920s. An alien – alien from what? – disguised by good English tailoring and living where you least expect him. With the blinds drawn.

Three thin sheets of Burroughs text in a blue airmail envelope. *He took some room with another gentleman. It was a long time ago. My brother he went crazy.*

Albatross never saw the light of day. Maybe fifty copies of the trial run were produced. They disappeared. Buff wrappers. Stapled. 81 pp. If this freely distributed magazine can be described as 'published' – and off they went to the copyright libraries – then *Albatross* would be around the fiftieth item in the checklist of William Burroughs contributions. And the first to appear in Ireland. The same text did eventually make the listings when I recycled it in Trinity College's official and long-standing literary magazine, *Icarus*, in May 1965. Maynard and Miles gave it the number C125 in their Burroughs bibliography of 1978.

The island of Gozo, 1967. Hot, dry, sand-coloured. Amenable to strangers. With the worst cuisine in the Mediterranean. Letters were exchanged with William Burroughs in London. And postcards. I found that it was possible to rent a house for a pound less than the cost of the room where we lived on Haverstock Hill during the film-ing with Ginsberg. After the ease of setting up a documentary organized around the Dialectics of Liberation in the Roundhouse, the logical step was to offer the Germans a follow-up, a film on Bur-roughs. Negotiations began, but I was still operating on hope rather than expectation when we moved into the property owned by the manager of the famous TV glove puppet Sooty. Gozo was agricul-tural, Catholic, a patchwork of small fields and extravagant churches. On Christmas Eve, a village woman knocked on our door, bringing a gift, a small live chicken in a brown paper bag. Its meat was tough as shoe leather.

Checking the holdings of that time, as listed by Barry Miles in *A Descriptive Catalogue of the William S. Burroughs Archive* (London 1973), I find that Burroughs kept six items relating to our potential film project. It's an honour to sit on the page between Terry South-ern (writer) and John Trevelyan (film censor). I follow on from Ian Somerville (systems advisor to WSB). And precede Kenneth Tynan (critic & writer), Tambimuttu (editor) and Alex Trocchi. A nice little snapshot of the era. My letters to Burroughs begin in December 1967 and finish in June 1968 (on my birthday). By which point, he had withdrawn into Scientology. And the Germans had decided that their interest in the counterculture ran out with Ginsberg. 'We do not know Burroughs in Cologne.'

I worked through the Gozo mornings on the Burroughs script. After lunch, we walked, or sometimes cycled, down a rough track to the sea. It was warm enough to swim well into December. The clarity of light, by day, and the starry dome, when we sat out on the flat roof in the evenings, played against negative visions of the spec-tral Burroughs, hunkered down near Piccadilly, exploiting English sets left over from Graham Greene paperbacks, Edgar Wallace B-features, and sepia traces of that merchant mariner come ashore in Stoke Newington, Joseph Conrad.

My sense of Burroughs – *photo falling, word falling* – was of a man in a room. Or a photograph of a man in a room: draining the colour out, tapping dead veins. In England, in Bayswater hotels, bars, the flat in Duke Street, he was visited by local disciples or enthusiasts, paying their respects. Writers – Michael Moorcock, J. G. Ballard, Jeff Nuttall – made contact with a figure they later recalled as an actor, a voice: a being as old and unforgiving as an Egyptian mummy. Burroughs is courteous, he responds, but he is not really *there*. Without moving his lips, he dictates the script. You find yourself ventriloquized by texts he has not yet composed or will never compose. The skin is made from a kind of liquid glass. Gazing into those mercury eyes, you are looking at a marmoreal version of your future self.

Ballard confirmed his Burroughs engagement through borrowed shifts of paranoid fragmentation, the forensic poetry of *The Atrocity Exhibition*. Moorcock composed *The Deep Fix*: 'a drug which takes SEWARD into a world that looks like Earth'. The printed dedication reads: 'For William Burroughs for obvious reasons.' Jeff Nuttall used his encounter with El Hombre Invisible as justification for *My Own Mag*, a stapled mimeo mass of cut-ups, riffs and routines. A man called Douglas Lyne, who invited the Hackney novelist Roland Camberton to tape a Burroughs monologue, relished this courtly American exile as a fellow spirit, a decayed aristocrat with clubland manners and a colonialist thirst for gin. 'For god's sake, I can't stand any more of this,' said Lyne's wife. 'I want to go drinking with Bill.'

Editing footage of Ginsberg, in August 1967, in a cutting room in Amsterdam, I began to appreciate how image pulls away from sound. We struggled to match unsynched recordings to mute pictures. Dialogue loops began to develop a life of their own, instructions from a parallel universe. To take a break, I suggested a run to The Hague, where they were screening the Conrad Rooks movie *Chappaqua*. The film is shot by Robert Frank. Frank was born in Switzerland, from where Rooks had recently emerged after detoxing in a private clinic. The deal felt like a cold-turkey nightmare running at whim through an autopsy camera, with a cast of expensive cultural quotations labouring to play themselves: Jean-Louis Barrault, Ginsberg,

Ornette Coleman. And of course Burroughs. Who emerges relatively unscathed. His prose was always about performance, perfect pitch. We jump-cut. A ghost dance around upstate New York. Swiss psychiatric clinics (trust-fund addicts). Native American burial grounds. He is never compromised, never discommoded. Give him the grey hat, the velvet-collared coat, and he's on. Tangier, 9 rue Git-le-Coeur. Duke St in St James's. The Bunker at 222 Bowery. 'Bill met very few people during his years in London,' said Barry Miles. 'He seemed to like it that way.'

'A poet is a spy,' Corso said. 'God's spy, you dig it? Like Keats. Spy for truth.' We cruised into Lawrence with Corso's story of the two hoods from St Louis in our heads. The small university town was so normal it was freakish. Kathy Acker, when we visited her in San Francisco, told me that, like all the other rock stars, actors, profile writers, she'd stopped off here, to pay her respects. 'Burroughs was the only prose writer I could find who was a conceptualist.' He welcomed her to his customized ambulance. They drove around town in winter evenings as the lights were coming on. It was Kathy's role to act as bait for college boys. There are a lot of college boys in Lawrence. This was a vampire show she didn't mind. She knew that it had potential as a future fiction, an anecdote. She was challenged once, she said, about the way Walter Abish lays out his text like a trap. Everything is calculated to such a fine degree in order to provoke a reaction from the reader. 'I can't do that,' Acker responded. 'The primary pleasure is not for the reader, it's for me. I came back to San Francisco because I planned to sail around the world. We were very excited. It didn't happen. We didn't know how to sail.'

There is a shop hawking New Age skateboards. PREPARE TO ENTER A NEW DIMENSION. Skulls in helmets. A university bookstore with racks of Algernon Blackwood and Arthur Machen. 30 MINUTES PARKING. DRUG FREE SCHOOL ZONE. I pull into an empty bay and, with malice aforethought, challenge Pavel to read the map and find the Burroughs property. He starts to bang his head against the window. An ambulance passes, lights flashing, siren on.

Dream Science

He was spending as much time now in the Land of the Dead as in Lawrence, Kansas. It was my impression that Burroughs chose this place in order to make that transition smoother; the twinned locations in the end were impossible to separate. Going out for eggs over easy, bacon, toast, coffee – and getting it, his order filled with a smile and a replenished cup – confirmed the fact that he was not yet in hell. In the dreams of beat hotels, bunkers with too many doors, trains like trains in Hitchcock movies (silver-smooth with back-projection lakes and snowy mountains), there were no breakfasts. It became an obsession: to score. To score even a cup of cold water with a shredded lettuce leaf floating in it. There are fast-food concessions in the Land of the Dead – of course there are – but they don't have anything you can eat. Sullen waitresses ignore the impatient old man in the grey suit.

Like Anna again, Burroughs dreams about packing. He's always cramming a suitcase with weapons he knows will be confiscated at the border by the same two officials; one paunchy, with gold teeth and a limp moustache, and the other in a white shirt and black tie; lean, mean, an ugly veneer of civilization. Charlton Heston in *A Touch of Evil* firing a cigarillo for that glinting shark's-bite mouth. The Orson Welles film, a Mexico of the mind fabricated out of Venice Beach, California, is one of the most accurate precursors of the Land of the Dead where Burroughs finds himself as soon as he nods off. *My Education* is a travel journal of expeditions in company with his suicided boys and Egyptian cats who can walk through walls. His relatives are waiting, his mother sometimes lodges at his side. He can *smell* her powder.

Apart from an interest in alien abduction (he pays a visit to Whitley Strieber, author of *Breakthrough*), and sexual encounters of the third kind, Burroughs was most concerned with proving that the dogmas of science were meaningless or totally misguided. He couldn't accept that nothing moved faster than the speed of light. He spoke of clicking a switch fifteen years ago and seeing lights come on in an unvisited room: *today*. Changing sets is a simple matter, he explained: Morocco, Martinique, Manchester, context is everything. The taste of a cigarette will do it, even a photograph of the cigarette, visible traces of rent-boy saliva. One line from a book by Joseph Conrad will import, or predict, meteorological conditions. You can read yourself into a storm. But you can't, when you're asleep, conjure up a decent plate of ham and eggs. The dead are starving, but they can't eat.

'I have seen weather magic,' Burroughs said. 'I have even performed it. I stopped rain in Seattle.'

Time is a politician's conceit. The reach of language, uncensored downloads from the third mind, is absolute: prophecy is never more than a statement of the obvious. Among the dream records Burroughs transcribes from 'scraps of paper and index cards and pages typed with one hand' are pre-vision/future-vision footage of 'air crashes'. That feeling of being enclosed, trapped in the seat. Over Manhattan. 'Very real.' Then they land on the street.

He's packing again. He has to escape. He thinks of: 'St Louis or anywhere west of New York.' Plague city. Hot dust. American smoke. *Photo falling, word falling.* Can't breathe without scorching the lungs. 'There is something terribly wrong here, some imminent disaster hangs in the air like a haze.' Get out of town, fast. If two men are following you, there must be an unseen third. Burroughs uses Wichita as the excuse; he's booked for a reading. As usual, he rehearses. His young assistants make the timings. 'James says he was proud of me.' On the road back to Lawrence in the ambulance: fridge, shower, toilet, bunk. Desolate country, burnt grass to sky for miles. Not one house. A few straggly trees, mulberry no doubt. The writer sits at his table, typing with one hand.

Suddenly, I'm hungry. It must be the Burroughs effect. We're entering his force field. Serpentine brain waves push out from a photovoltaic scanner, a radio mast. We must not arrive one minute early on Lear-nard Avenue. (*Lear* again: nothing comes of nothing.) We pull in at the EZ Food Store, a service station that doesn't serve. The woman at the till stares open-mouthed at these black-suit Euro aliens. I feel like a funeral director who has rung the bell before the sheet has been pulled over the patient. She spoons gritty pink goo from a tub. Shoppers pick up their gun magazines and cases of root beer. If you are granted access to the washroom, you are given a key attached by a chain to a wooden ball. The thickest turd I have ever seen, a steaming green truncheon, is curled around the crusted bowl like a dead python.

I buy a street plan and pass it to Pavel. Who dates it, notes the price ($2.25), before hiding this latest horror deep inside his black satchel. The folded map, published in Wichita, has a Mormon graphic: a many-spoked yellow sunburst over a temple-mall called *Lied Center*. We don't need maps. From this point, the car navigates itself.

We park across the street from the red weatherboard house with the neat white balcony. The most perverse writer in America has come to rest in a dappled Douglas Sirk avenue, where nothing moves. In our dark-windowed hired car, I pictured us as the two characters from Don Siegel's film of *The Killers*, the odd-couple hit-men, Lee Marvin and Clu Gulager. And that becomes the motif of my memory-tape. We are not implicated in the complex weave of personal relationships in the ever-expanding Burroughs biography. We are accidental bureaucrats, hirelings in town for an afternoon to do a job. *Get the shot*.

But Burroughs is far too canny, too long in the game. Pale sun-light across the table where he sits, waiting for the hour when he will take his first drink. Nothing to be said that has not been said a thousand times before. He talks property prices in Boulder and Lawrence. He reminisces about meeting Samuel Beckett in Berlin. Beckett stared at the wall. He had nothing to offer, beyond acknow-ledging that, yes, William Burroughs was indeed a writer.

The voice never rises above a gravel whisper. Time-travel has drained the man of superfluous social energy. There will be no more readings in Wichita, no more film cameos. He can't understand why every city he has visited in the last few years, when he comes to describe it, turns into Seattle. If there is an interview to be done, he'll manage it on the telephone. The red house is the closing set. The Toronto trip, to promote David Cronenberg's film of *Naked Lunch*, was a mistake. Nice hotel, no sleep. Excruciating pain, radiating down the left arm and up to the jaw. Popping nitro pills. 'No way to detach yourself since there is no place to detach yourself to.'

On the occasional table, I notice a copy of Gore Vidal's *Palimpsest*. I'd forgotten how Burroughs wrote about taking a fancy to the cocky young buck in the author photograph on the wrapper of *The Judgment of Paris*, back in 1952. 'A nice clean Ivy League boy.' They spent a session drinking together in the San Remo. This was before Kerouac's one-night stand with Vidal in the Chelsea Hotel; which was fictionalized, in different registers, by both men. Norman Mailer, reading everything in lurid post-Hemingway psychosexual terms, said that when Vidal 'removed the steel from Jack's sphincter', he buggered him into a vortex of booze and self-pity from which he would never escape.

Even in dream journals, Corso appears with his hand out. Burroughs complains of being tracked by bounty hunters. 'What am I worth? Gregory always wants to borrow money.' I pass over the letter Corso gave me in New York.

'Humpffff.'

Burroughs slashes the envelope with a ceramic knife. 'Best there is. Cost me a hundred dollars.' He scans Corso's message, snorts again. Flicks the letter across the table.

We get the standard heritage tour: the shotgun Nagual paintings with demon faces, and the books, which are mostly science fiction, serial killers, UFO reports. Along with unsolicited gifts left, pristine, on the shelf. Burroughs keeps a King James Bible close at hand: 'for the language'. He re-reads: Hemingway ('good on death'), Greene, Conrad. Denton Welch above all. And books with hard information.

A large ginger cat is sleeping on her master's sun-spotted single bed. Outside there is a feline cemetery with headstones, names and dates. Tasty snacks are prepared for the OAs (the outside animals): raccoons, possums, feral cats. Who do not stay outside, but who infiltrate the kitchen. If Bill gets up in the night, numerous rank and furry things press against his thin legs. He rescues wounded rats. And tolerates visits from Dean Ripa, the snake man, who has been known to set a king cobra, a gaboon viper and a fer-de-lance loose in the living room. Sacks of Tidy Cat deodorant powder are required to combat the fetid reek of the cat litter. All of these creatures, like Lawrence itself, like America, are dying. Becoming projections, Ariels and Calibans of the Midwest. 'Not even a rat left behind,' Burroughs says. 'That's my religion. Read Beckett. You identify and kill alter egos to get to the bottom: the unnameable, the abyss. Silence.'

He set a mirror in the goldfish pond to catch his ally. Weed cataracting a silver eye. Razored cloud-strip bandages. The rain-stick is broken and his magic is done. He pokes his cane among sluggish fish, stirs the leaf-thick muck. And talks about the time drunken Indians came over the fence from the Native American college. Guns are in the basement. There is a feathered wand in the bedroom.

The cats are tapping the old man for psychic sap, milking him, stalking through rubbled dreams of the coming Land of the Dead. On subsequent US visits – to Bastrop in Texas, and Phoenix, Arizona – I learnt about the fellowship of those internal exiles, the hardcore writers: Michael Moorcock, Jim Sallis. Like Burroughs, they kept cats and guns (Mike's was a replica). Cats infiltrate mystery fiction: men with coffee habits, ex-drinkers, post-traumatic spooks solving crimes the hard way. Moorcock uses cats like a scarf, like Peter Sellers in *The Wrong Box*; their claws scratch runes into his easy chair.

Burroughs measures out his day between methadone hits, calls to the vet, and the ever-earlier hour for that first tumbler of vodka and Coke. Once the slow drinking starts, it doesn't stop. Early to bed. When he eats – knowing there is nothing on offer in the Land of the Dead, that border country of extinguished volcanoes and limp-cock sex – he snorts an extra hit of sea salt, like snuff, between every bite. As if he is preparing himself for a return to the sea.

The orgone accumulator looks like an outdoor privy. 'Watch out for the black widow spiders,' he says. We pose for the ritual shot. Burroughs slips his left arm around Pavel. With that smooth face, disconnected smile and buzz-cut hair, Coen reminds Bill of a medical orderly. A keeper of liquids. In a few years, Burroughs will fade from the photograph. There will be two strange men standing, yards apart, around a scarecrow absence on a patch of Kansas grass.

Back inside, books inscribed, drinks poured, Burroughs comes to the revelation. *He doesn't write any more.* He paints, shoots cans. He collects his prescription from Kansas City. The last set worth recording was a landfill dump on the Kaw River, outside Topeka. Debris, cottonwoods, wild turkeys. Burroughs sat, unmoving, through the afternoon. He recognized an opening for his get-out novel, *The Western Lands.* 'Gradually, as he wrote, a disgust for his words accumulated until it choked him and he could no longer bear to look at his words on a piece of paper.'

A sweat-lodge ceremony with a Sioux medicine man revealed, and then exorcized, the ugly spirit that had oppressed him for so many years; a spirit in the form of a winged Vietnam War helmet. A spirit representing the karma of American materialism and invasion guilt. A spirit smelling of chicken-fried steak and napalm. This spirit was the curse laid down at the moment when he shot and killed Joan Vollmer in Mexico City in 1951. A curse that could only be ameliorated by dedicating his life to writing, taking the dictation of the old ones. And now the job was done.

The way was clear to the western lands, a dream cinema without horizons, space that contracts to a single point of light but never ends. 'I am forced to the appalling conclusion,' Burroughs said, 'that I would never have become a writer but for Joan's death. I live with the constant threat of possession, and a constant need to escape from possession, from Control. There is no way out.'

He stared into the abyss and the abyss stared right back. Michael Emerton, a curly-headed carer, boyfriend of James Grauerholz, one of the business managers of the Burroughs estate, shot himself in November 1994. Burroughs was very fond of the boy and made him the dedicatee of *My Education*. With Emerton at the wheel, there had been a high-speed crash in a BMW two months earlier. The driver lost control. The vehicle aquaplaned, bounced off a crash barrier and skidded across the turnpike. Burroughs got out, unscathed, leaning on his cane: 'I need an ambulance.'

Youths appeared all the time, wanting to see or touch the old man in the red house. Some were taken on to help with domestic duties or to run necessary errands. Most were photographed. Many had adolescent problems or projects to discuss with the junk-fed sage. Quantities of opiates were ingested, regular hits of dope; Kansas evenings softened with vodka and Coke. George Laughead arrived from Dodge City, trailing a high-school senior called Daniel Diaz. The boy's mother had threatened her son's life on two occasions.

'Shoot the bitch and write a book. That's what I did.'

The Burroughs sentence from a vodka session in Lawrence,

posted on a local website, was soon notorious. It had the kind of subterranean afterburn I found when, searching for traces of Pavel Coen, I played the *Beat* DVD I found in the Croydon charity pit.

The replay of a double-death memoir was hypnotic. Much truer to source than Cronenberg's respectfully overimagined account of *Naked Lunch* or any of the implausible translations from Kerouac into Hollywood. A palpable lack of budget pared Gary Walkow's film down into rigorous close-ups, brown rooms with low ceilings, a script made from quotations. And postcards from Mexico: an empty road, a river, the distant volcano.

Walkow's *Beat* was my passport to the Land of the Dead. A slim plastic wallet with a pixilated portrait of a man in a hat, who looked about as much like Burroughs as I do.

The actors, none of whom resemble their originals, sleepwalk with listless conviction, repeating lines they appear to have received under a general anaesthetic. Keifer Sutherland makes a pass at that cryogenic Burroughs voice of world-weary cynicism, hot ash in the throat: a man who has come back from the abyss with grumbling haemorrhoids. The tapeworm of raw-meat sex stays at the bottom of the mescal bottle, untasted. Too much human flesh at the end of the fork.

Here is a narrative framed between the formal austerity of Bresson and the rum psychosis of Jim Thompson. Lucien Carr, the blond boy of New York, stabs and kills his stalking predator, Dave Kammerer. A paradox frames my sense of America: impossible spaces, claustrophobic cabins. Kammerer is actively on Carr's tail (rubbing him with cashmoney, booze), while Burroughs, implicated in every action, plays witness and confessor. I'm back again in Gloucester, staring at Leon Kroll's painting of the two women and the sun-drowned man. A configuration in which the rape or betrayal or act of liberating violence has not yet happened.

Two deaths. Kammerer as he tries to mount Carr. And Joan Vollmer, the glass on her head, challenging Burroughs to accept his fate and become a writer.

'Do they have ruins in Guatemala?'

'It's all ruins.'

Sutherland's pastiched Burroughs likes a drink, but he's not Malcolm Lowry. He suffers the same tick, the compulsion to find the right word. 'Did you see the *flock* of vultures?' But is 'flock' the best collective noun? Bevy, covey, flight, gaggle, brood, hatch, litter, shoal, swarm? Like Lowry, he is on the Mexican bus with the chickens and the *people*.

Burroughs, his boyfriend (a version of Lewis Marker, with whom he visited Ecuador in search of the hallucinogenic drug yage), Joan Vollmer: eternal triangle. Vollmer, Carr, Burroughs: 'Too bad you're not a man.' Ginsberg, Burroughs, Vollmer: dry hump. Ginsberg, Kerouac, Neal Cassady: poetry. Cassady, Kerouac, Carolyn Cassady: confession. And on. And on. Until one of them strikes out for Mexico. Walkow's budget version has the mathematics of catastrophe absolutely pat. Maya plus Los Alamos. The pyramid of black smoke.

'No Mexican really knew any other Mexican, and when a Mexican kills someone (which happened often), it was usually his best friend.'

The miracle of *Beat* is Courtney Love, who is nothing like the febrile Joan (who had two small children and was too smart to write). Love is embedded in her performance, emboldened by sofa lips, harvest of hair, the supreme physicality. At moments she looks like a shire horse in scarlet lipstick and a wig. She's better than Kim Novak in *Vertigo* – where awkwardness of performance reaps dividends. She should be painted by Kroll.

'Lucien can write a song about anything.'

'Why don't you write us a volcano song?'

Walkow references everything from Malcolm Lowry to Billy Wilder: 'nobody's perfect'. Love's husband, Kurt Cobain, visited Burroughs in Lawrence. There were rumours that he spent his last seventy-two hours staring into the flicker and strobe of a Burroughs/Gysin dream machine. He died of a self-inflicted gunshot wound in Seattle.

Beyond the dust of the Mexican road, as the Ginsberg actor and the Carr actor carry Courtney Love towards the cone of the distant volcano, is the shadiest, coolest river. They strip, plunge, drift. Love vanishes. She is sitting in her damp underwear in a wood. All the good westerns have a version of this scene. Peckinpah liked nothing more than crossing the border; a respite in a green place, before red death.

That was it, I thought. Walkow had summarized it for me, broken the complexities down. I couldn't imagine where this DVD came from or why it could be found in Croydon for £1.50. And then the name rang a muffled bell. Alongside the director/performer Andrew Kötting (who had the look of Lowry and a major swimming habit), I was invited to talk about our project of taking a swan pedalo from Hastings to Hackney. We were in Trinity Buoy Wharf at the mouth of the River Lea, the precise point at which, months later, when a budget had been secured, I would come ashore, quitting the swan before she completed her voyage by disappearing into the tunnel in Islington. The swan reminded me of somebody: Courtney Love. White lady of destruction, shredder of myths.

After the event, a man approached. He knew my work and said that, if I were willing, he'd like to present me with a DVD. It was a film he made in 1995, a version of Dostoevsky's *Notes from Underground*. I remember sending this person a few words of thanks and I tracked the email down.

At first I found the shift from 19th-century Russia to 21st-century California disorientating, but all that soon settles. Sometimes limited means (budget) does create a useful tension. It was good to meet at the river's edge.

The man's name was Gary Walkow.

Mountain

She had just returned from a book tour in Canada. In Canada? I didn't know they were interested in Mexican writers.

– Walter Abish

Ripe

O come to me again as once in May.

We were spending more time, as much as possible, on the south coast, a flat in St Leonards-on-Sea. Attempting to evaluate boxes and files of hopelessly disconnected research material from journeys made in the wake of other journeys, I felt the need to put a brake on this headlong momentum and to strike out afresh from where I was: swimming or walking from the shingle beach on the far side of a busy road. The self-consciously quaint hill town of Rye – cobbles, teashops, silted harbour – had its overloud cultural associations, from Henry James and the early modernists to E. F. Benson and the two Pauls, Nash and McCartney. The young Malcolm Lowry was rusticated to Sussex, to be dried out and tutored by the fleshy American poet and novelist Conrad Aiken, who lived close to Lamb House on Mermaid Street and the garden where James paced out his leisured paragraphs.

I knew all that, but I'd forgotten or didn't arrive at the one fact that mattered until I returned from Los Angeles, having shadowed Lowry down the Pacific Rim from Vancouver: the author of *Under the Volcano* was boxed and earthed, on my doorstep, in the village of Ripe. The thing you are searching for is within touching distance, but you are obliged to cross oceans, witness forest fires, take open-top bus tours around the Hollywood Hills, before you are allowed to contemplate the names and dates on a local headstone.

Dark as the Grave wherein My Friend is Laid is culled from diaries, multiple drafts, cancelled starts, by Margerie Lowry and Douglas Day. It is, on one level, a remix of *Under the Volcano*; an author's cut made without the author. Lowry comes back to the nightmare of

Mexico with his second wife – who is seeing the significant locations of the troublesome book for the first time, in order to absorb and exorcize the pain. Along with scented traces of Jan Gabrial, the model for Lowry's bolter, the faithless (with good reason) Yvonne. A return is the most volatile of bad journeys, black spots of mescal-induced dementia flaring into new life. 'Perhaps the sensation of writing was related to a half memory that seemed now to come to the surface, as if indeed he were writing this down or as though somebody else were writing it down, or writing through him.'

It is madness to revisit actual bars, imagined towers, butterfly-crusted swimming holes, crowded buses, once they have been tainted and transformed by the act of fiction. You are undoing the spell. Words, and the order of words, obey the laws of magic. Everything is risked. And lost. Lowry invokes Emanuel Swedenborg, a traveller who made little distinction between the realms of the living and the deceased of vanished centuries. The terrain of Swedenborg's undead is as sober, industrious, hygienically free-loving (and dull) as Lowry's is carnivalesque, firecracklingly loud, peopled with blind old women putting dead dogs to the dried-out teat. Swedenborg, in austere black velvet, having breakfasted, envisioned 'a gymnasium where young men are initiated into various matters pertaining to wisdom'. Lowry took his seat among the *borrachos* in an Oaxaca dive called the Farolito, and tried to talk Spanish to dedicated drunks who, if they were in a good humour, might mangle a few phrases of cinema English.

'Nobody has written an adequate book about drinking,' Lowry said. He scorned that chart-topper, Charles Jackson's *The Lost Weekend*. Barometer set for a spell of riot.

Under the Volcano begins as an image: a dying man, an Indian, at the roadside, seen from a bus on the way to a bull-throwing. A fellow passenger steals money from the victim's hat. The incident provokes a short story. But there are so many aspects to this, so many details of what led up to the desperate excursion. 'There used to be a waterfall.'

As he discourses with a black magician in a white suit, a doctor who is not a doctor (but who would have been, given time, a major character in the novel), and a Mexican called Eddie (policeman and bar-owner with pistol), Lowry boasts: 'I am all the characters. They are all me.'

The crazy expedition pivots, Lowry says, on the search for his great amigo, a swordsman and horse-runner. A bank messenger who also acted in Eisenstein's staged documentary, *Thunder over Mexico*. We understand that Fernando, Lowry's Dr Vigil, is long dead. Even though the author has been sending unanswered letters from Vancouver for years. Those letters are trial runs for the book. The Eisenstein film is abandoned, aborted. I will play what's left of it, over and over, to locate Lowry's phantom drinking partner. Without success.

The other doctor, the Haitian from the new fiction, chuckles: 'Once, in Port-au-Prince, I saw a headless woman dancing outside the Hotel Oloffson.'

Ripe is the setting for a classic English murder mystery: a somnolent hamlet, an accident of crossroads, farms, railway tracks, more violent, repressive, suicidal – by implication – than anything Lowry squeezed out of the lemon-and-salt poisons of Cuernavaca. His Sussex arrival, none too fresh from his latest cure, bearded, raw, a stopped writer of mislaid reputation visited by an aristocrat (Lord Peter Churchill), and married to a former Hollywood actress, is the standard pre-credit sequence – it scripts itself – for orthodox mayhem from *Miss Marple* or *Midsomer Murders*.

Ripe is Margerie's copyright as much as Malcolm's: she outlives him, outdies him. Rewrites him. She is fresh from the saddle as a performer in B-movie westerns. She tried to teach him the geometry of the stars (celestial and Beverly Hills). Their meeting at the intersection of Western and Hollywood Boulevard has the force of fable: he arrives by bus, she comes by car (being with Lowry will end all that). She waits at the bus stop, he steps down. They embrace. They hold each other. They stay, motionless, frozen, until Jack King, Margerie's former lover, who has been detained by business, arrives.

*

Flying back to Mexico from Vancouver in 1945, drowsy with booze and pills, Lowry dips into Yeats: 'The living can assist the imagination of the dead.' He senses, Arizona beneath him, 'an organic turning of oneself inside out, the setting to work of all the headlong down-driving machinery of a colossal lethiferous debauch'. Reality comes close: Malcolm's crack-up. Outside animals are revealed in the absence of drink. In-flight coffee, untouched, tastes like mescal. Antabuse. Flash forward to the hideous therapies of suburban London asylums. Denied water, Lowry is doped, fed salt. Rage of Death Valley thirst. Until he sucks and swallows with bleeding gums from his chamber pot. Until the complacent, fat-whiskered medical man brings a bottle of whisky up to his pursed mouth: a telescope filled with urine. Until he agrees that they can cut a fistula from his brain; carve the bolus, the vegetal core. He can't put pen to the surgical contract. He's shaking too much. He writes standing up; blue veins harden in his legs. Margerie holds the trembling bone hand, guides his wrist. A Sussex culmination of that Hollywood embrace: she authors his books. She digs a novel out from the grave. He has written his Mexican friend, drinking buddy of the bad places, back from death.

All their bad journeys are reduced to the dregs of the last bottle: Margerie Bonner transports Lowry (after Vulcano, the Lake District, the Farne Islands) to Ripe. To choke and die. He can no longer lift a glass without support. Books that appeared under his name, having been mangled and scribbled over until they were almost erased, are edited and improved by the brave survivor, his wife.

'Conniption' is the word Lowry repeats, a chant to keep the plane in the air, as he heads to another border and all the waiting ghosts and policemen. 'Consulates. Customs. Conniption all over again. Double conniption. Bribery and conniption. Treble conniption. It is going into hell.' Conniption is hysterical excitement or anger.

Readjusting after our Canadian excursion, we spent a few days on the south coast. Our eyes had been peeled and polished by travel. I thought that a visit to Monk's House at Rodmell, with a walk down to the river where Virginia Woolf went in, would combine nicely with a first pass at Ripe, paying our respects to the graves of Mr and Mrs Lowry.

Anna, in her short white coat, on the chalk path between the Woolfs' garden and the River Ouse, framed against telegraph poles, the shoulder of the Downs, a high-cloud sky, looked American. The river was low, the sludgy banks sheer and lacking in handholds. We carried away an impression of beehives, droopy tendrils of wisteria, lichen-crusted statuary, lawns yellowed at season's end. Virginia Woolf was a torso on a pedestal, a votive presence in bosky shadows. Without literary suicides, drownings, gin and sodium amytal binges, Lewes and its sylvan satellites would be intolerable. *¡Evite que sus hijos lo destruyan!* It is difficult to wander permitted paths along the borders of corrugated fields, through tumbled graves of yew-shaded churches, without picturing combine harvesters ploughing into picnicking toffs at Glyndebourne, or squadrons of Hell's Angels on invalid-carriages roaring among the outside tables of heritage pubs declining to serve a sandwich after 2 p.m.

Ripe sits on the wrong side of the frantic A27, the humble cousin of that Bloomsbury outstation, Charleston. Charleston has its pond for naked frolics, its easy access to the Downs (Virginia bumping along on her bicycle). Its craftily defaced plates and chairs. Its book-bound importance. Its gift shop and festivals. Ripe has a couple of buried ghosts, a suspicious death, and a healthy resistance to outsiders.

This was the story of the Lowrys' last voyage, as I understood it: the road to Ripe. Malcolm on the island of Vulcano in an American shirt and heavy sunglasses. Clean-shaven, hair managed. He stands at the extreme left edge of the surviving photograph, shoulder sliced away. A thin but assertive tree spoils the effect; a modest flat-roofed building, a dormant volcano edging into mist. The photograph says: 'I'm dead. You can't see my eyes. Nothing to report.' A foolish Mediterranean detour to humour Margerie's late whim for tourism. And Lowry's sentiment for volcanoes.

It's a movie. But they don't make it. Nobody does. Antonioni could: Jack Nicholson and Monica Vitti. Dubbed by Dirk Bogarde and Shelley Duval. Booed at Cannes.

Next slide: Lake District. Grasmere? Lowry's hands clasped in lap. Seated on wet rock in implausible Mediterranean outfit. His clothes are always one journey, one continent, too late. Behind him, if you print without cropping (as Feltrinelli does for the Italian translation of *Under the Volcano*): a canvas rucksack, a box of matches. Ruffled lake and backdrop hills tease memories of Vancouver's Burrard Inlet. 'My trouser bottoms are scuffed and shredded like a Mexican beggar. Is this the right place to leave my ashes?'

Then London, the inferno. Hospitals. A living corpse, pipe wedged between tight lips, transported to Ripe. Where it all unravels like an orthodox English mystery.

SHE BROKE GIN BOTTLE. FOUND HUSBAND DEAD. MEDICAL EVIDENCE SHOWED THAT MR LOWRY DIED FROM ACUTE BARBITURIC POISONING ASSOCIATED WITH A STATE OF CHRONIC ALCOHOLISM.

The White Cottage. Writing impossible. Barred from the pub at the end of the lane, the Lamb. They walk out in the early evening of 26 June 1957, beyond the village, to the Yew Tree in Chalvington; a mile or so from their rented home. The soused Lowrys sit head to head at the public bar. Margerie, it is reported later, when such details are magnified, and a summer cold becomes a premonition of disaster, weeps for her lost Dollarton shack. She knows the world of stars and creatures in ways her husband never will. Beaks tapping at the window. A bear coming to the beach for berries. A swimming deer. Margerie's mystery novel, *The Shapes That Creep*, published by Charles Scribner's Sons in 1946, is as telling an account of life in the squatter community on the Burrard Inlet as Lowry's more celebrated tale 'The Forest Path to the Spring'. Margerie is no supporting artist in the Lowry legend. She encodes her stories and her scripts, produced to keep this shaky couple afloat, with lunar caustics of her own, crossword puzzles and references to Shakespeare's little performed play *Timon of Athens*. Her blotched, red-faced husband, a grouchy and hibernating bear of the woods, is the misanthrope. A foolishly fond dispenser of largesse in bars and Vancouver hotels where women are not permitted. Timon's death and his unvisited memorial will be a footnote to the last act.

A woman (not unlike the author) is the mystery solver in Bonner's fiction. She finds the first body and the book beside the corpse. Lowry's memories, like those of a drowning man, are nets: he speaks of coming on deck, mid-ocean, to find a flock of owls caught in the rigging.

A bottle of gin is purchased. To calm Margerie, Lowry claims. In their weatherboarded Ripe retirement, she keeps him company, glass for glass. They argue, as before. And worse. Margerie sets off down the darkened lane with its high hedges, the shrine-like alcoves in which farmers leave eggs and murdered crows. Lowry stumbles in her wake, touching trees, bottle wedged precariously under his tweedy arm.

Back at White Cottage, he staggers upstairs to catch a Stravinsky concert on the radio. A cold collation is prepared. Lowry is crouched in his corner, head on knees, gin half drunk, and Russian music sawing out of the crackling flesh radio. Margerie turns the volume down. Who narrates these events? The principal suspect. Margerie has good reasons for culling Malcolm. He is a serial suicide: threatened, attempted, now achieved by other means. Throw the dead dog, after him, in the ravine. *Le Sacre du printemps.* That much is true. Check the alibi with the *Radio Times.* Too much detail. The man is faithful to his flaws.

Mrs Lowry said her husband had been treated in a hospital for alcoholism, but was discharged as incurable.

'When he hit me,' she said, 'he was under the influence and in a bad temper.'

They wrestle. Over Bakelite knobs. Stravinsky's savage rite swelling and fading. Over the gin bottle. She smashes it against the wall. He curses, chases her down the narrow stairs. She retreats to the house of her landlady, Mrs Mason. Where she spends the night. On her return, next morning, Lowry is gone: dead. Supper all over the room. Beside him on the floor, the final insult, a bottle of lurid orange squash.

Remember how, in *Dark as the Grave*, Wilderness/Lowry signals his love for Primrose/Margerie, when everything in their relationship is in ruins, by drinking a foul beaker of some fruit concoction, a *refresco*, from which the serving girl has to pick the flies? Every cell of his being is screaming for beer, mescal, tequila: the worm.

He chokes on her pills. Sodium amytal, three-grain strength. Bottle missing from wife's drawer, her underthings. He has stolen her death. This is the final volume in the trilogy of mysteries she has no need to complete: Burrard Inlet (present), Southern California (past), Ripe (for ever). Before the funeral can be arranged, conspiracy theories start in whispers, before becoming scholarly papers and future blogs.

On that first Ripe visit, after Vancouver and the Burrard Inlet, and lunch with William Gibson, we found the graves, located the Lamb, wondered about the White Cottage, failed with the Yew Tree, and achieved little beyond some primitive empathy for how it must have felt to be exiled to a small English village that had no use for your presence or past achievements. The Hollywood *Rebecca* model, with Margerie as the innocent second wife (the Joan Fontaine part), at the mercy of Jan Gabrial's exotic original (the first Mrs de Winter), made immortal by *Under the Volcano*, was hard, then impossible, to sustain. Californians live through quotation, a remake authenticates the status of the first attempt. Ripe was not Manderley.

Lowry's name on a curved slab, a granite postcard buried in an extension of St John the Baptist Church, is not in deconsecrated ground, but this garden strip, close to a low wall, has a detached aspect. Like a recently abandoned allotment. Margerie is not beside him or with him. The salient facts are faded but visible. Combing back untrimmed blades of grass, I discover a glazed tablet with a Spanish inscription: *¿Le gusta este jardín? ¿Que es suyo? Evite que sus hijos lo destruyan!* I have a notion where that comes from but I'll have to check. Also buried are several empty mescal miniatures. And a Guinness can. The grave is thoroughly libated. Wild roses thrive.

Margerie proves harder to find. A little notice in the porch of the locked church offers a guide about as reliable as the spelling of Mrs Lowry's name. MARJORIE B. LOWRY. JULY 1906–SEPT 1988. O COME TO ME AGAIN AS ONCE IN MAY.

A visitor, researching Margerie's film career, and fresh from Gordon Bowker's article in the *TLS*, which detailed questionable aspects of Lowry's death and the subsequent inquest, became frustrated with the difficulty of confirming the proper memorial above her grave. 'I couldn't make up my mind over Marg's guilt.' As he speaks, a shaft of sunlight breaks through the clouds to reveal a stone from which all traces of Margerie Bonner are lost to orange spores, weathering and bird lime. She could not be planted further from her husband without striking off towards Charleston.

She met him in Hollywood on 7 June 1939. He died on the night of 26 June 1957. Or early the following morning. On 2 May 1946, the Lowrys were sent to 113 Bucarelli, reputed to be the least pleasant jail in Mexico City. After dark they were driven to the station in a taxi and removed to Nuevo Laredo and deportation from Mexico. The garden gates closed. And never opened again.

With Anna rested, and restored to Hackney life, a second attempt on Ripe seemed appropriate. I had been reading a series of four strange western novels by the Oxford academic Brian Catling. His *Amerika* was like Kafka's, better than the real thing; a hallucinatory construct out of *True Grit* and Cormac McCarthy's *Blood Meridian*. The series ended with a phrase that haunted me and set the tone for our return to Sussex: *They were buried the same afternoon in separate cemeteries. Nobody asked why.* I returned to source, the Lowry texts.

Jolted at the back of the bus, when he brings his second wife to Oaxaca, Lowry catalogues a priest in mufti travelling with his brother, and some kind of lawyer with a briefcase. He registers them as clots of words, unresolved sentences; descriptions he can't be bothered to transcribe (but he *is* transcribing, he is calibrating his own impotence). A writer without curiosity is a straw man. This landscape of organ cacti and varieties of red earth is nothing more than a smear of shop-soiled phrases, typewriter ribbons flapping against the window. Vultures in the washbasin. *Darkness, and strange lights were moving in the hills.* Friendship is played out, love has died. Lowry's myths are lies, no sailors were rescued from the sea. Every acquaintance is a potential character. Margerie is required to fill in the physical details, to give him the correct names for the plants and planets.

I tell Anna the story of the last Ripe night, to see if her instincts can identify the clues I missed. Studying my outdated Ordnance Survey map, she spots a PH that might be the Yew Tree Inn. We drive there and recapture something of the *Straw Dogs* atmosphere of the Lowry sessions. The locals, mid-afternoon, are established in the back bar; boisterous, work abandoned, or suspended in the drizzle, in no hurry to return home. The landlord is a turn and knows it. The notion of coffee at this hour is impossible to sustain: 'Machine's on the blink.' He manages a couple of large white wines, slops them over the table, and takes himself out to the yard. Where he fails to light a fat cigar. But almost fires his brandy.

It needs Professor Catling to do justice to the slow theatre of the pub, the hours required of looped anecdotes and unsynchronized laughter, before violence erupts and murders are carried back to curtained cottages. Pub time is no time, liquid relativity When he'd done with the American West, the Oxford don scripted a tale set on the Isle of Man. A Lowry connection. Lowry wrote about the Manxman they couldn't hang and how, neck scorched, he came back from the execution pit to accept free rounds for ever from his burnished seat at the bar. A friend and protector at the Burrard Inlet, Dollarton, through all the fires and troubles, was the Manx boatwright Jimmy Craige. The Isle of Man was another Vulcano, a site of exile and madness, fishermen eager to be elsewhere. And convenient for Liverpool, city of the Lowry family business. Museums of syphilitic horror.

After the Yew Tree, we took the road to Ripe: puddled tarmac, no verges, a high-hedged narrowness with a single kink. The village is unpeopled, the shop shut. The White Cottage, where Lowry died, is decorated with a blue-and-white heritage plaque the size of a satellite dish. There is a hinged mirror with its wooden back turned to the upstairs window, the room where the novelist sat in a heap listening to *Le Sacre du printemps*. You can see the attraction; the village inn, the Lamb, is at the end of the lane. Faint lettering on pink brick. A hanged white sheep. OMNIBUSES STOP BY REQUEST. A good place from which to be barred.

The Lamb Inn features a many-spoked wheel with three conjoined gulls' wings pinned to the hub: an echo of the Three Legs of Mann, the symbol of Lowry's first island. The spokes of the wheel represent the rays Sigbjørn Wilderness watches from his Cuernavaca tower as the day dies and he decides how late he can drink before it counts as a morning start. The three-legged device was well known on Sicily and Vulcano. Wings and wheels recall Ezekiel: 3.13. '*I heard* also the noise of the wings of the living creatures that touched one another, and the noise of the wheels over against them, and a noise of a great rushing.' William Burroughs carries his King James Bible, unopened, to Mexico City.

Le gusta este jardín. Somebody literate has left this Mexican tribute in the grass. A decorative plate of thick ceramic leaves and cobalt sky with yellow sun-face. Sun as volcano. 'What is the book – is it a sort of detective story?' The Oaxaca drinking pal, Eddie, asks Wilderness.

A translation is made. 'Do you like the garden which is yours? See to it that it is thus: that your children don't destroy it.'

Lowry wrote the words on a crumpled scrap of paper, so he claims, from a wall in Oaxaca. 'We evict those who destroy.' When they arrive in Matamoros, on the night before the return to Oaxaca, City of Death and candles, the bus deposits them beside a hotel called El Jardín. 'So dark this Mixtec city, absolutely and so utterly dark and sinister it was almost beyond belief.' The notice from a public garden – *¡Evite que sus hijos lo destruyan!* – is as much part of the quest as the figure of Lowry's one true friend, Fernando.

The turf of the burial ground is soaked with evening dew. The heavy pink roses are like the petticoats of fire victims. Who left this message? Julian Barnes, talking of Flaubert, asked: 'Why does the writing make us chase the writer? Why aren't books enough?' Alberto Rebollo, president of the Malcolm Lowry Foundation of Cuernavaca, came to Ripe and was photographed kneeling in homage at the grave, pouring a mescal libation over the hidden plate with its quotation. His account of this visit is like so many others: he is disorientated, lost. He asks for directions (a mistake). 'I was about to cross the threshold, I had the feeling of being an actor in a film or in a dream.' Another scholar told him that it was a waste of time talking to the dead.

Rebollo, like the Sussex painter and friend of Conrad Aiken, Edward Burra, understood borderlands, conversations made over cigarettes in cemeteries. Burra, the most Mexican of English watercolourists, visited Lowry in Spain and then in Cuernavaca. His carnivalesque images are the best windows on the Lowry labyrinth: ghost dances of outside animals and late-humans grinding bones in subterranean bars. Feathers and fruits in ornate glass coffins. Voodoo eyes made from bottle-stops. Zoot-suit skeletons fleshed in labial folds. Barbiturate jazzers eating their own tongues in El Greco delicatessens. Delicious fur collared Harlem whores dealing tarot cards in all-night cafeterias.

Burra called Rye: 'Tinkerbell towne, an itsy bitsy morgue quayte DEAD.' His painting of the churchyard, now hung in the Jerwood Gallery in Hastings, parallels or makes play with events at Ripe. A defeated woman, back against the flint wall, contemplating the graves. A man, kept apart, down in a heap like Lowry in the bedroom at the White Cottage, his head leaking nightmares. And this narcoleptic couple duplicated in a hobbled pair creeping along the wall: a black widow, a sexless mannequin as grey as the inside of a glove. Lowry and Burra did not bond. The large watercolour was produced a year or so after Lowry's burial in the Ripe church dedicated to John, the decapitated wilderness prophet.

Anna's energies were fading fast. She strolled the perimeter of the primary school and retreated to the car. I inspected a hole in the wall in which spiders had left a smoky web sagging with husks of flies. Then I retreated, for the last time, to Lowry's grave. Two fat rabbits with fluffy white tails were nibbling. As I approached, they bounced away into the undergrowth. Lowry had a thing for rabbits. It was a symbol he laid down with care. 'Everything is to be found in Peter Rabbit,' he said. Mexican painters riff on the eternal argument between hare and coyote. Hare climbs a ladder to the moon. He gets away.

Back in St Leonards in time for an evening swim, I discovered a newly stencilled graffito on the wall beside the flat stone table on which William the Conqueror was reputed to have dined after coming ashore at Bulverhythe. It was a rabbit. It was *the* rabbit. Ears cocked, whiskers bristling. A symbol too far? No matter how enthusiastically he bounds, this phantom animal, made from black marks on a white surface, will never experience the sea.

Vancouver

'Canadian cities looked the way American cities did on television,' William Gibson said. I could see what he meant: a widescreen economy of rinsed light that was profoundly satisfying in a superficial way. My theoretical Scottish roots were refreshed by the sharp-edged, lung-scouring clarity of the waterside set, a prodigious end-stop of snow-capped mountains. The sweep across the First Narrows Bridge from Siwash Rock in Stanley Park was like a Hollywood studio logo from the days before films were financed by more production companies than there are categories of hepatitis. Or like that anonymous mural you spend much of the meal exploring in a deserted Chinese restaurant in Aberdeen. 'Anti-buzz,' Gibson concluded. 'Definition by absence.'

It was 6 a.m. and I was throwing off the longest flight of my life by making, as I'd always intended to do, a two-hour walk through wherever I found myself on the Pacific Rim. The walk would be a flattened loop, a prison circuit like Albert Speer in Spandau, or Henry James worrying a single sentence into a turn around his enclosed garden in Rye. Later, in a hotel in Paris, a few lines in the *International Herald Tribune* would remind me of my self-imposed Vancouver ritual. There was a man they called 'the pacer'. He kicked up the dust of his secure compound, erasing or complicating his own traces. This exercise regime or period of solitary meditation was rebranded as an event, an artwork, without his knowledge or permission, by a covert American surveillance crew. Curious strangers hidden in neighbouring properties. Remote technicians evaluating 24-hour drone cinema feeds. 'They were never able to confirm the man was Bin Laden.' But they sanctioned his execution.

That first morning circuit I picked up a *Metronews*. TWO CANADIAN

PLANES JOIN LIBYAN MISSION. TWO CANADIAN CF-18S WERE TASKED WITH AIR-TO-GROUND ATTACK MISSIONS. NEITHER SORTIE DROPPED ANY BOMBS. On the ride in from the airport, Kim, who had arranged my reading, said: 'Goldie Hawn lives there.' In a free paper, skimmed over a substantial Chinese-Canadian breakfast on Nelson Street, Goldie yapped about Elizabeth Taylor, 79, who had just died (congested heart failure), and the problems of celebrity. 'She was gorgeous in her prime. I don't know the titles of any of her movies.'

There is a fir tree on the roof of an apartment block. A dark, rather melancholy woman, in a borrowed camelhair coat with collar turned up, scuttles out from a shop with a blinking sign, carrying an empty violin case. PAYDAY LOANS. PROFESSIONAL NAILS. HOUSE OF TOBACCO. Gallery-quality light-tube signage in red and green. When I try to cash a cheque, after my reading, the post-office operative in the local mall tells me that they don't keep cash on the premises. But they'll get it in and ring me at the Sylvia Hotel. Poverty and courtesy go hand in hand. White pleasure craft in the marina. Golden towers of glass along the waterfront as the sun rises. Prescription regulars waiting for their plastic thimbles outside locked offices. Inukshuk: ancient symbol of the Inuit. On Deadman's Island, the tribes buried their honoured corpses in the trees. John Morton, a settler, made the observation in 1862: 'hundreds of red cedar boxes, lashed to the upper boughs'. The Squamish Nation: 200 dead warriors roosting among the leaves.

The path around the rim of Stanley Park offered me a credible account of where we were, by means of evergreen slopes, a pleasing succession of views: cormorants on black rocks, container ships riding at anchor. Tamed metaphors of wild nature lifted my spirits by invoking not only my circuits of Victoria Park, back home in Hackney, but also the opening movement of Lowry's *Hear Us O Lord from Heaven Thy Dwelling Place*.

The first story in this posthumously assembled collection, 'The Bravest Boat', has a morning-after flavour about it, the topographical shakes; Lowry can't quite trust his rhythms. He reaches out, to touch place, in the act of leaving it. 'Far away over in America the snowy volcanic peak of Mount Hood stood on high, disembodied, cut off from earth, yet much too close.' The mountain vision is the prolegomena to a Mexican return; volcano tourism, the bad journey by way of the Panama Canal, Rome, Naples, Sicily. To Ripe. But Mount Hood, now cited, is also a bridge towards the poets of the Beat Generation, Jack Kerouac and Gary Snyder: *Desolation Angels*, *Danger on Peaks*. Lowry establishes the model for cross-border escapades, disappearance into the ash. His poems, for which no other publisher showed much enthusiasm, came out, alongside Ginsberg and Corso, as a City Lights pocketbook. But Lowry remained unvisited by the coming generation, missing in action, a Mexican-frontier casualty like Ambrose Bierce. Alive but past recall.

Kim Duff, who described herself as 'the one with red longish hair wearing blue jeans and black boots', offered to pick us up at the airport. 'The Sylvia is the perfect place to stay in Vancouver on bright spring days.' London was not so bright. In pursuit of the background to Professor Catling's western novels we took ourselves, just before packing for Vancouver, to a boutique cinema in Shoreditch where they were showing the Coen Brothers' unnecessary remake of *True Grit*. Which was closer to the book, if that is a virtue, than Henry Hathaway's crusty original (which found room for a wired Dennis Hopper, who was given the part as a calculated affront to the tank-driving Republican John Wayne).

The Rooster Cogburn of the Charles Portis novel is more complex than John Wayne. As Donna Tartt said, when she introduced the reprint: 'Rooster is somewhat younger, in his late forties: a fat, one-eyed character with walrus moustaches, unwashed, malarial, drunk much of the time.' Cogburn is a veteran of the Confederate Army, one of William Clarke Quantrill's notorious border raiders. The darkness in Rooster, unexorcized, is never taken to a sweat lodge. It belongs in a massacre; one of the grimmest episodes in a war of violent extremes. It happened in a small Kansas town known to be a nest of Abolitionists: Lawrence. Final shelter of William

Seward Burroughs. Out of the Wichita Vortex come the rough riders of the Apocalypse.

The whole Shoreditch area was now a fashion feast where major designers rented pop-up cubbyholes to appear like rough trade. Hunger drove us into a basement of clinking City folk. Around 2 a.m. Anna felt the cramps and was violently sick. In shallow sleep I heard a crash, but didn't wake enough to investigate. Crashes on the street outside were a commonplace. This time, as I discovered, my dehydrated wife had fainted and slumped to the floor, damaging her neck. She was in enough pain to consider pulling out of the American trip. How she would endure a lengthy transatlantic flight, when every move was agony, I couldn't imagine. She fired down the pills, finished her packing, and got in the cab.

We were pulled out of the line, our attempted check-in aborted. Asked to report to the desk, with fears – among an irritable conga of Orthodox Jews, Indian traders with large cases, extended Chinese families, students and returning backpackers – of being bumped, left to sleep at Heathrow or made to return another day, we were upgraded for the first and only time to business class. After which, everything was possible. We were put to sleep, like effigies on a marble tomb, in pods, but reversed, feet to partner's head. The unwatchable film I watched was Oliver Stone's *Wall Street*, bad money chasing worse investments. Mountain ranges far below dreamt us back to life. Icelandic volcanoes bided their time.

Kim Duff was all that she claimed. Her partner was a star tattooist with artist status. They delivered us to the Sylvia Hotel, a place now favoured by senior citizens with mannerly dogs. I liked it at once.

We talked about the jet stream. And the Fukushima Daiichi nuclear meltdown. Kim said that the Canadian government had ordered pharmacies to stop selling potassium iodide because people were bulk buying. The Japanese disaster, much closer here, was a boost to drug companies who are always trading on scare-shock newsreels, world-ending horrors countered by an upgrade of vitamins.

The Sylvia bar was an aquarium of brandy light: dark wood, low couches embroidered with floral patterns, and a wide window on English Bay Beach. Better far to drink than to eat in such a place. Lowry spent many hours in the permitted limbo of the clubbish Sylvia, such a short step from the street. 'This is the most hopeless of all cities of the lost,' he said. As an inducement to Dylan Thomas. When they slumped at this bar in April 1950. Their ghosts never left. The fourth trip to the North American continent was the killer. And this was mine. William Gibson, who moved through airports with such familiarity that he barely registered on their surveillance systems, saw Vancouver quite differently. 'Strangely clean, lacking in texture, like video games before they'd learned to dirty them up.' Kim was excited, at a modest Vancouver pitch, about the rumour that Gibson might appear at the anarchist bookshop for my reading the next night.

The hotel, a solid commercial enterprise, has no more right to its position than the squatters' shacks at Dollarton. Posing beside the Burrard Inlet, before or after a swim, Margerie Bonner blesses the forest and the water with a glow of entitlement that is somewhere between post-coital and quietly astonished.

The evening sun burnishes Kim's long red hair as she drives us downtown for the reading. There will be a meal first, close to the financial district of Gastown, where Kim used to work, before she declared as a poet. I have a chance to connect with some of Vancouver's Olsonians. The Gloucester man's conference visitation, the gathering of the clans in the summer of 1963, left an indelible stain. Creeley, Ginsberg, Robert Duncan, all the high geographers of projective verse were in town: performing, yapping, seizing the day. Olson, according to Tom Clark, set up court on a balcony 'overlooking the majestic peaks of the North Coast range'. Cigars, jumbo milkshakes, three-decker sandwiches: he ordered everything. And he delivered, so he thought, the best reading of his life: four breathless hours, before the janitors closed the building. Such a performance is shared with an audience; they feed it and make it happen. In Vancouver the listener-participants were trained to the task; here was a city much visited but otherwise indifferent to culture, saving their riots for ice hockey, Stanley Cup results that went the wrong way. Conrad Aiken, reporting from Granada, where he attended a bullfight with Lowry and his temporary roommate Ed Burra, got the dynamics of performance just right: 'The audience an important factor – almost more than the bull.'

The poets, at our communal Lebanese table, suffer agonies of choice; a menu card is a minefield of possibilities. Rituals of anticipated digestion – swift beers, disallowed cigarettes, dope postponements – make for a warm but edgy occasion, with the event at the Spartacus bookshop hanging over us all. A visit by the English poet Tom Raworth, the last of the transatlantic men of the 1960s, is fondly recalled; his performances on and off the podium. How *fast* he was, in delivery and witness. 'The view is again unapproachable.'

The significant moment for me is the meeting with Miguel Mota, a Lowry scholar at the University of British Columbia. Miguel solves, without my asking, the logistical problem of getting across the water to search for traces of Lowry's shack at Dollarton. This, after all, was the underlying motive for my trip to Canada. Back in Dublin, when I was making contact with Burroughs and immersing myself in Kerouac and Snyder, the idea of Lowry diving off his rickety pier into the cold waters of the Burrard Inlet was more potent than my reading of *Under the Volcano* and *Lunar Caustic*. The nature of that healing retreat, with Margerie Bonner, after the madness of Mexico, was as seductive as anything I managed to extract from the published texts. And yet, although I lived alongside the Forty Foot, the rocky swimming place in front of Joyce's Martello tower in Sandycove, I never swam in Dublin. Now Miguel will pick me up on Saturday morning and drive me to the creek.

The Spartacus shop, in which I experienced, immediately, the thermal glow of time-travel, was the sort of generously overstocked, musty cave that London no longer possessed. The attendees, many of whom, I'm certain, lived in the place, had aged with the books.

A new voice was an acceptable intrusion on the permanent party. An earlier version of Spartacus had burnt down, like Lowry's shack – and, like the shack, had risen again. The area was called East Hastings Street. Which was spot on: drift Hackney, collectivism, used books, used people. These are the brave ones who turn a merciless urban highway into a seashore; by scavenging, slumping against buildings to watch the race of clouds; by walking as if they are swimming. Remembering only what needs to be remembered.

There is a man who is filming, forty-four years after the event, a documentary about the Dialectics Congress at the Roundhouse. I am called on to dredge up memories of the 1967 Ginsberg shoot. There is Peter Quartermain, a friend of Patrick Wright, once a Hackney neighbour, now a distinguished cultural historian. Patrick, who lived here as a postgraduate, stressed that the north–south orientation was far preferable 'to any engagement with Winnipeg and the prairies and beyond'. Like so many others, Patrick succumbed to the romance of crossing the border, heading for California.

'You could sense something of Ken Kesey's world, with that mixture of down-home conviviality and know-how with home-brewed psychosis.' Patrick made his retreat to 'a tin lawnmower shed fitted with a woodburner and planted in a juniper forest in Siskiyou County'. 'Not much to visit there,' he told me, 'although the big volcanic mountain – Mt Shasta – is like a marvellous Fuji for Northern California.'

A latecomer, tall, bespectacled, light-boned, took up his position near the door. He was noticed by some, but they didn't pester him or come at him with the typescripts and privately printed booklets that professional event-attenders carry in plastic supermarket bags to every reading. William Gibson. I met him, once, at a talk he gave at the ICA in London. Now we arranged to have lunch.

I thought of a character described by Gibson in *Spook Country*. 'He looked a little like William Burroughs, minus the bohemian substrate (or perhaps the methadone). Like someone who'd be invited quail shooting with the vice-president.' Or even out to Hollywood. A complimentary bungalow at the Chateau Marmont. This happened to Gibson, he had the right profile at the time. He was working on *Pattern Recognition*. A fancy magazine asked him to attend a private festival of films that were shot without film, outtakes from Godard associates in the Dziga Vertov Group. 'Garage Kubrick,' he said. YouTube, Gibson decided, signalled the end of print publications putting up novelists in Hollywood suites. We were coming into the age of assembly. There was nobody better qualified to launch my journey south than Gibson. When the sort of objects shelved in this shop – and the people who grazed on them – vanished from the chart, William Gibson would still be operating. He knew both worlds so well.

When Bill was staying in London, at a book-ballasted flat in Camden Town, his host pointed out of the window at an eccentric figure, horseshoe-spined under a rucksack bulging with the sort of small-press poetry Spartacus regulars carry in their anorak pockets, tramping north from the Tube towards Compendium Books. That was me. On the street, of the street: absorbed, burdened. And Gibson's gaze from the high window was a superior brand of pre-Twitter, pre-iPhone surveillance. *Pattern Recognition* opens on Camden High Street. Accidental pedestrians are fixed between hard covers.

Dollarton

Miguel led us down the forest path to the spring, a well-kept track only lightly heritaged, and attracting, on this crystalline morning, no other pilgrims. The pine resin, the cone-crunching footfall, the glitter of the inlet, did not unpick or intrude upon an imagined terrain so thoroughly colonized and adapted to purpose by Malcolm Lowry and Margerie Bonner. Notice the affection in her voice, many decades after leaving the burnt shack, when she is recorded, remembering the birds, the animals coming to water, in Mota's film, *After Lowry*. If a pleasant beachside recreation zone within fifteen minutes of the city can be defined by absence, Miguel has caught that spirit in his DVD tribute. You marvel at the courage or desperation required to self-assemble an inhabitable hut from driftwood and sawmill lumber. Lowry was in most respects a handless man (as Robert Louis Stevenson knew the term) He wrote standing up and was punished with varicose veins. But write he did, compulsively; or rewrite, layer after layer, postponing resolution. He prepared the bolus, as he called it, of an arcane, interlinked structure (as rickety as his shack and as magnificent), for the coming fire. Unfinished books were safe from public exposure. Like the Wyndham Lewis of *Self Condemned*, Lowry was an English author who found in wartime Canada the perfect retreat, hell as paradise. Lewis was trapped, in company with his long-suffering and barely acknowledged wife, in the stifling claustrophobia of a small hotel: until, as with the Lowrys, they are 'blasted out of it by fire'.

Lowry flirts with Margerie's pills. Lewis, reading about the successful felo-de-se, a double event, of the refugee Stefan Zweig and his wife in their apartment in Rio, is rather envious. The post-war world, Zweig reckoned, would demand more effort than he was prepared to make. Lewis, that hard-shelled crab, puts his newspaper

aside, to acknowledge the spectacle of recent frost on Toronto back-
yards. Lowry delights in the oil refinery on the far shore, where the
S has fallen from the SHELL sign.

Mrs Lewis, Froanna, is a backroom presence, hidden from visitors to the studio, a hand in a serving hatch. Lewis, photographed
in his round spectacles in 1940, looks much like Dickie Attenbor-
ough playing John Reginald Halliday Christie, the Rotting Hill serial
killer. Margerie Bonner, at the lowest estimate co-author of the
Dollarton idyll, is feeding Malcolm, channelling Malcolm, reading
his pages, making suggestions, confirming his role as doomed
(barely functioning) poet-genius – while, at the same time, drawing
on aspects of their shared hibernation for her own murder mystery
The Shapes That Creep. And retreating, when the drinking is too
extreme and the pinch of poverty too tight, into a perky,
highball-snifting, Laguna Beach novel of her Los Angeles past: more
The Thin Man, William Powell and Myrna Loy, than the existential
delirium of Humphrey Bogart and Gloria Grahame in Nicholas
Ray's film version of the Dorothy B. Hughes novel *In a Lonely Place*.
The brittle weirdness of *The Last Twist of the Knife*, Bonner's fantasy
return to La La Land, is not helped by the fact that her publishers
managed to leave out the last chapter.

'Eridanus' they called their small paradise. The tolerated huddle
of fishermen's shacks has now vanished to facilitate a parking zone,
memorial stone and clearly flagged trail. In Lowry's day he was
attacked by the Vancouver press, when he was noticed at all, as a
wealthy, freeloading scrounger, celebrated by fools elsewhere. Tourist boats on the Burrard Inlet jeered at the squatters and threatened
to burn them out.

There is a plaque to honour the years, 1940–54, when the Lowrys
lived on the beach. The 'aluminum retorts of the oil refinery' are
mentioned. And 'wild ducks doing sixty downwind'. After quitting
this paradise, Lowry never stopped dreaming of his return. The
mayor of North Vancouver, Marilyn Baker, put her name to the fading metal tribute.

Miguel, effortlessly hospitable, as so many proved in this town, picked us up at the Sylvia, to make the drive over Second Narrows Bridge and down the Dollarton Highway to Cates Park. He had given up on the England football game at half-time, they were already two down. We parked and he led us to the spot, or as close to it as he could calculate, of the original shack. The one in the photographs. Margerie spoke in Miguel's film about how Lowry would dive off the jetty at all seasons and swim out for an hour, sometimes two, over to the far shore. After the news of his father's death he was gone so long she wondered if he was coming back. I thought of Andrew Kötting in Hastings, another deepwater man. The English Channel is a poultice for incipient psychosis. Kötting was known to chase the tide as far as the De La Warr Pavilion in Bexhill. Watching the film-maker emerge, to hobble over the shingle, I understood the interspecies mutation of being too long in water: red eyes, upper-body bulk, salt-white lips, throat like sandpaper. A compulsion to freeze at the transitional point between land and sea. Chest out, balls pinched like wizened grapes. Arms folded for team photograph. Lowry, who was sent to the Leys School in Cambridge (where J. G. Ballard would go on his return from Shanghai), was a burrowing, bullocking scrum-half. He was also, in his youth, a golf champion. One of his respectable, stay-at-home brothers, Wilfred, won an international cap for rugby in 1920.

It is when they stagger from the water, after a long haul in choppy conditions under white mist, that these boys, Kötting and Lowry, talk in tongues. What they have just experienced, the out-of-body hallucinatory state, dredges up a rush of uncensored memories, their own and those of the drowned, along with stutters and rattles of cold. They are in a different place. It is hard for towel-holders to understand. The late prose of *Dark as the Grave* is as close as we can come to one of those swims. Go with it, go under; fire back the whisky.

The winding path through the woods, between the site where the shack had once been and the general store where the Lowrys collected water and purchased their necessities, is a topographic fiction for both Malcolm and Margerie. For him, a locus of confrontation.

An opportunity to think through his work in regress. For Margerie, the store is society, with all the challenges of emerging from her impoverished retreat: after ugly rows in life, the storekeeper is appointed villain, the killer in her mystery novel.

MALCOLM LOWRY'S CELEBRATED SHACK STOOD ON THE BEACH EAST OF THIS SPOT. HE CALLED THIS STRETCH OF SHORELINE ERIDANUS. ITS MYSTERIOUS SEASONS, HE WROTE, ARE 'LIKE THAT WHICH IS CALLED THE TAO'.

A tablet of stone set in November 2004. I'd like to swim, the water is strobing gold. I take off shoes and socks and wear the bottoms of my trousers rolled. The clear, cold water of the Burrard Inlet, across from the blue, wooded shoreline, and the aquamarine tanks of the refinery, dissolves complexity. Eridanus is anti-Mexico: stillness, silence. Ice on the breath. Long winters. Neighbouring fishermen heading back from Alaska. Months of woodchopping and night jazz.

From among the sharp stones in the shallows, I pick up something that glints like a coin. It is a yellow-gold beer cap, CORONA LIGHT, with rusty serrated rim and a black crown. Nothing to do with Lowry; a token of some summer visitor, one of the conference attendees off the bus. I carry it away.

AMPUTEE HAS PROSTHETIC LEG STOLEN FROM CAR. LEG IS DESCRIBED AS HAVING A FLESH-COLOURED FOOT WITH A SILVER CLAMP ABOVE THE ANKLE AND A LONG ALUMINIUM ROD WITH A BLUE FINISH. *Metronews*.

My morning circuit expanded; Anna needed rest to counter the pain in her neck, the aftermath of travel. The Sylvia was the best kind of haunted hotel. Keys disappeared and reappeared. Dim corridors were barely illuminated with flickering EXIT signs. Walls bend and warp, blotches appear like a catalogue of forensic stains. You acquire that sense of belonging that comes when you know you'll be moving on in a couple of days. W. P. White the architect had pulled it off, a valued retreat nobody found good reason to burn down. The performance artist at the desk felt no obligation to come out of his trance to clock me, at whatever dark hour I took to the streets, with cap and camera.

The idea – and it was barely that – was to absorb the loop of ground, Stanley Park to Coal Harbour and the Vancouver Convention Centre, or, the other way, by Sunset Beach Park to False Creek; to burn fresh neural pathways, to make my plodding steps into a proper architectural conceit. My circuits, coming out of sleep, would stretch, as we drove down the coast towards San Francisco, into a straight line, an unfolding concertina of images, sounds, headlines from free newspapers, words on walls. The Gothic S of the Sylvia, hanging on a shield above the entrance, was the missing letter from Lowry's refinery hell. And a better shape to walk, a snakier symmetry. Pink light tubes, in a dark window on Nelson Street, spelled ESTHETICS: the S and the T and the I burning brighter than the rest.

A Pacific city of this size was, as William Gibson pointed out, a major port and a distribution centre for drugs. Mountain ranges were deforested for Chinese furniture; heroin flooding in, by way of a return, with collateral damage visible in the doorways of Hastings Street East. Beyond that, there would be grand-project remnants, Olympic legacy in the form of an unoccupied athletes' village, posthumous public art. The 2010 zone and its satellite Paralympic Village, much like London's Lower Lea Valley and the Royal Docks of Silvertown, floated in a limbo of stalled investment. A fenced encampment of white tents with Moorish peaks and curves, like Kent's Bluewater supermall rendered in canvas, was hosting a Russian horse circus.

NOW PRE-SELLING. PINNACLE LIVING FALSE CREEK. A Sikh family talk into competing cellphones, trying to find a cab to get them out of there. The pizza-delivery boy has a T-shirt three sizes too big: I RAN THE MARATHON. The old sawmills of False Creek carved up 1,000-year-old Douglas firs. Nothing has arrived, but everything is promised. COMING SOON: LONDON DRUGS. EDGEWATER CASINO. LEGACY LIQUOR STORE.

My ultimate Vancouver loop, before the lunch with the Gibsons, undid me. I came all the way round, after English Bay Park, Sunset Beach Park, False Creek, the giant BC Place Stadium, Downtown, Gastown, to the Waterfront Centre, IMAX, seaplanes, post-Olympic Media hub. All the psychogeographic energy lines were feeding into an understated mall: 100 YEARS OF SHOPPING & SERVICES. A granite Calvinist ghetto: HERITAGE DISTRICT. Galleried floors with stone-clad walls. A panopticon for discriminating (but invisible) consumers. And its name was: THE SINCLAIR CENTRE. SINCLAIR WELLNESS. DIAMOND DEAL JEWELLERY. THE PERFUME SHOPPE. SHARING THE SPIRIT.

A Sinclair could claim credit for all this. James Sinclair, Minister for Fisheries, had a vision: 'the redevelopment of heritage buildings'. And he sucked me right in. To the one Vancouver construction that drained my sap. I took a bus out of there, back to Central Station, to secure our tickets to Seattle. I gave the only beggar who approached me on any of my walks all my change. He was so self-effacing in his muttered request, it felt like an obligatory toll for free passage. The station was lit like a German opera house.

Without really thinking about it, I assumed that William Gibson was the numinous presence in Vancouver. Like Lowry he came from elsewhere, in part to avoid war. Thereby volunteering for combat status in quite another field. His bad journey seems to have been endured with admirable stoicism and processed into books that surfed all kinds of hip currents. He played the gap between technologies, eco systems, video games, outlaw subterraneas. He chose this place, rather than Mexico and the volcanoes. Some of the Gibson pitch was an evidence swab taken from Burroughs. Burroughs said that his goal was to make it into space with a customized aqualung. Gibson blended inner and outer multiverses, crime and consumer aesthetics, in cyberspace (his term). Name it and you own it. Schooled in Arizona (Burroughs was in Los Alamos, New Mexico), Bill acquired the impressive childhood traumas the best writers need. Teenage angst with Beat paperbacks: life with mother in a monoculture. Everything conspired towards that moment when he crossed the border, on the drift, with no specific aim, as it was later rationalized, of evading the draft for the Vietnam War. Toronto was too blatant in its mash of runaways, psychedelic head-bangers and career depressives. Gibson managed a shop peddling drug paraphernalia. He was lucky enough to meet a woman from Vancouver, Deborah Jean Thompson. Together, they travelled. 'We concentrated,' he said, 'on European fascist regimes with favourable exchange rates.' Greece was good (DeLillo made telling use of Athens). And Istanbul, that stretch city, a storehouse of future images. 'We couldn't stay anywhere that had anything remotely like hard currency.'

In Vancouver Gibson learnt to scavenge and deal (as we all did). And to meld aspects of this transitional life into his fiction. In photographs he looks adequately creased and troubled, with laughter lines too, but behind the thin spectacles the eyes avoid the camera's interrogation and notice whatever is coming through the door or the wall.

Guu Garden Izakaya is the restaurant William Gibson chose for our lunch and it was a smart choice. We had a walk uphill through the cherry blossom of Nelson Street, overtaking natives, to the corner of Hornby. Finding the right block, a recent mandala development, oval within square, the One Wall Centre, was not to find the restaurant. The place where we would meet Bill and Deb was behind slatted windows and it felt a little like an office extension, or executive canteen for a wealthy but covert television franchise. At home it would be situated on London Wall, not far from the Barbican, close to money but not feeling its hot breath. Customers very much like ourselves, in striped shirts, without ties. The Guu Garden was not a garden and it didn't have visible lumps of a Roman wall. It was clean, above all, with plain wood tables, perfectly square, and soon covered with round glasses and bowls. The food was good, but not alarmingly so. We let Bill order. I hoped I wasn't drawing the Gibsons away from work in progress. If so, they showed no signs of impatience. Bill said that he never liked to travel when he was parturient with a novel. They were closer to Japan than Europe.

We talked a little about Ballard. Gibson remembered Jim, from the old days, as a John Bull figure in a gold waistcoat and funny Hawaiian shirt, genial and very sure of his ground.

The Gibsons found that Vancouver provided adequate cover and distance, a strategic territory in which to operate without too much doorstep interference. 'A place where it is always Sunday night,' Bill said. Which is not to say that nothing happens. A local restaurant critic, enthusing over Guu Garden, apologized for the delay in publishing his review: 'I've been helping out at the warehouse with the online Olympic Store. Now I'm back to my regular eating schedule.'

The restaurant sat nicely with the subtle, cross-Pacific vortex of investment. Money in downtown Vancouver is always in transit; new developments were appearing, fully formed, with no dusty, crane-heavy construction interim. The malls, banks, residential towers were changed overnight like sets for touring musicals, try-outs for Phoenix or São Paolo. There was enormous enthusiasm for the *concept* of rebuilding. A dangerous addiction. It soon becomes the critical state, evidence of progress, positive employment statistics: whatever is being made at a given moment is *work*. A successfully completed apartment complex is waiting, as soon as the launch party in the penthouse is concluded, to be torn down. In the marina there are lines of yachts for sale. Seaplanes tout flights to the islands, second homes for fixed migrants.

Deb Gibson grew up around Dollarton with a view over what is now Cates Park, the forest path to the spring. Lowry's account of stumbling, crazed with thirst, through this community, in search of the house of the local bootlegger, is wildly off-balance and fired with hurt: 'Gin and Goldenrod'. A highway it would be death to negotiate. Felled trees. Ditches. Sewage pipes. Real-estate offices. A new schoolhouse: 'a great concrete block of mnemonic anguish'. The Lowry figure, Sigbjørn Wilderness, remembers a night drinking with Indians. Deb remembers, as a child, the stories of the English writer in his squatter's shack. She couldn't wait to grow up and get into town. The community above the park knew little of

Lowry's reputation, books written for foreigners, but they mistrusted him. It was said that he stole booze from the only shop. He was a man to be watched, a bad lot.

When Burroughs came to Vancouver on tour, Bill Gibson met him for dinner at the Sylvia, where the countercultural hero was established in a suite. They had one of those institutional meals nobody mentions as a selling point for the legendary hotel. The advantage of the low lighting and the windows on the bay is that you don't spend much time trying to identify what's on your plate. Afterwards, upstairs, Burroughs offered Gibson a choice of pharmaceutical pick-me-ups and a hit of vodka from his white plastic flask. Gibson waited for his moment, and in a lull excused himself, as the police manual instructs, to visit the bathroom and have a quick nose through the Burroughs kit. Along with a primitive razor from the 1950s, there was a rusty flip-lip Elastoplast tin, looking as if it had come safely through a combat zone. Inside were two black coins stamped with Nazi insignia. Curiosity made Gibson take his chance, when Burroughs was out of the room, to ask one of the minders, the young men in white tennis shoes, about the swastika coins. 'Bill takes them everywhere. They're going into his eyes when he passes over.'

Seattle

The train slides slowly backwards into the Expo city, allowing us plenty of time to appreciate the giant black gladiatorial portraits on the side of the Seahawks Stadium by Union Station. It had been a famous ride from Vancouver, despite the loud and unbroken yatter of a group of matrons heading for a shopping spree in Portland. I kept the pocket camera rolling on smudgy-windowed shots of ripped hillsides, sawdust alps, lumber yards; narrow creeks with fishing boats crossing the frame at the optimum moment. Anna's hero of the day was our train captain, the feisty Crystal, who licked us into shape for the customs routine at Bellingham. Which passed smoothly after the initial 5 a.m. shakedown, before we boarded the Amtrak Cascades in Vancouver. Empty all satchels and cases on to the inspection table and pay a premium for infringing on sacred American soil. Out in the main concourse, so wired you could smell it at twenty paces, a grunge hippie couple are sending paranoid telegrams through their nervous systems; checking and rechecking every soiled item of fancy dress in their bulging plastic sacks, every odd sock, psychedelic tin can and pouch in their fat rucksacks.

Bill Gibson told us, with relish, that the border country of tumbledown shacks, scrawny rivulets, stands of scrubby trees, was acknowledged as prime serial-killer terrain; proud redneck folk, self-sufficient, keeping relationships strictly in-house, as incest or worse. There were some very nervous cattle in wet fields. But that was the cartoon version, the Robert Crumb head comic. There were also pioneers, migrants, survivalists. Gary Snyder, I knew, grew up on what he called 'a stump farm', north of Seattle. From the train, we could choose between the ocean and, from the other window, the North Cascades with Mount Baker. The landscape of Snyder's earliest inspiration.

'A walked line,' said the artist Hamish Fulton in a retrospective show at the Turner Contemporary in Margate, 'unlike a drawn line, can never be erased.'

Our hotel was midtown, between the busy interstate and the Alaskan Way Viaduct. It was hedged by generic blocks, car parks, warehouses, mall buffets and a sex-aid wholesaler. Grey dawn light flattered illuminated gantries advertising GOODYEAR and FM local radio shows: OLDIES ARE BACK! It was hard to shake off the *War of the Worlds* tripods and the quaintly sci-fi Space Needle spike of the 1962 World's Fair. The detritus of that ambitious civic project hung around as an entropic tourist attraction. Half-closed conference halls with Jimi Hendrix fused-guitar memorials, Native American neo-totems, branded ephemera from *Star Wars* and peace gardens serviced by the Alweg Monorail were somewhere to shelter from the perpetual rain of Washington State. The Seattle Center, as it was now called, blended the melancholy of Margate's abandoned Dreamland funfair with one of those yards where they store the unwanted statues of Lenin.

Wherever I walked, on my first damp circuit, I couldn't shake free of this horizon of skinless steel armatures and bare trees; Seattle's enduring tribute to the transitory, to boosterism, the space race, Boeing. A persistent microclimate of downloaded gloom referenced Jack Kennedy's conveniently 'heavy' cold, the one that allowed him to duck out of attending the closing ceremony. (He was otherwise engaged with the Cuban Missile Crisis.) Taking a detour through the deserted park, I appreciated what they still had on offer: a ticket to another planet, the past of unadulterated Darwinianism, lunar colonialism, Mob politics in high places. And Jimi Hendrix.

The whole town, from the container ships and grain silos to the office women puffa-swaddled like Inuit, to the freighters, to the softly spoken junkies making their approach between the red hand

and the white leg of the WALK DON'T WALK sign, had been translated into a Danish crime film. Into recovery trauma: Korea, Vietnam, Bosnia, Iraq. Into leisure-dressed corporations with impossible-to-satisfy global ambitions operating out of anonymous business parks. Into grunge rock stars in Cape Cod-look mansions fondling trophy weaponry in the room above the garage.

This was the Denmark of Céline's exile. As haunted as Elsinore. The presiding goddess was Courtney Love, playing the murdered Joan Vollmer: and she wasn't at home. I watched her, legs crossed, little black dress, grey boots, being interviewed on YouTube about Seattle. The woman was a miracle of intelligence expressed as manifest physical being; every move, every gesture. Hair flicked back. Hands making that elegant teapot-handle shape on her hips. She said that she didn't come from here, she was a runaway kid. But she would *never* send Kurt Cobain's ashes down the coast to LA to be buried in that big cemetery with Jayne Mansfield.

Coming away from the hotel, where Anna tossed and turned in restless sleep, it took an act of will to spin from the interstate, the older smarter properties that spoke of green spaces, Japanese tea gardens, museums, universities, to the rain-slicked shopping centre and the working streets that offered a lift of harbour light; Pike Place Market and Elliott Bay. Vagrant figures were on the move with me, keeping dry in doorways; asking for nothing. Bill Gibson recommended the market and it was everything he promised. Heroic metaphors of excess: oceans of fish as performance aids to barkers in white overalls and white rubber boots; Kew Garden jungles of flowers; fruits so waxed and fat they looked fake; breads, sweets, biscuits; herds of raw red meat. Even bookstalls were piled high with maps and magazines and newsprint: the final deposit of the printed word before leaving the homeland for some Alaskan wilderness. READ ALL ABOUT IT. ARABIC. JAPANESE. CHINESE. OUT OF TOWN. The big clock is set to New York Time.

My usual tactic, which I shared with Lowry, was to make my tour, early and alone, sniffing out potential breakfast bars to share with my wife on a second circuit; hazards of transit smoothed over.

Seattle was a challenge. We had to steer very wide of the first Starbucks, retained in its original form and now operating as a major waterfront attraction.

'Primrose was asleep,' Lowry wrote. 'It was about six-thirty. He woke her up, and they took the same walk he had made.'

Towards breakfast, respite; porridge, orange juice, green tea. Palliatives to take the edge off what I sensed was becoming a challenging frontier for both of us. I was not looking forward to the long drive south. It had to be done, or I'd be stuck here for years. All my instincts were for a ferry across Puget Sound and then to start walking through the Olympic National Park. Like the Lea Valley on steroids.

Seattle as I understood it – very little – was not a place designed to make you feel comfortable. How could we expect that within the active magnetic field of Starbucks, Boeing, Bill Gates and Microsoft, Amazon and Kindle? There was, as Gary Snyder said, in a book I found in the Pike Place Market, danger on peaks. 'Give up! Give up!' Where else could you imagine Sven Nykvist, Ingmar Bergman's austere photographer from *Persona* and *Hour of the Wolf*, shooting a romantic comedy for Nora Ephron? *Sleepless in Seattle* is what Anna would call 'the ultimate ironing film'. There was a quality in Expo town that implanted or sustained the germ of Pacific Rim odysseys, epic hikes, hunger marches as driven as that of Cabeza de Vaca.

In December 1957, while working as an oiler on a tanker ploughing through the Aegean Sea, Gary Snyder wrote to his friend Will Peterson. 'Visualize long thousand-mile walks. I've even contracted a notion of walking from Seattle to San Francisco by devious rural and woodland routes.'

It wasn't just Snyder, the native, the mountain man. Seattle was a notable pit stop in the dream cycle of William Burroughs, in his Kansas exile of cats and shotgun paintings. 'Why do I keep saying "Seattle"?' The old man, asleep in his narrow Lawrence bed, finds himself translated to a dirty grey loft occupied by a messenger in a slovenly blue uniform. He doesn't have the Elastoplast tin in his fist.

There are no Nazi coins to seal the eye sockets. 'Cities are being moved from one place to another.' The coins are the fee, initiating Burroughs into an occulted geography.

It happened to Lowry; he was given the map, the cabbalistic chart. Margerie helped him manage it, she collaborated in his delusions: if this hopeless drunk was not a genius, it was all for nothing. Reynal and Hitchcock (perfect name for it) agreed to publish *Under the Volcano* in February 1947. Too late, too late. As disastrous, this public triumph, as the long delay of Kerouac's *On the Road*. A chorus of approval. No way but down. And out. The rest is a painful obituary. The New York publishers will pick up the tab for a trip east (wrong direction). Margerie removes the galley proofs before they are reduced to sodden pulp; she returns them. Lowry, premature psychogeographer, sets himself to plotting the worst route between the Dollarton shack and the world city on the Hudson. Try this: plane to Seattle, bus across the States to New Orleans (uneasy rider), converted Liberty ship carrying bauxite to Haiti (one step ahead of Graham Greene), up the East Coast to New York. Lowry said that he now understood why Hart Crane jumped overboard.

The road trip intersects with Kerouac. 1947: Kerouac plots a ride to Hollywood, then Tijuana. By way of Oregon, Washington, Idaho. 'The great unknown Montanas, the mysterious Dakotas, the undiscovered places of America.' Or else: visit Burroughs. Arizona, New Mexico, Texas. A huge work *must* emerge. He mentions Céline. 'The only thing I'm worried about is the inevitable Siberia.' Bad journeys take on their own momentum, an irresistible illogical logic. The traveller witnesses his dissolution, only to confirm the potency of place. Lowry in Cheyenne, Wyoming: 'Just like the cinema!' Lowry in Kansas City. The notebook fills with uselessly monumental sunsets, slag heaps of vanished industries, the same automobile fatalities on empty desert highways noticed by Robert Frank; mammary billboards, toilet bowls in dry-retch bus stations, heavy breakfasts like jukebox headaches. Shreds of graffiti are broken sentences from a magical primer in a foreign language.

Malcolm can't use this stuff. It will be franchised to Kerouac. Lay your head on another bottle, brother. Make it a compass.

Dylan Thomas wasn't the only Welshman Lowry saw in Vancouver. The saturnine figure of Charles Stansfeld Jones, a census-taker for voter registration, turned up at the shack door like a refugee from John Cowper Powys's *A Glastonbury Romance*. Jones was an adept. Lowry had dabbled in Swedenborg and Böhme, in Blake, and systems of correspondences. But this accountant and minor council official was Frater Achad; cabbalist, magician; a former initiate of the Golden Dawn and Ordo Templi Orientis. He was the mystical child of Aleister Crowley and Jeanne Foster (Soror Hilarion): the collateral aftermath of a period of sex-magic rituals. He came to Lowry carrying the black spot, in the form of a chart, huge as Kerouac's teletype roll for *On the Road*: the Sephirotic Tree. Here was the occult vocabulary for Lowry to factor into the latest draft of *Under the Volcano*. Permission to undertake astral journeys, expeditions to islands of the dead, by taking dictation from Beelzebub, Lord of the Flies. In company with Jones, long evenings were passed in Eridanus, doling out tarot cards, casting divinatory sticks, reading MacGregor Mathers. And contemplating the unravelling of the great scroll of the Pacific, the plane ticket to Seattle.

Jones took the 'Oath of the Abyss', an attribute of his cult grade as Magister Templi. Lowry tumbled, wrecked on mescal, tequila, habanero, after the poisoning of two pets cats, and a 24-hour binge, into an irrigation ditch flooded with raw sewage; the barranca where his fictional consul would be thrown with a dead dog. Writers are such literalists. In the rented Cuernavaca house, the cook Josefina, who despised Lowry, this foreign drunk who was not even an American, put a whole rabbit, ears, eyes, teeth, cotton tail, paws and fur, in a large pot of barely simmering water. They ate by candlelight, having no idea what was on the end of the fork. They gummed and tongue-probed with care, spitting out bone and pelt.

Crowley wrote to Stansfeld Jones congratulating him on the ritual he had devised. 'You create a vortex of force which will suck in all the people you want. Treat death as an ordeal, an initiation. In short be the founder of a new and greater Pagan cult in the beautiful land which you have made your home.' Jones went mad. He fulfilled the fantasy of his sozzled compatriot Dylan Thomas: he wandered Vancouver naked under a raincoat, which he would throw off to declare that he had crossed the Abyss, having divested himself of all the Veils of Illusion. Crowley cursed his former protégé, calling on the Demon Servitors to destroy him utterly.

Burroughs made several entries in his dream diaries noting how the European cities of his past were grafted on to the American wilderness. Like Kerouac in 1947, and Gary Snyder in 1957, Burroughs saw himself trudging impossible miles on nightmare journeys through real but transposed continents. Nazi coins, made into blind spectacles, badged him through sinister frontiers. 'I have walked across Siberia. It took two months. I had to kill five people. New York is gone.'

I was astonished to see how closely the somatic diary of the Beat senior citizen, with his cats and his canes, duplicated the model for the looped walks I was trying to undertake, every morning of our Pacific Rim trip, as a way of rolling up the deranged invasion path tramped and recorded by Albert Speer in the prison garden at Spandau. 'I have, it seems, walked westward from the Bering Strait,' Burroughs wrote. 'Across Siberia and Northern Europe.' Speer, Hitler's architect of ruins, having successfully concluded a trial hike, Berlin to Heidelberg, set out, through the long years of his imprisonment, having confirmed the length of his stride, to calculate a pedestrian progress across Germany, Siberia, the Bering Strait, to America. Then down the Pacific Coast to Mexico, achieving thirty-five kilometres south of Guadalajara, before they let him out into an afterlife of self-justifying interviews. Speer's activities were viewed with disdain by his fellow prisoners, a numbered rump of high Nazi officials, admirals, diplomats; delusionists who were fortunate to escape the noose after the Nuremberg Trials. Spandau was a sinister holiday camp for ghosts, policed by bored (and bribable) soldiers of the occupying powers.

The last prisoners left, numbers not names, were the compulsive fugue walker, Speer, sweating out his swollen fantasies, and Rudolf Hess, Deputy Leader of the Party, survivor of a brain-cracked flight to Britain. Their relationship, hostile, jealous of history, a grudging alliance of shared solitude, was Beckettian, absurdist. The pacer of dirt circuits and the watcher in the long coat, madman or cynical sage. It was Hess, the witness, who suggested the beans. That Speer should measure each circuit achieved by shifting a bean from one pocket to another, like a cricket umpire tolling the number of balls bowled in an over, or one of Beckett's Cartesian pebble suckers on an Irish strand. 'My memory loss was faked,' Hess boasted, faking it again for Speer, the ultimate faker, the man who almost convinced himself.

Speer is 5. Hess is 7. Numbers are painted on their backs like stencils on packing cases. A snatched photograph of Speer in the garden has him leaning on his hoe like William Blake's engraving: 'The Traveller Hasteth in the Evening'. A long-striding walker is being walked by his furies into a dark night. I came across this image as a cover illustration on a pamphlet issued in 1971: *A Defence of Sacred Measure (such as the foot, mile, acre and other units of British metrology, and of the ETERNAL and HUMAN values inherent therein)*.

And in this spirit I trudged my loop through Seattle's weather and winking signs and concrete levels and sodden Indians with polystyrene coffee beakers filled with more rainwater than coins. What Speer became, his daily circuits an energizing device for memory, was a writer. Continents tramped and mapped were provocations for text; a terrible freight of words, private diaries crabbed and scribbled. An archive of 25,000 pages was smuggled from the cell on illegitimately defaced toilet paper. A monster novel in which the satanic opera of the Reich would be deconstructed by way of meditations on cinema, landscape, fine art and the absent, ever-loving family.

'My only previous acquaintance with such prison cells has been in American movies,' Speer wrote in October 1946. He recognized, very early in his fractured autobiography, that the one thing the

Nazis were really great at was inventing euphemisms. Miles were devoured in the shadow of high walls and guard towers in the north-western Berlin suburb. He crossed continents. A singular invader. An army of one. By the time he reached America, I was tracking him, but Spandau time never became my time. As with Speer, the daily plod – witnessed by surveillance systems – was nothing more than the assembly of a shaky outline for a work of unreliable fiction. New quotes invented to fix the past.

When Speer introduced his daemon, Hitler, he spoke of the Führer's obsession with Karl May's invented Wild West and the exploits of his noble backwoodsman, Old Shatterhand (the Aryan version of Fenimore Cooper's Leatherstocking). Newsreels of fire, burning cities, erupting volcanoes, induced in Hitler, as Speer recorded, a sexual rapture.

'Lacking a tape measure, I measured my shoe, paced off the distance step by step, and multiplied the number of paces. Placing one foot ahead of the other 870 times, thirty-one centimetres to a step, yields 270 metres for a round. The project is a training of the will, a battle against the endless boredom; but it is also an expression of the last remnants of my urge towards status and activity.'

The Beckettian other, Estragon to his Vladimir, Rudolf Hess, sits mute on his bench, watching, muttering to himself about doctored food and stomach cramps. But Speer spears on: 'Today I walked eighty-nine beans.' As he passes the spectre with the Gothic skull and heavy black eyebrows, he whispers: 'I am going to an island beyond Sicily. I can't go any further.' His audience, his goad, the Deputy Leader in the threadbare greatcoat, says something. And repeats it on the next lap: 'Why not go by way of the Balkans to Asia? To the United States of America. The lands we have yet to conquer.'

The itinerary of the ultimate bad journey was established, or channelled. While concentration camp surgeons, slave masters, bureaucrats of genocide, interrogation experts peddling their dubious skills, decamped for Bolivia, Uruguay, Speer trudged through Siberian winters towards the necrophile carnival of Mexico.

'After the despair of the past weeks I have resumed my tramp. This morning I left Europe and crossed the pontoon bridge to Asia. Sometimes I think about death.' News from the world outside arrives like a trailer for a film by Fritz Lang. Speer recalls Wernher von Braun fantasizing about flight to the moon. Now it seems he has helped the Americans launch a satellite. 'I think of new potentialities for annihilation.'

Hitler used Karl May as proof that it was not necessary to know the desert in order to direct the movement of troops across North Africa. 'The people are as foreign as American Indians.' With imagination, you do not need to travel to know the world. 'I am still 3,300 kilometres from the Bering Strait. Endless forests of larch and fir, with gnarled silver birches in the highlands. Grass often over my head.'

Hess stared at him in astonishment. An ant crawled through the hairs of his drowned hand. He gestures. In his triumph at reaching the coast, Speer has forgotten to transfer his bean. 'My respects, my respects,' Hess whispers. The walker sits, for a moment, beside the watcher. They discuss the old regime's love of forests and the philosophy of the beauty of highways, as developed by Todt, and manifested in the vision of the Autobahn. When they part, to return to their cells, the sky is red as a blood orange.

Insomniac, feeding on contraband pills, Speer, the author of this insane journey across the world, evaluates his rivals; he reads everything from Walser to Böll as a lamentation. 'Today I passed Seattle on the West Coast of the United States. In sixty days, despite cold and high winds, I have covered 560 kilometres.'

'I'll tell you the difference between you and me,' Hess says. 'Your follies are contagious.'

And so they were. I was invited to Berlin to lead a walk across a city I didn't know, from east to west, Alexanderplatz to the 1936 Olympic Stadium; a walk made in the precise footprints of a journey documented in an earlier book, *Ghost Milk*. It was a redundant concept, but I accepted it as a way of taking a look at what remained of

Spandau. I would be met by the film essayist Chris Petit, who had some experience of the city, and who was presently engaged with his Museum of Loneliness, an unrealized project for staging minimalist interventions in the narrow gaps between blocks of social housing. A young woman called Lisa agreed to drive us to Spandau, a failed supermarket behind inadequate fencing, alongside a former redbrick barrack block, and premises occupied by peddlers of alternative medicine and garden furniture.

Parking slots were reserved for ARCADIA BERLIN, which seemed about right, a wink at Speer's attempt to lay out a garden in this dark place. And a reminder that Speer had once corresponded with the Scottish poet and garden-maker Ian Hamilton Finlay. Finlay's stern arcadias were structured from ruins: 'The World Has Been Empty Since The Romans.' Spandau was an accidental Hamilton Finlay, an informal conceit with no gardener, no artist.

The sun was dropping, flaring in the windows of structures that had once been part of the prison. We squeezed through a gap in the fence beside the wreck of a WURTMAXE sausage stall. Among the unloved shrubs, the yellowing and riotously fecund firs, we poked about for traces of Speer's walked circuit. We compared the present ground, like an abandoned retail park on the fringes of the M25, with covert black-and-white images of the Nazi crocodile around the high-walled enclosure in the published Spandau diaries.

Did Speer plant the tree hanging over the boulder painted with a white number? The former exercise area was now the site of a neo-Nazi cult shrine. The grey rock with the painted 7 was dressed, blasphemously, with a collection of small white stones like the ones traditionally left on Jewish graves. A freestanding metal plate was decorated with the cardinal number, a horizontal line through the middle in the European fashion. A wreath of straw, like the wheel of a symbolic chariot, was laid around the crudely painted white number in a memorial gesture. There were further hidden 7s all over the sunken garden area.

And of course I found myself booked into room 700 on the 7th floor of my hotel in Mitte, the old East. When, tired after the flight from London and the Spandau excursion, I went upstairs for a rest before the evening's inevitable talks, performances, late meal, my bed was stripped back, and a strange couple, the man gaunt, the woman generously proportioned, were fucking vigorously on the floor. He was wearing a black leather vest and a pair of polished shoes. She was naked. She glanced at me, and then they carried on. Through the window I could see the ball and spike of Fernsehturm, the TV tower overlooking Alexanderplatz.

It was Hess who was remembered. He was 7. Speer was no longer part of this. At the event, which had been pitched as 'women talk, men walk', I sat behind a man whose leather jacket was customized with a snake swallowing its own tail: TO LIVE IN DISCONTENT. As we suspected, dinner was late, in a fashionable restaurant decorated with V2 rockets and foxes with bandaged paws. The waiters were unhappy actors. The bar was full of stylish Russian hookers. The building had once been a Jewish Girls' School. There were photographs in the corridors recording some of the tragic history. Everybody was waiting for Veruschka, who never arrived. After an hour, when a bowl of salad came around for the second time, Petit pushed back his chair. We had a beer in a beat bar that traded on the fact that Charles Bukowski had once visited town. It was too late for food. By now Speer had become an anagram for Spree, the river along whose bank we would soon walk, in search of a hollow tree from which I could deliver my lecture on the symbolism of 7; on Malcolm Lowry, William Burroughs, Beckett, Céline. And the eternal recurrence of bad journeys.

When Lowry arrived at his Taormina *pensione*, struggling in the wake of D. H. Lawrence, as I was now stalking him, he expressed his delight at the notion of collecting another volcano. He would soon be sailing to a barren island. All the signs were auspicious. They had given him Number 7 and the villa was called the Eden. He unpacked his typewriter. It was the Day of the Dead. 'I swim to and fro,' he said. 'And I contemplate a story of this place.'

He was the story, it was never written. *Tremor in Taormina*. Seven was the number waiting for him in Mexico. Names and numbers are candles. In *Dark as the Grave*, Lowry searches for his friend, the descendant of Zapotecan kings, a man who ran for twenty miles beside his horse. 'Fernando had helped to make this life fruitful and good as men should have had it in the Garden of Eden.' Another garden, another oasis. Another *pensione* from which he will soon be expelled. It was the Garden of Eden. *Le gusta este jardín? Que es suyo?* The inscription on the ceramic tile in Ripe. 'And it was of Fernando too that he thought as, following the guide, he descended into the dark tomb number seven, where gleamed the guide's one candle.'

Forks

'Travelling makes you ill,' said Roberto Bolaño. Sometimes my insensitivity has consequences. I noticed, of course I did, that Anna was struggling with the fallout of the fainting fit that left her dehydrated and sick after that Shoreditch cellar meal and the plush viewing of *True Grit*. But grit was part of her Englishness, her upbringing. Pain was managed. Days of high energy, bolstered by vitamin D, were exploited. If Anna could manage the morning walk, it was assumed that all was well. I was aware that Seattle was problematic. So I found a better breakfast bar with granola and green tea.

But all was not well in our high tower. Anna had peeled to the pulse of the city. She lay awake on the huge hard bed trying to work out how to tell me that she was going straight to the airport in the morning, returning to London. The difference quantum had become critical. This was as remote from Hackney, children, grandchildren, as it was possible to be. The old dream of driving down the Pacific Coast came with too high a premium. I needed it for my book, which is to say my continued existence. Anna supported the fiction, but another few days in Seattle and she would be left without shape or substance. The myth, in any long, close relationship, is of common ground. That memories can be truly shared and refined by repeated tellings. That anything overrides the brute imperatives of the work in hand.

We took a slow, convalescent boat trip around Elliott Bay. And it helped. We would be leaving Seattle soon. Meanwhile, I had one last expedition to undertake: a bus ride to a special place on the other side of the water.

After visiting J. G. Ballard in Shepperton, as part of a walk around the fringes of the M25, London's orbital motorway, I noticed how the celebrated writer's name invaded other cities, and always as a marker of outer limits. On a busy promotional trip to Paris there was no opportunity to tramp, as I'd planned, to the end of one branch of the Metro, the station called Balard. (Jim Ballard, like Anna, would never discuss surgical procedures he had undergone. The amputation of a single letter was a private matter. Health, like his current work in progress, was not a suitable topic for conversation.) What I'd forgotten was that Ed Dorn had once lodged in the Ballard district, as somewhere 'to keep costs down'.

My concept was overburdened with symbols: a day's stroll around the curve of the mauve track from Bastille (known) to Balard (mysterious). The writer Philippe Vasset, who produced *Un livre blanc* as an investigation of all the blank white spaces on the map of Paris, and who supported himself by making regular trips to the City of London to tease out information for a subscription-only bulletin on the latest rumours from the Secret State, told me that he knew Balard. It was where the French tested underwater defence systems. On the other side of the road, they planned a holding camp for economic migrants.

'Où est votre place? Comment habiter ici? Malgré la couverture satellite permanente et le maillage des cameras de surveillance, nous ne connaissons rien du monde.'

Seattle had its own remote Ballard. We found the No. 15 bus and climbed aboard with a motley of the decent poor, an underclass of the physically disabled, Native Americans, cleaners and short-order cooks returning home. We crossed the bridge. Under the shelter of a flyover, a man stood holding up a cardboard sign: I WILL DO ANY WORK. GIVE ME A JOB.

The rain was in temporary remission. It was easy to see why Seattle was chosen as an objective correlative for the Danish gloom of *The Killing*, a television series saturated in weather; a melancholy parade of hooded coats, agitated windscreen wipers and crumbling human physiology. The shards of the World's Fair offer a backdrop for the title sequence of a slowly unravelling murder mystery. We walked away from the safety of the departing bus like slouched

TV-noir characters heading straight for an encounter with a float-ing corpse, the woman with one shoe and no pants in the shrubbery of a twilight park.

Anna was recovering well in this version of Shepperton on Sal-mon Bay. We ate in a Vietnamese café and then continued down a straggle of pet hospitals, storage facilities for geriatrics, boat build-ers, to the Ballard Locks and public gardens. HEALTHY FOOD FOR DOGS & CATS. MUD BAY BALLARD. GIVING UP KNOWLEDGE EVERY DAY. BALLARD JAM HOUSE. In the photograph, Anna is smiling, but there is a fine mist over her sore eyes. The smile is tight. And she has a mouth filled with broken wine glasses.

Ballard is the Pacific Scandinavia, the former world leader in the manufacture of shingles. The first mill, completed in January 1888, was the Sinclair. Here was established a town of wood, fish, iron. A new place populated by Norwegians and Swedes, many of whom drifted down from Canada. The first whites arrived as homestead-ers in 1852. Before that, land was occupied by the Shilshole band of the Duwamish tribe. Captain Ballard won 160 acres of land along-side Gilman Park on the toss of a coin.

The park was a civic imposition; walking there we recovered some residue of our old familiarity. The neat wooden houses on the other side of the inlet reminded me of sailing down Norwegian fjords. Confident incomers, women in hats and heels, used to pose for portraits at the junction of 85th Street and 32nd, where there was a sign saying CITY LIMITS. Beyond the dirt road, the forest began. And the source of their prosperity. Fire-food. In 1889, a raging inferno consumed every lumber mill, wharf and warehouse between Union and Jackson in Seattle. Materials to rebuild the city came from the yards of Ballard.

The car they had for us was a Chevrolet Impala. It was solid, com-fortable, silent. There were no manifests or manuals. 'Just get in and go. You can leave the keys in LA. Have a great ride.' I didn't want to crunch against a concrete pillar getting out of the subterranean gar-age, but the woman was right. This boat drove itself, even if it took us three days to work out the radio. And we never succeeded in finding anything worth listening to, a steady diet of messianic hucksters, tired country and western, adverts for furniture stores.

We cut downhill towards the ferry. I was surprised at how smoothly this was going, fifteen minutes in and we were on the water, crossing Puget Sound towards Bremerton and the Olympic National Park. I remembered another Danish take on the West Coast, the migrant director Nicolas Winding Refn's film of the Jim Sallis novel *Drive*. The stunt driver in zipped windcheater who moonlights as a professional getaway man is checking out possible motors for the night's business. The limping mechanic tells him he looks like a zombie and offers: 'Benzedrine, Dexedrine, caffeine, nicotine.' The boy, played by Ryan Gosling, doesn't smoke. He's more of an existential gum chewer. Like a Jean-Paul Belmondo part regraded to Robert Macfarlane, the respected British academic, author, climber. Lean, contained, easy-moving, but with a dangerous glint in the eye. 'There she is,' says the gimp. 'Chevy Impala, most popular car in the state of California. No one will be looking at you.'

As we bumped down the ramp, rain became torrent. Anna was navigating, but I had nothing better to offer her than a laminated map of the Pacific Northwest with bruise-blue mountains drawn in three-dimensional form, and seen from a migrating bird's point of view. The Olympic National Park is as negotiable as our own Victoria Park in Hackney, with a few more hills. We could skip around the whole promontory in an afternoon; then on down 101, the snaking coast road, to San Francisco. And, ultimately, Los Angeles.

An hour of streaming traffic, military bases, hunger pangs, took us off-highway in quest of a convenience store, proper roadmaps – and 101 itself, our route out. With a bag of Gary Snyder's books in the back, I wanted a quiet evening in which to read and re-read, in preparation for the visit to his Kitkitdizze retreat in the Sierra Nevada. I'd missed Snyder on the previous Beat odyssey with Pavel Coen. And somehow, given the Zen discipline of his approach to life, his reputation for not suffering fools gladly, or at all, the mountain poet seemed the most challenging of my American assignments.

Gary's varied approaches to the roads between Seattle and California unspool like Kerouac's scroll for *On the Road*. He is constantly on the move, making notes, employing humour, *noticing*. 'Two pigs in a pickup sailing down the freeway.' He favours the more direct Interstate 5. He sketches off-highway signs: hexagonal DENNY'S, starry CARL'S, loopy MCDONALD'S, eight-petalled SHELL, MOBIL with a big red O. The soft roar of flow.

We don't overtake, we are part of the necklace. Under black clouds, with densely wooded or stripped hillsides banked around us, the afternoon closes in. We drive the drive. Miles of snaking road with occasional rigs lurching towards us, stacked with peeled forests; a Dunsinane of Ken Kesey hard-hat lumber out of *Sometimes a Great Notion*. I read 636 pp of the Panther paperback, only to find the last page missing. *Viv closes the large book. For some time she has been turning the pages in silence.* 'I still *don't understand what happened.*'

We have to get off this road. The urge to walk through the forest is too strong. I will try to find a track to the lake. The rain has released some of the wet-tobacco, primeval rot of the fallen trees; tangled roots, green mulch, heavy, boot-sucking red clay. There is a shuttered cabin. We push on for a few minutes, enough to know that another half-hour and we are not coming back. Anna's face is so white she seems to be in a pioneer studio with drapes of ancient grooved bark behind her. The drooping moss-encrusted branches, ferns and crocodile logs are another element entirely. Trees not only cut off the light, they absorb intruders, devour memory.

When Tom Clark re-imagined the crazed French author's flight and Danish imprisonment in a novel called *The Exile of Céline*, he said that all the natives talked about was 'faster forests'. Trees are sourced industrially and marked as furniture before they can put down anchors into the ground. Nothing of that here. This forest pre-dated the first migrants across the Bering Strait. Tourists were stumbling through the fringes searching for a cobweb on which to rest, husks for some spider's larder. Everything since we accepted our voluntary imprisonment in the Impala was as Céline said when he described a faked Pompeii with a plaster Vesuvius puffing out smoke. His friend Jacques Deval took him on a tour of a Hollywood film set: 'eerie, spectral and somehow staged'. Like the submarine pens of Washington State. And the psychotic marines who bring their invasion traumas home. Frontier survivalism is horribly rewired.

We found a motel and, coats over heads, made a run for shelter. The town, a mean strip of shops and bars alongside the highway, close to a logging camp, was called Forks. Gary Snyder told me, when we met, that he had written two poems here. Or that he'd revised one poem and made it new. The bed was substantial; the noise of the traffic splashing through water on 101 was soothing. Natives liked *mass* on their plates. I had grilled salmon and a tub of salad; enough to feed us for a week. The surface of the table was inset with images of grizzly bears. Several fellow diners were tubed to oxygen cylinders, which they hauled around on wheels. They tucked away deep bowls of steaming meat with no hindrance.

My morning circuit, which left me sodden but exhilarated, wouldn't play back into any Spandau mapping. It was everything Speer would find impossible to project by drawing on orthodox sources of reference. Monster rigs were parked all the way down the narrow strip, glistening in a psychedelic spectrum of green-and-red reflections: commercial signage, rain-slicked petrol-station windows, fuzzy haloes around light poles. A narrow gap between the high backs of the lorries and the electrified noise of the cafeterias and convenience stores revealed a startling, deep-blue gash of sky. Our motel was low-level, down-lit, set against the silver lake of a parking lot. White weatherboard cabins shimmered in pink bounce.

VAMPIRES WELCOME.

There is a sinister trade-off here; blood-bite solicitation alongside lists of combat veterans who made it home safe from Iraq and Afghanistan. Many of the names are Mexican in origin. Any space left is given to the cult of wood: Native American art, eagles, leaping fish. A new moon shines on DIE TWILIGHT SAGA. Coach tours bring Germans to the forest feast. To windows of stag skulls. And non-ironic US flags.

All is explained when I get my coffee. This obscure halt between Mount Olympus and Destruction Island was chosen as the ideal setting for the globally popular *Twilight* vampire franchise, about which I knew nothing. Stephenie Meyer, author of the four dark romances, didn't drive around to locate this place. She googled her way to the perfect nest for teenage plasma addicts. The pitch is a young girl called Swan who falls for a 104-year-old Dracula; a Forks man fastidious enough to drain the blood of animals rather than humans. Another character shapeshifts as a wolf.

Around the breakfast bar, where I digest this information, a couple of loggers in baseball caps and plaid shirts are carrying on the card game that has run through the night. The oxygen cylinders have wheeled themselves home. The good old boys are talking about how they can fix things for a grandkid done for drunk driving in possession of a case of beer and an armoury of handguns and hunting rifles.

Albert Speer: 17 April 1962. 'Endless forests surround me; in the distance are smoking volcanoes.' When the Nazi architect learnt that he was, after all those years, to be released from Spandau, he violated prison rules for the last time by sending a telegram to an old friend. 'Pick me up thirty-five kilometres south of Guadalajara. Holzwege.' Holzwege was the pseudonym Speer used for clandestine correspondence. He took it from Heidegger. And it has a nice double meaning: 'wood roads' and 'wrong ways'.

Kitkitdizze

Coming down through the woods on a soft winding track, two minutes shy of the time when we have been instructed to arrive, 10 a.m. on a bright Sunday morning, we see the man already out there in the clearing, his right hand on the dog's collar. Two minutes later, you feel, and he'd be gone. But this is the right person, without question, the one we have come to see. The one we have talked about and quoted on our ride down the coast, through Oregon, into California and the foothills of the Sierra Nevada.

The man in the clearing, silver hair lit from behind, unstructured French-blue workshirt over pink undershirt, over black T-shirt, is lean, of modest height, and steady as a post. The dog is more enthusiastic, a superior hillbilly poodle. She bounds forward to lick the passenger window, avid for society. As the man is not: he can take it when it comes, assess a situation, shape unshapely events to a predetermined programme, and deliver what's required, before returning to his proper business, a measured life in a portion of territory he has made his own.

The dog is called Emi. Beyond that pointy elongation of nose, and the wet welcome, this promiscuously affectionate, warm-breathed female is a canine in sheep's clothing; a tumbling knotted rug of a thing, all flapping ears and thumping tail. Emi has a supporting role in *The Practice of the Wild*, a documentary featuring her human companion and the writer Jim Harrison, shot on Hearst property at San Simeon; a leisurely senior-citizen conversation on wilderness, Native American myths, the Beat Generation, mortality and memory. 'Nature is not a place to visit,' the man says, 'it is home.' The film is a long weekend of walks, meals, chat. The subject of all this attention is courteous. Talk is the price he pays for hospitality. Some of the figures I have tracked down in America, after so many years of visibility and fame, are playing themselves, wired to well-grooved reflexes, seeing ill-matched Hollywood infants ape their mannerisms, so that they no longer possess their own copyright. They have become spooks, flown in for publicity shoots, tolerated visitors to the set. The man in the clearing is not like that. He has always stood his ground, questioned the easy fables.

He is Gary Snyder: poet, bioregionalist, teacher. And now, having bought out his early partners, Allen Ginsberg and Dick Baker, the sole proprietor of this estate, a hundred acres of manzanita thickets, with open stretches of ponderosa pine, black oak, cedar, madrone, Douglas fir, bunchgrass – and one of the most seductive houses in America, self-conceived and self-constructed. The land was purchased in 1966, after Snyder returned to California, following periods as a Zen Buddhist monk in Kyoto; in the engine room of an oil tanker; travelling through India with his second wife, Joanne Kyger, in company with Ginsberg. And then revisiting Japan. Participating in the 'Gathering of the Tribes', that finger-cymbal, Dionysiac, hippie rally in Golden Gate Park, San Francisco. And establishing through conferences, lectures, readings, a solid reputation as a direct and inspired spokesperson for a new ecology based on pushing the ceiling back to the Palaeolithic and beyond.

A hundred acres of ground is a substantial mind-map for a poet. Snyder's friend and colleague Lew Welch saw eternity in an inch of lichen on a rock. 'These are the stamps on the final envelope,' he wrote, zooming from his alcohol-fired metabolic extremity to a yellow-green cluster of organisms existing at a speed accessible to red-eyed witness. And accessible to this driven and difficult man, who looked, as many of the Beat originals did, like a not-quite movie star. Like, say, Steve Cochran. Or Rory Calhoun. Or Scott Wilson as one of the killers from *In Cold Blood*. Like someone who might have got a ride in an early Peckinpah western. Welch, a career drinker, was tall, red-haired; a cross-country driver of legendary finesse (an upmarket Neal Cassady), a military-trained marksman. He had been at Reed College in Portland with Snyder and Philip

Whalen, a formidable Pacific Rim triumvirate of youthful poets. Heavily dosed on Gertrude Stein, and inspired by a chance encounter with William Carlos Williams, Welch was confirmed in his destiny as an outsider: cab driver, fisherman, backwoods hermit.

The poet Charles Upton, who has written about Welch's shamanic Buzzard Cult, about suicide as a journey towards being ingested by a native predator, said that the essence of this teaching was: 'Kid, don't end up like me.' All the seekers we encountered on our drive down the coast, from solitary forest dwellers to Californian communards, faced the Pacific. They lay down, after spiritual exercises, on their sides, the chain of mountains as a spine. Whatever Europe left them, by way of poets, mystics and visionaries, was tested against the particulars of local knowledge, the practice of tribes who had been culled, pensioned off. Welch wanted language to work as magic. He alerted Upton, by way of 'Sufi Sam' Lewis and Carlos Castaneda, to a 'lifelong sensitivity to dark psychic forces'. The Buddhism of China and Japan had to be fitted against the rituals of frontier life: making space, getting by in the military-industrial state. Gary Snyder, attending Philip Whalen's memorial service at Green Gulch Zen Center, expressed the view he shared with Welch: 'Face it, Charles – Buddhism is *atheism.*' What troubled Upton was the seductive nature of the death cult he located as the underlying theme of Welch's poetry. 'Meat is rotten meat made/sweet again.' Devoured is reborn. Immortality is a memory-system encoded in the rhythms, breaks, silences of achieved poetry. Upton mentions the Mexican Day of the Dead, tortillas and tequila laid on the grave to feed hungry ghosts. Disaffected wanderers travel south to salute, but never quite reach, dormant volcanoes. This is where the Buzzard Cult thrives. After Welch stepped away from the jeep, two copycat suicides were recorded.

Unlike Snyder, Lew never found his place. One day, according to rumour, he walked into the forest, and he didn't come back. I'd forgotten where this happened, but I thought about it as we drove for days through the overwhelming shade and eternal drizzle of the Olympic Peninsula and the Oregon coast. We had to take the ocean on trust, hearing the roll of the breakers, but seeing nothing, blinded by the spray of enormous rigs carrying logs to rail-side wood yards.

Taking responsibility for a portion of Sierra ridge, once occupied, river valley to densely forested upper slopes, by Indian tribes, was a major statement of intent from Snyder. 'We were cash poor and land rich,' he said. 'And who needs more second-growth pine and manzanita?' Alexander Pope, in his upstream exile at Twickenham, laid out garden and grotto as a conceit, an extension of his work into the world, and a powerful attractor for patrons and lesser talents. To fund the Sierra reinhabitation, as Snyder saw it, he took on reading tours and an academic position at UC Davis, fifty miles down the road in the state capital, Sacramento. He called his land, this place where he had lived for forty years, Kitkitdizze, after the Wintu Indian name for the aromatic shrub known as 'bear clover'. Sliding down the electric window of the Impala, to give Emi's snout the opportunity for a proper greeting, you get that smell; what the actor Peter Coyote, visiting the community, called 'witch hazel'. It drifts in from the surrounding bushes.

To maintain his 'permeable, porous life', the dissolution of artificial barriers between homesteader and terrain, Snyder rides out, driving down the track for research, pleasure and duty. He spends time in Alaska, in Portland with his son Kai, and in San Francisco. Kitkitdizze has become, he reports, 'a well-concealed base camp from which I raid university treasuries'. This Thoreau-inspired wilderness encampment, real as it appears, is underwritten by the requirement to present itself as a topic for thesis writers, a reluctant paradigm. A magnet for approved visitors, students, localists, or anyone needing to understand if this thing can be managed: a self-funding, functioning centre that is not a retreat, but a resettlement, in a land Snyder calls Turtle Island. Turtle Island is that old America, mountain and desert, before the European colonialists and exploiters, before strip logging and the rapacious industrialism of the gold-mining operations. Or the present hunger for natural gas.

A lot of public land,' Snyder told me, 'has to be converted, in the most organized fashion, into hundreds and thousands of gas wells.

It's like the original oil era. They've tricked a lot of public land by offering inducements that haven't been followed up on. It's rocks and hard places for everybody, in terms of energy, from now on.'

Anna drove the first hour, sitting stiffly, managing the pain in her neck, while I did some filming and tried to absorb the sounds of my early-morning walk. Sights lacked outline in the downpour. That rock on Cannon Beach might be a stranded whale. I bought a name-check cap to wear on the future swan pedalo voyage with Andrew Kötting, and a bag of oranges (most of which were confiscated when we crossed the border into California).

'Great joy in camp, Ocian in view.' Wrote William Clark on Dismal Nitch at the mouth of the Columbia River, having, in company with Meriwether Lewis (and a fifteen-year-old Shoshone woman, Sacagawea), reached the Pacific at the completion of a two-year transcontinental expedition launched in 1804. The hunger, beyond journals filled with reports on topography, plant and animal life, Indians encountered, was for new territory to exploit. The swan voyage with Kötting was an absurdist homage, in reverse, ocean to city – as a means of making contact with England's riverbank, woodland tribalists and runaways. Clark was trapped on Dismal Nitch for five days, waiting for the weather to relent. Unlike Kötting, he didn't know about red wine libations.

After Port Orford and a night's roost overlooking a small harbour where fishing boats were winched from the water, we saw the sun for the first time since leaving Vancouver. I was ready, like Lew Welch, to worship the pale eye of fire; pink striations, feathery cloud discriminations above banks of mist shrouding the beach and the coastal hills. 'Orford,' said Charles Olson, 'is a peninsula none try but Cyclops.' The hours spent inside the car, working our way slowly south, creeping through coastal settlements and over a procession of bridges, cantilevered, double leafed, steel trussed by Conde B. McCullough, Oregon's master engineer, were the only reality. The evening halt, meal, sleep, and the morning walk, were soon forgotten, swallowed up in the miles driven.

For Roberto Bolaño, the car, by the time his literary executors are breaking open computer files for fragments to publish as *The Secret of Evil*, is revealed as the ultimate instrument of fate. 'They tell Bolaño about his death, how he was run down by a mysterious car, a black Impala, and they talk about his life, a succession of legendary drinking bouts, as if the bars and rooms where Ulises Lima got sick and threw up were the successive volumes of his complete works.'

The windscreen of the Impala detaches us from the road. A steady beading of rain, the swish of the wipers, confirms the Pacific Rim adventure as a memory-movie, a sequence of prompts and quotations unpicking what we think we know; making us wonder if, in truth, we ever made it out of the thunderhead depression of that first drowned Oregon city with its skeletal World's Fair.

Gary Snyder was justifiably proud of his childhood on a stump farm just north of Seattle. He delivered milk for his father. He learnt to chop wood, how to use a two-handled saw. Tools were important to him, the right kit for the right job. In Kitkitdizze, there are tools everywhere, racks and stacks of them, useful objects respected like artworks. Blades, chisels, axes, boots, helmets, guns. Peter Coyote remembers Joanne Kyger laughing 'about how much stuff Gary had to store so that he could go off to Japan and live simply'. The novice monk insisted that his future wife clear her credit card debt, which had climbed to $1,000, before she travelled out to join him. On arrival, she discovered a list Snyder had compiled, numbering her faults and the ways she could improve her presentation. The big difference in Japan, Snyder explained, was the necessity of having the right manners. His fourth wife, Carole Lynn Koda, was Japanese-American. But in Japan, she got everything wrong. 'I walked too fast,' she said. 'I swung my arms too much. My stride was too long. I looked at people in the eyes. That marked me out as American right away.'

Snyder talks about the 'long view'. The vision of Pacific America privileged from high peaks. He was, from the start, a skier, climber, trail walker. These activities took precedence, as a schoolboy and young student, over academic studies. At the age of fifteen, in 1945, he completed the ascent of Mount St Helens: 'Step by step, breath by breath – no rush, no pain.' The newspaper he read when he came down from the hike, on 13 August, was a day-old copy of the *Portland Oregonian*. It carried a photo spread of the aftermath of the atom bombs dropped on Hiroshima and Nagasaki.

Learning from Chinese scroll paintings at the museum in Seattle, Snyder adopted a linear continuity of narrative, everything happening at once: the pilgrim with his staff on the mountain, the bridge over the stream, the forest and the ocean. Diary fragments, named persons, conversations in roadside cafés, bars, truckstops, prayers, chants, native shamanic lore, myths of place: they enjoyed an equal status and emphasis. The delivery was crafted to move like natural speech with a leavening of slowburn humour. This was a country-smart poetry, beautifully balanced between frontier transcendentalism and the long gaze of Asia.

After the first hour, I took over at the wheel. We talked about Gary Snyder, whom I had never met, and Michael McClure, whom I visited with Pavel Coen, in the house above Berkeley. Both poets read at the Six Gallery in San Francisco, when Ginsberg exposed 'Howl' to an appreciative audience for the first time. We tried to define the attractive otherness of Forks. The *Twilight* aspect of the town was no more intrusive than the traces of Elgar in Malvern or Hardy in Dorchester. Being on the road, spatially limited, loosed from time, imposed a Pynchonesque or Philip K. Dick reading of the world and its conspiracies: pick any wavering thread, follow it, and all the characters interact, exchange roles, climb out from the grave. Films and books are coded. In different languages. Watch out for Number 7. For Seattle. Vulcano. Guadalajara.

The girl who moves to Forks for an inappropriate relationship with a centenarian blood guzzler is played by Kristen Stewart. Who reappears as Marylou, a version of LuAnne Henderson, the first Mrs Cassady, in the Walter Salles film of *On the Road*. She folds into the timeless Beat scroll of American bad journeys. Critics are excited by the episode when Kerouac, Cassady and LuAnne, driving naked through Texas in the Hudson, smear each other with cold cream. Kristen Stewart's *Twilight* character is called Bella Swan. When we reach Bodiam Castle on our swan pedalo voyage towards London, a girl from Moose Jaw slips into the water. She pedals, naked. Her name is Kristen. (Anonymous Bosch, the photographer on the *Swandown* project, sends me a postcard from the Canadian wastes with a J. G. Ballard quote: 'Moose Jaw is quite a place to be.') Researching this river, the Rother, I find in a memoir of Lowry's old Rye acquaintance Ed Burra an incident from the late 1920s: the celebrity addict, Lady Brenda Dean Paul, caused a local scandal by stripping and plunging, at the point where Kristen would follow, on impulse, many years later. One time is all time. The scroll unravels. Burra, this memoir reveals, reads Céline, Ken Kesey, Flann O'Brien, *The Dharma Bums*. He adores H. P. Lovecraft. And is sick in Mexico.

In cafeterias and gas stations, we picked up rumours of trouble ahead. A mudslide had blocked 101, north of Eureka, forcing us to divert for more than a hundred miles over the Klamath Mountains on 299. No cars, steep banks of snow. The marker seemed to be a solitary tree with branches as thin and grey-green as an old man's arms. I stopped for a closer look. The tree was heavily cropped with single shoes; ripe trainers in red, white, blue, with very clean soles.

When Anna tried to draw the curtains in our Red Bluff motel, they came away in her hand, along with a substantial portion of the wall. I was too tired to care. The token swimming pool was more of a septic tank, its petroleum jelly surface thick with polystyrene coffee cups, cigarette butts and scum like week-old bean soup. The town, on my morning Speer circuit, was a desert of fellow pensioners escaping from rest homes, abandoned car lots with lines of fluttering pennants. Unknown knotweed plants were breaking out of the riverside embankment and invading the tarmac.

We left early for Sacramento, gold country, and Grass Valley. A quiet Great Western hotel was like something out of Stevenage:

new, ambitious, hedged in by trees. The highway audible and the bed large. A good place to prepare for Snyder.

A week on the road had been enough to confirm my instinct that the western strip, all the way from Canada to Mexico, with barely registered climatic and ecological shifts, is a different consciousness. Our west is their east. The frontier myth of pushing across prairies and deserts, over mountains, dissolves into Pacific haze. There are new orthodoxies. The poets, with varying degrees of rigour and scholarship, are Buddhists. 'We are on the edge of the East,' Snyder wrote in his essay, 'The Etiquette of Freedom', from *The Practice of the Wild*. 'So where do we go next? Naturally, we look west, to the East. That's where we go.'

Our route to Kitkitdizze read, in the email Snyder sent, like one of his poems: 'Crossing the Yuba river in the gorge, climb up out of the gorge, and about 12 miles from Nevada City you turn right (east) up the first highway of consequence.' After that there are signs nailed on trees, dirt roads and Jackass Flats. We were also advised where to get breakfast and which was the best Chinese restaurant. Nevada City trades on its history, gold. In bookshops, hovering between antiquarian and crafty, they have signed copies of Snyder's books in glass cabinets at New York prices. Weekend tourists take brunch in revamped saloons with sepia photographs of the mining days.

The man in the clearing stays just where he is, his back to the house, as we clamber out of the car and walk towards him; Emi butting against our thighs, nudging us on. Snyder is a fit octogenarian. He has presence before language, in the outdoor way of taking the temperature of a situation before acting. He's had his brushes with the shadows that come with age, but he's sharp, narrow-eyed; skin creased and printed like a proper manuscript of mortality. Jack Kerouac, in *The Dharma Bums*, took Snyder, in the person of Japhy Ryder, as the second American hero of the Duluoz Legend; a scholar-poet of the mountains and Pacific west, after Neal Cassady's transcontinental road rat, hard-cock energy vortex. Ryder is first encountered in a Berkeley cottage among prayer mats and orange-crate bookcases.

Under interrogation now, Snyder is both open and guarded; the difficulty being that he doesn't understand what I want, what I'm after, making this long trip. What he is very clear about is that Kerouac was a fabulist; actual events such as the ascent of the Matterhorn Peak in the Northern Sierra were accurately reported, other aspects were romanced. Back in Hackney, I received an email from Snyder: 'I am as you know a reluctant beat icon – and have never considered myself a beat writer.' In London bookshops, Gary is more widely represented as a wilderness essayist than a poet. 'I'm particularly interested in talking around *The Practice of the Wild*,' he said.

Talking around was the essence of our encounter. While we stood where we were, Snyder discoursed on logging. 'They used to have bigger trees when I was a kid,' he said, recalling the dairy farm, and the stumps, ten feet high and twelve feet in diameter, on the hill 'back of where the pasture was'. That forest was logged in 1890. As a boy Snyder made expeditions, walking and camping, into the surrounding territory.

The focus of our conversation, as we remained between car and house, shifted from Oregon to the recent nuclear meltdown in Japan, and the practicalities of sustaining Kitkitdizze. Snyder was no Amish-style purist. His practice, through meditation and spiritual discipline, was rigorous, but it was programmed to sustain rather than deny the realities of life in this scattered community of the woods. Snyder's son Kai, who 'knows about computers', pointed out that the best coverage of Japanese nuclear horrors came from al-Jazeera. 'How do I find out how to get al-Jazeera?' Snyder asked. 'Just google it.'

The electronic world, which Snyder recognizes as a thief of time, is tolerated. 'I resisted, but I found how useful it could be.' The house, built from the forest that surrounds it, by students and friends, is a graceful blend of two cultural paradigms: the pioneer home-stead out of *The Searchers* and a traditional Japanese structure based around a central fire pit, a hanging pot and an open roof. The roof sweeps low, skirted with pinkish-red tiles and clumps of moss. Gary is in no hurry to move inside. There are other buildings, barns, meditation halls, going back further into the woods. Until the right model for conversation is identified, we will stay where we are, listening to a leathery croak of native life forms somewhere in the trees.

'What are those birds?' Anna said. 'Frogs,' Snyder replied, 'bullfrogs.' It was hard to talk over their throaty, repetitive chorus. 'How do you put up with it?' 'I shoot them.' They are a non-native species, these bullies of the green pond, and they eliminate the local yellow-legged variety. It's like a shockingly obvious solution to a Zen koan. *Bang!* I recall Jack Nicholson's cameo in *Easy Rider*. The manic white-gleam orthodontics at the campfire, before the redneck attack that will kill him. Jack mouths Terry Southern's dialogue against a racket of cicadas and lone dogs. 'You ever talk to a bullfrog in the middle of the night?' That Cheshire-cat grin in the dark. Then the thump of clubs and boots. And the career-defining moment of shifting from Roger Corman B-features to offbeat, independent adventure, to global celebrity and perpetual self-impersonation. *Croak! Croak!*

The pond, dug by Snyder's early construction crew, is chlorophyll sludge, picking up the colours of the surrounding evergreens. The bullfrogs sound more like turkey buzzards. Lew Welch, down the coast, in his cabin near Mount Tamalpais, talked of Zoroastrianism and 'buzzards that eat the dead'. He registered the forest as a regiment of vertical coffins, giant redwoods waiting to wrap their bark around humans who stand still too long. 'The trees are just passing through,' he said in a letter to Snyder.

Poets on their far-flung travels, their neurotic migrations, kept in touch with letters, discussions of craft and influence. When Welch corresponded with Charles Olson, on the East Coast, he said that he had 'finally taken to the woods, I hope for ever'. Like Snyder, Lew kept a gun. There was a bad moment when his companion in solitude, a cat called Stanley, dragged himself back to camp with deep scratches and two legs missing; forcing Welch to shoot and bury the beast. There had been some talk about Lew building a home at Kit-kitdizze, but Snyder felt that in the remote cabin beyond Forks of Salmon, where his friend worked on his *Hermit Poems*, he 'really achieved the meeting of an ancient Asia sage-tradition, the "shack simple" post-frontier back country out-of-work workingman's style, and the modernism of modern art'. Like Snyder, Lew had to deal with the shadowy duplication of being a character in Kerouac's fiction.

Kitkitdizze was no simple retreat for Snyder. The land was rela-tively cheap because nobody had much use for it; the scars of industrial mining came close. The community to be supported included: 'two grown sons, two stepdaughters, three cars, two trucks, four buildings, one pond, two well pumps, close to a hun-dred chickens, seventeen fruit trees, two cats, about ninety cords of firewood, and three chainsaws'. The bees were destroyed by black bear. The kitchen garden went dry in winter and was raided by deer. The chickens were taken by northern goshawks, red-tailed hawks, racoons, feral dogs, bobcats. The forest was full of noises. When visitors arrived in the early days, it was to a set that might have attracted the *Easy Rider* crew or Antonioni's picturesque hip-pies from *Zabriskie Point*.

Helpers shared a work roster, freeing Snyder to write and research. The manner of the man now, when he is alone in this place, is dignified, unhurried, pedagogic. He instructs, he remem-bers, he references: books on fire by Stephen Pyne of Phoenix, Arizona; a text called *Forest Primeval* by 'a biology guy' called Chris Maser; articles from the *Nation* on food-stamp policy. Snyder trades in specifics, hard evidence. When he gives public performances, events like the Berkeley Poetry Conference of 1965, the reading is carefully constructed between translations from the Japanese and Chinese, short sharp squibs, and longer, serial compositions that have been cooking for decades. Listening to recordings, you can hear the big audience being drawn in, the warmth of the laughter. Snyder spoke about the sequence *Mountains and Rivers, Without End*. Journey after journey, down 99, from the Northwest to San Francisco. He borrows an epigraph from Lew Welch about being 'forced by poverty to move with leisurely grace'. Returned from Japan, he discovers that the old road is no longer there; Highway 99 is now Interstate 5. 'Pine trees coming up through asphalt . . . see what happens when you try to be country.'

When I try to bring the practicalities of composition, the gossip of craft, into the conversation, Snyder misreads my questions or veers sharply away. In letters he wrote, to Kerouac and to his friend Will Peterson, during his six-month voyage as a 'wiper' in the engine room of an oil tanker, the act of poetry is rarely mentioned. Inspiration is fugitive, like a 'rabbit with horns'; it comes, when it comes, as a chimera, a freak. Aware of the depredations of the corporate energy pirates, the strip miners, the dynamiters of forests, the leaking wells and supertankers, Snyder delivered polemic from the unusual position of having experienced strange hallucinatory voyages across the world's oceans. His letters are about boredom, drudgery, clouds, money earned, bars, prostitutes, thefts, marine tourism. He makes temporary landfall in Robert Louis Stevenson's Samoa: 'volcanic green flowery hills . . . lotus-eater land, a buddha-realm of flowers and delight which is really like old captain cook and herman melville'. Money is stolen from Snyder's pocket while he swims; he doesn't care. 'Other guys lost money too, but it's all so good-natured.' Wild pigs. Gauguin horses eating flowers. The tanker spews out its oil, before the return to the West Coast of America. San Francisco. Rice wine and Buddha texts.

When we move inside, for green tea, at the table that has replaced the authentic but inconvenient fire pit, there are dried fruits on small saucers. 'Shall we talk?' Snyder says. 'How much time have you got?' Meaning, quite reasonably, *when will you depart?* We settle for another hour. There is much to be done on a Sunday. Jim Harrison, in the film shot on the Hearst estate, asks if Gary felt the need to retreat from the world after the loss of his wife, Carole. The answer is immediate and considered, in that style the poet has: it was no melancholy fugue, but a necessary three-month period in which he simply didn't want to see, or deal with, other people.

Contemplation of the fact of the thing: death. Carole's presence remains here in the house, and more especially in the barn, which has been converted into a library. Her books and papers, the projects with which she was involved, are spread in her adjoining workroom. The house itself is uncanny in its relationship between interior and exterior; how, quite unexpectedly, it feels as if you are back outside; or how the beams fold into the forest like smoothed branches, and narrow alcoves expand to fulfil their purpose, for storage or prayer. The daily routines can be set by the weather, the winter snows and the months when cooking, and eating at a communal table, moves to an open-sided kitchen-shelter. We come at a quiet time. But the spirit of the naked bathers, the woodchoppers, the chanters, the poets who gathered or passed through, is strongly felt. Snyder was sitting here in March 1997 when he got the call from Allen Ginsberg in New York; the gloomy prognosis, the liver cancer. He had climbed with Ginsberg in the High Cascades, travelled with him in India, and together they had bought this land.

While Snyder was waiting for the formal interview to begin, my instinct was to keep quiet, drink the tea, look around. Standing outside, by the pond, we covered plenty of back territory: how the FBI blacklisted the young poet and ordered the senior forest ranger to terminate Snyder's job as a mountain-peak fire-watcher, simply because he had been a member of the National Maritime Union, which was perceived as a Communist conspiracy hell-bent on strikes. 1953. 'That was the last government employment I ever had.'

We discussed edgelands. He had seen photographs of the huts of the Manor Garden allotments in the Lower Lea Valley in East London, before they disappeared to make way for our great Olympic Park. 'It's money for basically nothing,' he said. 'It's the global against the local, absolutely. Semi-urban wilderness is valuable. What about Epping Forest, have they left any of that? Epping Forest is too valuable to touch.' It was *touching* to have Gary Snyder take notice of developments in Hackney, and to see him align the recent enclosures with grander landscape sweeps in Canada, Alaska, California. He spoke of his love of John Clare, 'The Badger' being one of his marker poems.

Driving down to his academic work at UC Davis, Snyder noticed another kind of urban edgeland. 'There is a big rice field, flooded paddy, near Sacramento airport. It used to have a sign on it: "This rice field annually feeds 40,000 people." That's export only. There are a billion people in China. The Japanese don't import so much rice, they have their own subsidized industry. But they import wheat from Canada. It goes out through Vancouver.'

'But we're reinhabiting the land,' Snyder said, his pinkies horizontal as he lifted the small cup between his two hands. 'This was a high-priority place to live for the Indians. They were wiped out, there's only a few left. They're around though. The valley was all marsh, wetlands. They go down there for the fishing and for duck. The valley is covered in tule fog for quite a few weeks in the winter. And it's very chilly. It's sunny up here. We're at the snowline. Higher up, there's deer all season. So the original inhabitants made their living in the rather benign foothills. Cooler than the valley too. This is a benign place to live.'

Snyder has a benign aura. I watched the humour lines around his mouth as he talked, unable to forget a remark in a story by Bolaño, who turned, in that way writers have, his own oral disasters into a metaphor. 'I even regarded the loss of my teeth as a kind of homage to Gary Snyder whose life of Zen wandering had led him to neglect dental care. But it all catches up with you. Children. Books. Illness. The voyage comes to an end.'

Gary, they say, was wild, if you caught him at the right time. There have been a lot of photographs over the years, from beards and sandals, to black collarless jackets and motorbikes, to alpine sunglasses against high peaks. A confident artisan of language, ripe with paradox, monkish austerities and early libidinous pleasures. The bathing pools and parties, as Kerouac reports, where San Francisco dignitaries, scholars and art patrons were entertained in a

Marin County retreat by naked hosts: Ginsberg, Peter Orlovsky and Snyder. The stud in the left ear still strikes a jaunty note. Narrowed eyes. Thin spectacles perched on creased brow.

The years press down a little, rounding the shoulders under the dark blue shirt, as we walk across to inspect the library in the converted barn. But the stride is sure. Snyder is undeceived. He was tempted to use horses to pull logs, but thought better of it. You can't live on this ridge without cars. People tell him, 'Nobody can afford to become a farmer.' You have to inherit the land. When young folk come down from these hills, they go to Portland to retire. 'Reinhabiting and biovisionary ideas are useful, practical and brilliant. But they don't catch on. It's not for the time. You cannot sell voluntary simplicity to people. And that's what we're talking about, voluntary simplicity. Or, in some cases, downward mobility.'

The barn, open to daylight, is stacked with information, books organized not fetishized. Snyder stressed again: 'I'm not a prose writer, I'm a poet. That means I write when it hits me. I scribble a few things. When I do my organized editing and classifying, rewriting, I do it here, mostly in the morning. But not real early. Because the first thing I do is that I meditate.'

Chatting with this man – hands in his pockets, Emi rubbing against his thigh – we appreciate that we have taken enough of his programmed day. The long drive down 101, which will continue to San Francisco, and then Los Angeles, has been about placing this meeting. We confront one another like polite but road-weary strangers, in the middle of nowhere, nodding across red Formica in some breakfast bar; big US flag outside, convenience stores shuttered, along with the brass-plate bank. There is a piece in *Danger on Peaks* set on the road we will drive. Snyder's sister, Anthea Corinne Snyder Lowry, noticed that a pickup ahead of her had lost a grass-mower from the back. 'She pulled on to the shoulder, and walked right out into the lane to take it off. That had always been her way. Struck by a speedy car, an instant death.'

*

The poets who survived the San Francisco renaissance of the late 1950s and early 1960s were the ones who created a successful brand. They were identified with philosophies or styles attractive to the media and the academy. Voluntary simplicity was never an easy pitch. 'There are books about that,' Snyder said, 'but many people looking for the simple life didn't do it well. They came out of the bourgeois background. They didn't have the cultural context with which to do it. But there are places that are flourishing still. Like Southern Oregon. And parts of Northern California. Or south of Eureka on the river basin. Not everybody knows about them.'

The seminal event at which poetry, or the figure of the male poet, first became visible, beyond the ghetto, was the Six Gallery reading in 1955. The gallery had previously been an auto-repair shop and a communal art venture called the King Ubu. Michael McClure, the youngest participant that night, recalled earlier performances by Gerd Stern: 'with belly dancers and bongo drums'. Ginsberg, who had moved from New York to Berkeley, launched 'Howl'. But just as significant, McClure felt, was Snyder's 'A Berry Feast', which closed the evening.

'Gary,' McClure told me, when I visited him, 'opens the door to seeing the heart.' The two major strands of much that would follow – urban apocalypse (the madness of cities) and a new interest in ecology, shamanism – were aired and made public. McClure read his elegy 'For the Death of 100 Whales'. Seventy-nine bored US servicemen from a NATO base in Iceland went out in four small boats, armed with rifles and machine guns, and massacred a pod of a hundred killer whales.

This line-up at the Six Gallery, under the chairmanship of the established San Francisco poet Kenneth Rexroth, had an historic aspect. The difficulty of sudden fame after years of benevolent neglect, and years to come of casual labour and occasional academic patronage, took its toll. If a viable persona could not be constructed, and *sold*, there was erasure, suicide, Mexico. The surrealist Philip Lamantia, declining to expose his own work, read the poems of his friend John Hoffman. Hoffman died under mysterious circumstances in Guadalajara. Ginsberg in 'Howl' has him disappearing 'into the volcanoes of Mexico leaving/behind nothing but the shadow of dungarees and the/lava and ash of poetry'. Snyder's friend Philip Whalen, who was also present, performed with his usual rather shambling grace. A Zen abbot with a taste for fast food.

But the third member of the Reed College gang was not there; he was out of town. In the hills. It has been suggested that Lew Welch's absence from the Six Gallery contributed to what happened on 23 May 1973. Welch wrote: 'I feel like an *outcast* often.' The confession of his identity as a poet, to fellow fishermen or cab drivers, was painful. It didn't matter that he came from a privileged background in Phoenix, that his grandparents knew the Goldwaters at the country club. He was handy; he drank, he fitted in. But as Welch remarked, 'It used to be just about worth your *life* – to say you were a *poet*, in a tough bar.'

Beat existence in the city must include the means of getting away, *fast*: the car. Walsh's vehicle of choice was a 'Jeep Station Wagon'. In 1959, he piloted Kerouac and the Japanese-American Albert Saijo, coast to coast, improvising haiku as they went. Mojave Desert, Las Vegas, New Mexico. Navel-fluff or belly-fleece from a stripper's costume in East St Louis attached itself to a memorial cross they plucked from the empty highway in Arizona, a marked road death. The cross was presented to Ginsberg in New York and placed on the wall above his bed. 'Lew was a fine poet who really couldn't be employed,' Whalen said. 'He was going for nothing. That was what was inside him.'

Turkey Buzzard dreams after he is gone. Friends making search maps of his last words. Gagging on Larkspur Root. Climbing into the Sierras. No roads, no visible rails.

Snyder, guiding us around his home at Kitkitdizze, demonstrates where inspiration comes from, if it does: as a natural occurrence, against the practice of daily life. 'He loved uncoiling his mind into a large inclusive loop,' Peter Coyote said, 'and expressing elegant formulations.' Lew Welch lived with western restlessness, at home nowhere but car and cabin. He looked for conclusions that were never to be found. 'This is the last place,' he wrote on Mount Tamalpais. 'There is nowhere else to go.'

As a settled poet, a homesteader, Gary is the supreme technician of the ordinary, relishing kerosene lamps, backup generators, benches of blades. When and how to serve tea. When to blast the frogs in the pond. The facial expressions you get, talking to him, or leafing through old photographs, are of quizzical challenge and certainty of purpose, developed on solitary trails and in high places. Snyder writes a poetry of statement: location, weather, movement. 'This life:/We get old enough and finally really like it!'

As Kerouac, Neal Cassady and Lew Welch never would. Kerouac, in tragically premature old-man Florida retirement, is hounded by visitors who possess some of the books (without having properly read them). He is beaten in bars by rednecks and blacks (without prejudice). He is glued to a chair inches from the TV screen with its featureless splatter of unreality (the migraine scroll of our time). He is drinking drinking drinking; to the last choked breath. A swollen-faced athlete of excess at forty-seven. Policed by nurse-wife and incapacitated working mother. And Cassady, heading south again, crosses the border, walking out along the railway track after a wedding party in Mexico. Heat haze, terminal exhaustion. Mortality is a competition. 'I wonder which one of us'll die first,' Kerouac wrote in *The Dharma Bums*. 'Whoever it is, come on back, ghost, and give 'em the key.'

Kitkitdizze is a forest-baffled absence of ghosts. Strategies are in place: for snow, bears, power cuts, or the collapse of the entire Californian economy. Snyder's sensitivity to time is geological. 'Our records only go back a couple of hundred years. We don't know what the past held.'

I'm still not sure what I was searching for, but I think I may have found it. I've always been fascinated by pests like Thomas De Quincey; the way he hiked to the Lake District and attached himself to Wordsworth and Coleridge, before 'betraying' them with gossip and mangled histories. When I travelled across the United States, fifteen years ago, making a nuisance of myself with the figures of my early reading, Ginsberg, Corso, Burroughs, I missed Gary Snyder. The writers I met, apart from Burroughs in his red clapboard Kansas bungalow, were in hot, cluttered rooms in cities. They had already answered too many questions, spent too many years in the echo chamber of old recordings. Snyder's engagement was more direct. He played a political role with the Californian Arts Council in Sacramento. He backpacked. He spoke at conferences. The only rule in politics, he reckoned, was to tell the truth.

We had returned to the footprints in the soft ground where our conversation started, the clearing in which the Impala was waiting.

'Where was Lew Welch when he went into the woods?' I asked.

'Right here.'

Welch had been staying with Snyder, camping, thinking about another move. His jeep parked up above the house. Snyder, going out in the evening to call him for dinner, found the note. The gun was missing.

I never could make anything work out right . . . I had great visions but never could bring them together with reality. I used it all up. It's all gone . . . I have $2,000 in Nevada City Bank of America, use it to cover my affairs and debts. I don't owe Allen G. anything yet nor my mother. I went Southwest. Goodbye.

The jeep was full of cans. Snyder with around forty neighbours and friends searched the forest for five days, crawling through the manzanita. They watched the sky: no turkey buzzards. Nothing. Gone. Signed off with a letter.

Charles Upton was just one of Walsh's circle to receive a visitation in the form of a dream. The dead float in our memories and sometimes in the streets; we see them when we need them. And we learn to let them go. Mothers, fathers, figures like Beckett or Joyce, come vividly, but never more than two or three times. They are mute as Ezra Pound, after the years in the Washington asylum, when he drifted like a hieratic head through Venice or Spoleto. Or the funeral of Mrs Yeats in Dublin.

'I went south-west.'

Upton, in troubled sleep, saw the suicided poet at a blackboard, doing something called 'Chalk Speak'. Which made me think of Charles Olson, his sweat and excitement; the squeak of a chalk stub, the whaling of Camels. 'After that dream I got a map of the Sierras, looked for some place that sounded like Chalk Speak, and finally picked "Spanish Creek". I was wrong.' In dreamtime, Lew was alive and well and settled in Milwaukee.

Upton writes a letter, gets no reply. Maybe Chalk Speak was Jack's Peak, a mountain in El Dorado County. South*east* of Kitkitdizze, above the south-west shore of Lake Tahoe. Perhaps the dead lose their sense of direction. If not their sense of humour. Turkey Buzzard as Trickster. A barren and inaccessible wilderness of snow and rock.

But there is another Jack's Peak in Monterey County, south-west (by south) of Kitkitdizze. It was the ocean for Lew, the far horizon where the sun sets. The dream he sent echoed something he told Frank Dieterich: 'Up in the Sierras there's these sheer granite crevasses hundreds of feet deep. You could balance on the edge of one, blow your brains out, topple right in; you'd never be found.' Bones too tough for buzzards to crack. Maps pored over, expeditions launched. Places that are not *those* kinds of places. As Kerouac said in *Mexico City Blues*: 'You just numbly don't get there.'

Snyder wrote a poem. He called it 'For/From Lew'.

> Lew Welch just turned up one day,
> live as you and me. 'Damn, Lew' I said,
> 'you didn't shoot yourself after all.'
> 'Yes I did' he said,
> and even then I felt the tingling down my back.
> 'Yes you did, too' I said – 'I can feel it now.'
> 'Yeah' he said,
> 'There's a basic fear between your world and

mine. I don't know why.
What I came to say was,
teach the children about the cycles.
The life cycles. All the other cycles.
That's what it's all about, and it's all forgot.'

Burbland

Three miles outside Nixon, heading north-east, getting away from Reno as rapidly as was practicable, Ed Dorn stopped to pick up one of the First (now Last) People, a man who said he was half Shoshone and half Paiute. And who was making a fifteen-mile hike towards Route 40, where he hoped to find a ride to a town run on gambling and drive-through divorce: 'The Biggest Little City in the World'. (You can see something of the bounce of light, the affectless hardbitten opportunism, in John Huston's film *The Misfits*. Wild horses as uncanned dog food. The name actors are doing it for the last time, nursing cancers and bungalow death wishes. Arthur Miller certainly wishes he had left his script as a *nouveau roman*. But he manages to locate a new wife among the throng of international photographers who have been hired to add class to a failing product. The portfolio of Magnum stills overwhelms the movie. And appeals to an entirely different audience of collectors and aesthetes.)

Questioned, as they jolt along, Dorn at the wheel, the black photographer Leroy Lucas beside him, the walker explains why his journey is necessary. He is going to sell a pint of blood for five dollars. Fresh blood is the only available welfare. The buyers don't discriminate, they're not like the Diners Club vampires of Forks, with their preference for free-range forest animals. 'They just mix it all up. Nobody knows where it comes from.'

Dorn reveals, by way of return, that in the pinch of his own early poverty, he would trade blood for twenty-five dollars a pint in San Francisco; after affirming that he had not travelled in alien lands. There were certain obvious territories carrying a freight of fear. Ed played safe. 'It was best just to say you had never been to *any* foreign country.' What this anecdote seemed to demonstrate was the

economic stretch between the Humboldt River, on the California/
Nevada border, and the promised lands around San Francisco and
the Bay Area. Where uncontaminated white life-juice carried a
value multiplied by a factor of five. The Black Mountain poet Cal
Shutter, for example, sold so much blood between 1966 and 1972 that
he found regular employment playing vampires in underground
movies for Kenneth Anger and others.

Coming from Kitkitdizze to Nevada City, it was tempting to follow Dorn east to Reno, and then into the unknown and challenging
geographies he describes in his finely crafted 1966 book, *The Shosho-
neans: The People of the Basin-Plateau*. Nobody I know can do the
angles of managed (and self-inflicted) awkwardness so well: to be
what and who you are, with no baggage; a clear eye on foolishness,
corruption of means and language. When you have to sit on a
smeared, sodden chair in the home of a 102-year-old Indian in a wilderness hovel, do it. Register the mechanisms. Make the trade in
cigarettes. Shape the episode into masculine prose.

There is no point of exchange now, even the names Shoshone and
Paiute are imposed. If you have seen enough westerns you know
how the structure works: the cops are muscle for the money, and
the prejudice they choose to indulge in the privacy of the jailhouse
is their own affair. Whoever or whatever arrives in town, without
invitation or bags of silver dollars to feed the stalled herds of
machines (like factory-farm hogs), is advised, in no uncertain terms,
with weighted and ironic formality, to keep moving. 'Step out of
the car, please, sir', it is understood, means its opposite: *drive.*

The dry heat of the Basin-Plateau was attractive after our
Impala-surf through the wet sponge of the Olympic Peninsula and
Oregon. Dorn was the ideal copywriter for the Badlands. 'Well
known only to a few gamblers, professional criminals, movie stars,
divorcees, and, of course, the people who live there,' he wrote: as
he journeyed, Reno to Pocatello, hanging out with a terminally
drunk rodeo rider who decides to mount a cow at midnight, wearing a set of boy's chaps. Or eating the sour-sweet glue of Chinese
slop under interrogation from the ancestors of the men who slaved

to build the railways. As the safest option in a settlement of culinary fundamentalism. And bars of workless working men where nobody moves for fear of falling over.

Swerving away from Dorn, from the potentialities of that special kind of intelligent abhorrence, was to reconnect with a simpler narrative: Sacramento, San Francisco, Los Angeles. *And the poet Tom Clark.* It began to look as if Clark, biographer of Kerouac, of Dorn, and his mentor Charles Olson, was the person to visit. All trails led to an address somewhere across the Bay that Clark was careful to keep private. And to the problematic physical and material circumstances of this underappreciated lyric poet: as he reported them. Things were bad and somehow Tom thrived on it. Not for nothing had he contrived a novel from the darkest days of Céline: the apocalyptic German night, the headlong flight under bombing into Denmark.

Tom did not encourage random cultural tourists, but I persisted. To the point where, between the lines in a flurry of emails, Clark mentioned the fact that Cal Shutter was still around, still with his wife of many years. If Shutter stepped outside his nest, which he rarely did, it was hellfire and damnation. Food had to be foraged. From time to time, Clark said, the veteran poet, bloodless and abino-white, begged on the streets. Solicited coin. He had Clark's sympathy. Tom had retired from the fray, but he retained the sharpest memories of old poetry wars and shifting alliances; the ways in which reputations are made and lost. He was the former poetry editor of the once-hip *Paris Review*, a colleague of George Plimpton and his ilk. There were numerous books to Tom's name: poetry, biography, criticism. Scholarship with punch. He had studied at Caius College, Cambridge, where J. H. Prynne was his Moral Tutor. He taught at the University of Essex in the high days of the 1960s. Now every excursion to San Francisco was an adventure. The pinch of these darks days left him like a desert father, a fiery monk defending a discontinued theology.

Triangulating other contacts in the Bay Area, including an English exile who lived in a communal house that once belonged to the

actress Tuesday Weld, I teased out an address, deep in Burbland, for Cal Shutter. After repeated calls, I managed to speak to Shutter's wife and protector, Veronica. By good fortune, it turned out that she had lived for a few years in east London. Someone sent her a paperback of *Hackney, That Rose-Red Empire*. She remembered a few of the faces from Montague Road. She would persuade Cal to let me record an interview. But there were strict rules and conditions attached.

Setting a time for our meeting wasn't easy. I would have to rise in the dark to complete my Speer circuit down California towards Chinatown, the Financial District and the Ferry Building. Shades of Spandau were starting to dissolve in weak sunshine as I relished a good walking city. 'Cal is nocturnal,' Veronica said. 'I am the reverse. Consequently the one time in which we are both relatively aware is the early morning.' It would have to be 8 a.m. in the foothills of Burbland, in order to find husband and wife upright. There was no mobile and an unlisted landline (which Cal would never touch). Even his emails slipped out under Veronica's name.

Driving down 80 from Sacramento, then over the Richmond–San Rafael Bridge, made me wish I had the camera not the wheel in my hands: San Quentin never looked better. The ugly prison was a castle of cheese, finely grated by the steel stanchions of the long bridge, while the waters of the bay twitched and flickered. It was a homecoming, our return to San Francisco: the Holiday Inn and the Greek café on Polk Street. I dozed that night within the grid of a familiar city rising to a ridge of towers beyond which you glimpsed the thick blue sea, a nervous morse of lights. Beside my bed was a copy of Tom Clark's new and selected poems, *Light & Shade*. His 'Message in the Fog' was stark: 'one solitary/roosting/sooty grouse/hoots'. I remembered how the poets in Colchester, English and American – Dorn, Clark, Tom Raworth, Cal Shutter – squeezed so much juice out of John Clare. Pure recognition. Fellow feeling. Joy for life.

Sally Vincent, when I mentioned my hope of visiting the Shutters in California, hissed. Bridled. Turned for confirmation to her husband. Ralph Vincent was giving a reading with Tom Raworth and Lee Harwood in a Brighton pub. The younger locals who packed the floor were surprised, and even grateful within bounds, to find these ever-alert veterans breathing, on their feet, and in good voice. They were part of the somatic drift to the south coast; a non-retirement or economic retrenchment much like the marine twilight of their London parents' generation, out of Streatham and Croydon to Hove and Bexhill-on-Sea.

But the point with Tom and Lee – the glamour, if you like – was the transatlantic gold card, the respect in which they were held by their peers on the far shore. Just as Clark and Dorn (like Clark and Lewis on their Mississippi raft) locked down in Colchester, to sample the mysteries of the English pub, boredom as a resource, so Raworth and Harwood headed west; reading, performing, socializing in Marin County, Boston, Portland. Writers' colonies in which to keep journals about not writing. Zoos and white galleries favoured by the New York School. Borrowed apartments where families could be lodged for a season against the endless peregrin-ations of the freelance life. They turned up, when the offers came, like grape-pickers. Much of this was a matter of basic friendship, con-tacts sustained during the last days of the postal service; letters, cards, enclosures, satiric collages.

The Vincents, in San Francisco on their first and last US adventure, were invited to pay a visit to the Shutters in Bolinas. Which involved, as Sally described it, a long hot bus ride with the kids. She found the house and knocked on the door. 'Cal's away,' Veronica said. The disconcerted English group, the children now restless and thirsty, poked around the fringes of the property. From a point among the trees, they spotted Shutter: on the roof, embracing a chimney, behind which he was trying to hide himself. It was a welcome worthy of Watts-Dunton keeping the curious from Swinburne's door at the Pines on Putney Hill. Sally never forgot or forgave this episode. She left an upper-case message in marker pen on card.

The younger Cal Shutter, naked or nearly so, tightly beshorted, cross-legged on a white wood throne, can be seen on the cover of his 1975 publication, *Pink Sand*. An affectionate domestic portrait by Veronica. The hair is conservatively tribal, long but unshowy; a pleasure-beach saddhu, lean to the point of statement. One of the fine young cannibals of the Slide Area: mind surfer more than wave-breaking narcissist.

Even the best intentioned and best informed of visitors can intrude. Until the hour of our meeting comes around, who knows if it's welcome, if it will work? Much of Cal's life is programmed by his remote viewing of the calendar of English Premier League foot-ball. But he also keeps a blog on what's happening in Mexico. Javier Hernández, known as Chicharito, the Manchester United striker with the supreme neck muscles, a steal by Sir Alex Ferguson, is therefore a figure of considerable interest. Cal rates poets like foot-ballers and footballers like poets. He also makes paintings. And collects anonymous yard-sale photographs of shorelines with no figures or narratives.

*

Anna, who doesn't like reading when the car is in motion, and who often makes her more telling discoveries after the potential detour has flashed past on the blind side, is much better with maps than Pavel Coen. Last time out, Coen dropped us deep into Oakland. Anna located the Shutter neighbourhood with fifteen minutes to spare. I could hear her stomach fluting gently. There had been no time for Bob's Diner; eggs over easy, crisp bacon, and leisurely coffee refills.

Breathe it: the distance from Colchester's winter damp. How much faster and more laconic the prose would have to be. How gladly naked and sun-kissed. The avenues were wide, unpeopled: proud, established, civic suburban. Anna put us in the zone, I zeroed in on the house. A lush crop of untroubled grass dense with bluebells. An enviable property, once; white with Arts and Craftsy windows in asymmetrical arrangements of narrow verticals and broad rectangles. External steps have to be negotiated with discretion, too heavy a tread will turn them into a mantrap. I checked the roof. Nobody was hiding there.

Veronica made us welcome, immediately. She was a beautiful woman whose thick red-gold hair fell to the shoulder. The table to which she led us was dressed with wild flowers and set out with decorative, gold-rimmed side plates. There was an inherited teapot, a waxed carton of Clover Milk, enhanced with vitamin D, and a selection of interesting rocky cakes on a shallow dish. A leaf-filtered sunstream flowed through uncurtained windows to backlight Veronica's abundant tresses. Dark wood. Glass-fronted cabinet. Wooden elephants. Plants in pots. Unframed paintings. 'The fading vestiges', as Cal has it, of the best kind of American dream.

We chatted. Would the man appear? Then, arriving at the table from some dark interior space, out of a cupboard, as it seemed, Shutter was among us. He was not only nocturnal, he looked nocturnal. If I didn't push our chatter forward with sufficient engagement, he would dissolve across the flower-patterned oilcloth in a puddle of Clover-flavoured milk. The internal clocks of the other figures around that Burbland table were set to morning alertness, while Cal was visibly winding down, shedding his nightskin. Those years of blood-draining made him glow like a fish who lives so deep within the ocean that it has to manufacture its own light.

Shutter spoke about the messy afterlife of his old friend Tom Clark's Olson biography, a book he admired without reservation. Veronica interjected: 'Ralph Maud's was a parasitical book. It couldn't have existed without Tom.' Which was certainly true: the Maud thesis, *Charles Olson at the Harbor*, was repudiation, line by line, of Clark's allegory of a poet's life. Such free interpretation offended Maud's proud sense of witness; it unmade a thriving academic industry. 'He is nibbling at Tom's crumbs,' Cal said. Our night-blogger could be peppery and gracious at the same time. But he was *on*, flying, catching Anna's interest, as he did the English voices, the Cambridge gossip: how he led Allen Ginsberg, sated on the Welfare State Rupert Brookes of the 1960s, bright-boy pick-ups from his reading the night before, to the locked double doors of E. M. Forster's rooms in King's. Tom Clark, so Cal reported, was the babysitter when Olson trundled into Colchester to see Dorn. 'Charles would go for three days, just talking. Then for two days he would sleep. Then he would disappear. Read Tom's Dorn biography. He lays it down, man. I mean he was really *there*.'

In profile, Cal is a porcelain mask of extreme delicacy, with not one superfluous crease or fold. The skin is powder pale and threatens to rub away like damp India paper. Eyebrows are raised in quizzical arches. Mouth a downward curl. Our host was prepared, like the naturalist Edward Wilson, a Caius man like Tom Clark, for overwintering in an Antarctic hut with Captain Scott. He wore leather fingerless gloves, a striped stocking cap and several layers of touchline wool. Unsleeping as the world snored in hoggish slumber, he fed his widescreen computer. Day after day, publication took the form of crafted pages of text and image: Dorn, John Clare, Kafka, Creeley, Philip Whalen, John Wieners, Walter Benjamin, Thomas Hardy. And of course Tom Clark. With shimmering photographs of mountains, mists, stags, oceans, streets. This epic free-service anthology took the place of the mimeo mags that once poured out of Essex. The labour of keeping the texts alive was monastic and involved a measure of dialogue with unseen readers who made their comments bright and tight.

Now, in pinched and increasingly desperate times, Cal recalled Clark's road trips, voyaging with Dorn across the upper plains in 1979, as a treasured memory. But no more real than a viewing of *The Magnificent Seven* in a clapped-out print in the Colchester Odeon. Dorn was driving back into his own deleted history, searching for evidence, in the shape of enduring restaurants or brokenbacked hotels, that his projection of self was here ahead of the present text. The two poets followed the Belle Fourche up towards the Badlands, for a circumambulation of Devil's Tower. 'It's a *long way* around Devil's Tower,' Cal said. Dorn, moving or at rest, was the finest reader of landscape the West had. 'Those two boys, big poet and his buddy, his editor, had the best of it. I travelled alone. Did you ever read Wurlitzer? *Nog*, man, that's how it was. Never wake inside the same head twice.'

Cal enjoys it so much, you can't call his pitch a complaint or threnody. Bad luck is simply a confirmation of status, being at the end of an honourable line. The house is falling down. Veronica is unwell. Cal's bones are as brittle as celery sticks. He mislaid his income when the college where he worked, a money-laundering scam, folded. He sued. They shifted all their assets elsewhere. He not only lost his pension, his resources were drained by lawyers. Darkness was kind. Cal hunched over the candlepower of his widescreen computer painting poems, tapping away in biker's fingerless gloves, like a miser of words, a secret alchemist of the old America (1948–78). Black Mountain, Beats, late modernism.

'Would you take on another biography, a road novel?'

'Nobody's asking. No one knows anything. It's all been rewritten. So a lot of people know a lot of things about other things they've been told to know about. Even though those things are very empty. And the experience of those things is itself hollow. When I try to resurrect certain things, I find that people are utterly innocent. I had a fellow telling me that the Czechs are embarrassed by Kafka. Good for Kafka. In a way, I find solace is not being visible.'

The dish of cakes was painfully visible, within reach, varnished, and speckled with raisins. Anna's eyes were watering, but she was too English to reach out. Or not polite enough, in this context of offered friendship and exchange, to ask. There was tea – or was it coffee now? – to lubricate our talk. The cakes were like family fossils, a badge of the social; when we left, they would be put away until the next time. An heirloom in superglued crumbs.

'Nobody has set foot in this house for three years,' Cal said. Overplaying it perhaps, by a month or two. Making this beautiful spectral pair of time-travellers seem like characters in a documentary by Albert and David Maysles. Like *Grey Gardens*. I had to be careful not to turn into Louis Theroux.

Shutter was the unofficial archivist, through his biographies of Douglas Woolf, Weldon Kees, Robert Creeley and Rudolph Wurlitzer, and now his nightly blogs, of the lineage of the living stream of American poetry. From which he felt unjustifiably excluded; attacked by new alliances, new academies; mistrusted by the keepers of typescripts, letters, journals. 'It's the same for all of us trying to do serious work. Everything was done to prevent Tom Clark having access to the Olson papers. To the extent of the bald-faced statement that there was no Xerox machine at the University of Connecticut.'

The man in the cap, racing away at the table – 'It's all so awful and *weird*, man' – was at risk of giving paranoia a good name. He lodged inside it, making the scene literal, manifest, a thing of wonder. The history of this handsome couple, courtship, flight, accidents of the road, was a self-perpetuating legend; backed by books and photographs. 'Don't touch the wall. Your hand will go straight through.'

Ed Dorn was the lamp, the inspiration. Shutter saw himself, by way of his friendship with Tom Clark, as the *Gunslinger* poet's back-up amanuensis, supporter, fall guy. There were evil times when Dorn came up against internet surges of reflex dogma in reaction to the whips and scorpions of his disaffected satire. Hysteria and an easy moral outrage are conditions of Pacific Rim technology.

After their time together in Colchester, after the road trips, the admiration Clark had for Dorn was absolute, so Shutter told me. And, in that sense, Olson, as Dorn's abiding mentor, had to be challenged, or made ridiculous. 'Those later years, man, when Olson hung around wearing nothing but a bath towel! Ordering up meals from the hotel staff downstairs. When he was out, his people cleaned everything. They took all his junk, coated it with dust, transferred it. Charles never noticed. Popes have never had that kind of service.'

And the last days of any of us? The work loses its potent illusion of edge and discovery, but it continues in Beckettian absurdity. Among the boxes and the dust and the pictures. And the impossibility of achieving shape. Memories sag, narratives sprawl, comfortably, like a drinker's belly when the muscles have gone. Eyes fail. Voice rasps on.

Shuttling between logging camps in the Northwest, cramped apartments in Seattle, driving truckloads of malevolent furniture from Arkadelphia to Pocatello, dodging the hungry bugs of the Hotel Dante in San Francisco, plotting escapes to Mexico City and Yucatán, Dorn's road trips echoed Kerouac, and reflected a restless post-war spirit. He said that he was not, initially, a man of the West: he passed through, by bus, or shared car, from Illinois to California (where he starved or wandered the streets like the ghost of his future).

'He was inflamed,' Shutter said, 'with a strong desire to travel down the spine of the continent.' Dorn spliced Olson's interest in Mayan glyphs against Wilhelm Reich's theories of psychosexual energy. 'Lima might be a mighty fine place to retire to.' There were no orgone accumulators in the garden.

The story always looped back to the three men – Olson, Dorn,

Clark – in Colchester. Helene Dorn, Ed's first wife, the one with the bad back, said: '*Do* something, Ed, you're not staying up another whole night with him.' Sunset to sunrise, Olson would ramble, growl, thump, burn: Clark reported. Shutter never forgot his description.

'In the morning, Helene would come down. "Oh no! God!" Before I got Charles to the room where he was supposed to be staying. It was so precarious. The kids had bunk beds. They were real light beds and Charles was huge. He was supposed to be going to Dorchester to look at the museum.'

The computer was pinging in an inner chamber. Cal rushed off, and came back, to continue, without missing a beat.

'Look, man, what did he do? As a scholar, Charles was out of it by about 1937. The best he could do was sit against a fence in a daze. After Melville, it was instinct and intuition. It was all *I Ching* and the Tarot. "I look therefore it's interesting." The subjectivity is all there is.'

At the time of the 1966 World Cup, Tom Clark commissioned football coverage from Dorn for his mimeograph magazine series. Dorn returned the favour, making Clark sports reporter for *Bean News*. They had some fun with the sanctimonious robot-speak of professional commentators. Football, they recognized early, was the new politics.

'Ed was a lovely guy, with that brilliance of being on the edge,' Shutter said. 'A writer. A good reader. He knew the world. And to travel with him, as Tom did, the landforms were a map he could read like a story. There is no comparison with Olson in terms of being able to understand these things. It was theoretical for Charles. It was all from books. Charles was Ed's guiding teacher, the one who taught him that the adventure of the mind was something that he should embark on. Charles encouraged him. And he loved Charles deeply for that, always. But he saw Charles with a true eye. And was respectful. And honest and objective. And a good and faithful student.'

*

Veronica topped up our cups. Then stood at Cal's shoulder, glancing rather wistfully towards the white light of the window and the street beyond. Our talk was live, a useful tying together of loose themes. Or the spur for fresh voyages. The devouring passion was Manchester United, that's where Cal's intensity cranked up. And this was what Veronica anticipated and feared. When the drama shifted, abruptly, from Olson to Wayne Rooney, it was time to let the morning in. A snort of honey-scented air before the retreat to bed. In preparation for another long night siphoning pirate feeds from Stamford Bridge and Old Trafford. Like impoverished Nigerians tapping mainline oil pipes in the delta.

'Poor kid. Some people are going to age better than others. Rooney's dad is the endomorphic boxer type. You saw from his dad what Wayne's going to look like when he's thirty. His touch is great, but his body's getting thicker. He's got this grudge against the world because of it. Soccer, for me, is the only theatre of interest. It's world theatre.'

We got to the inner sanctum, the shaded room where Cal replays, with commentary, Rooney's hat trick for United against West Ham at Upton Park. *This is unreal.* I'm standing in the half-dark, on the far side of the world, before we've enjoyed a bite of breakfast, watching a balding young Scouser's demented assault on the camera. Expletives undeleted. And listening to the last American poet's interpretation, as he plays the illegitimate clip over and over.

Cal produced a tall ledger, pages ruled, script in red and blue, recording – like the BBC's sheepskin-coated John Motson – every goal scored in the English Premier League: marksman and assist, pattern of play. It was occult: the gematria of triumph and defeat in Blackburn, Stoke, Norwich, West Bromwich, Swansea.

While we were witnessing the Rooney goals, Veronica showed Anna the way to the bathroom in the basement. An adventurous descent. This lightless vault was glaciered with the usual books, papers, correspondence; boots, shirts, scarves of a lifetime. Against the wall rested a number of warehouse-scale paintings. They were by Shutter. And depicted spot-the-ball freeze-frames from decades of English football.

Veronica gets her wish. Cal plasters exposed skin with thick white ointment; he's like a Venetian aristocrat protecting himself against the contagion of plague-threatened streets. He limps. Anna moves slowly too, in sympathy, feeling the crimp of travel in neck, back, knees. This is a *wow* moment for all of us, an expedition to the summit of Indian Rock. Veronica is in fetching, broad-brim Bloomsbury hat, Cal in a soft-blue fisherman's cap. We zigzag across old grey stone, above the trees, the red roofs, the sea. 'The fog on the Bay,' Cal says, as he pants up the last few yards, propelling his slender weight on a stick, 'is pollution from China.' He points to the neighbour's house where the cops shot and killed a man after a domestic argument. 'They call it suicide.'

When we returned to Hackney, still haunted by the afterglow of this hallucinatory encounter, Shutter kept in touch by email. He was busy, he said: 'writing weekly reports, for a fellow once of Manchester, now a resident of Buenos Aires, on the subject of Argentines playing football in Mexico'. It was of course 'an entirely onerous chore'. As surreal but apposite a form of patronage as I could imagine.

Then Veronica took over. Cal had drained himself with nocturnal research, chasing a bad-journey trail of fugitive images, mountain to mesa. He forgot to tell me about the little thing he had with Julie Christie in Bolinas. Our walk to Indian Rock must have encouraged him to venture, once again, among the quiet suburban streets.

Early one evening, on a pedestrian crossing, Shutter was struck by a car driven by an elderly, half-blind woman, suffering, so Cal later implied, from dementia. He was dumped in a hospital in Oakland in an ER ward, among numerous gunshot victims, drug overdoses and indigent asthma sufferers.

'Bit of a bad patch,' Cal reported, after he discharged himself. 'Many body parts bent out of shape and could use magical replacement. Still one skulks on beneath the coverlet, stubbornly breathing.'

And still those illuminated night-pages are forged and Argentine defenders in Mexico are tracked. Pages of poetry, fresh as paint, wait for an appreciative audience, every morning, on the blog. 'The body of the beast seeks its elected donut.'

Berkeley

Seeking our elected donut, or better, a late breakfast among the broad avenues of the university encampment of Berkeley, we came unexpectedly on a door familiar from our previous trip: Serendipity Books. A serious temptation always. Superstitiously, fearing the power of being drawn back into that particular undergrowth, I had avoided used books, and used dealers, on this trip. But Peter Howard of Serendipity was the man. It was my belief that the whole trade depended on the energy of Howard's operation, the way he sopped up libraries, swallowed discounted stock (with the good taste to rescue Douglas Woolf from oblivion). He was never afraid to back a hunch, to pay for the unique item, the annotated script of a significant movie, and to sit on it, if necessary for ever. And now, shockingly, we learnt that for ever had come.

There was a small handwritten notice on the door: Peter Howard had died. I was reminded of a like message on card pinned to a musty book dormitory in Hastings. 'Regret. Closed morning for wife's funeral. Open 2 p.m.' There was a light inside, a woman in lime-green polo shirt and blue shorts was working at the heaped desk. Her name was Nancy and she happened, by some extraordinary coincidence, like a Nancy in a childhood adventure story, to be cataloguing one of my books. Could it have been *Slow Chocolate Autopsy*? While we were chatting, the phone shrilled. And I found myself talking to my old colleague Martin Stone, who was in Paris, his current base.

Many years ago, at the period I describe in *White Chappell, Scarlet Tracings*, I introduced Peter to Martin, driving him from Hackney to the treasure-trove hideout on Cannon Street Road. Peter had spent three or four hours going through my shelves – most of them in our bedroom – evaluating *every* book, every pamphlet. Having filled a couple of boxes for shipping, he took off his baseball cap (he was a season ticket-holder for the Giants) and joined us for dinner. There was an indentation in his head, as if he had used it to stop a bronze baseball. 'Meningitis,' he told Anna. 'My wife diagnosed it.' A lump of his brain had been cut away. I realized that this man was something out of the ordinary and that Martin, with his magical eye for sleepers, his fabled history in rock music, his way of forming collections around drug literature or M. P. Shiel, would be precisely what Peter required. They became friends. Peter packed more boxes for shipment. They were still under the table in Cannon Street Road when he returned on his next scouting trip the following year. Peter became a patron. He induced a reluctant Stone, anaesthetized by booze and pills, to fly west, to cruise the USA, teasing out lost libraries in trashed cities and remote prairie towns. Serendipity published a tribute to Martin, written by Peter Howard, to be accompanied by a set of commissioned art photographs; including one of Stone lying, as if in Poe-like cataleptic trance, in his coffin. The special edition was offered for sale at many thousands of dollars. After twenty years, I believe, one copy was sold.

The overwhelming book heaps, the compact shelf system, the mounds on desks, chairs, blocked aisles, the chambers within chambers, provoked memories of Ed Dorn leading Tom Clark into 'the complicated lower-level underworld of the old Pike Street Market' in Seattle. Clark sketched Dorn as: 'a restless, obscurely driven young seeker in the lonesome days of 1952 or 1953'. The two poets excavate the caves where I found books by Gary Snyder and delirious pulps by David Goodis. They emerge 'out of bright subterranean illumination into soft luminous-gray daylight underneath a low, thinly weeping sky'.

When Helene Dorn returns to the city where she began her affair with the poet, she feels somehow disquieted, out of herself. Dorn, when he was making his way towards hard labour in a logging gang, explored the secret spaces of the market and the bars of 1st Avenue with the man he called Bill Elephant; the tough utopian backwoodsman and sardine fisher who took the poet under his wing. Seattle was the edge city: a cluster of cultural possibilities around the university, fishing fleets heading for Alaska, charity shops kitting out trail crews in hard hats and heavy spiked boots. The Pike Street Market, as I interpreted it, was the point of exchange between William Gibson's form of scavenging as rough trade, in a place where he patented a new language from the electively non-verbal technologies of the silicon-chip wizards and the global coffee franchises, and the frontier romance of young Ed Dorn, devouring Wyndham Lewis, reading Conrad aloud with his wife; a survivalist shack life on the edge of the Cascades. Seattle, Dorn reckoned, was like Hudson Bay. You bought what you needed for the Arctic winter, the gold fields, the frozen forests.

Peter Howard met his wife, Alison, in Alaska. They were up there, their daughter, Kerry Dahm, said, to build houses for Eskimos. When the project was done, they constructed a moss-covered raft and floated down the Yukon in the general direction of Berkeley and Serendipity: the book-rescue operation. A mausoleum of Americana with documents of the western lands, important first editions of Henry James, D. H. Lawrence and Ernest Hemingway. Howard, on his travels, amassed more than a million volumes. Beyond the shop, now in the care of Nancy, was a Berkeley warehouse, and the family home to which Peter finally retreated. 'We all die,' he told an interviewer, when his pancreatic cancer was diagnosed. 'Businesses end.' In the opening game of the season, the Giants were performing on the big television beside the bed. They were beating the Dodgers. 'He died at the bottom of the sixth inning,' Kerry said.

I drifted among the stacks. There was no obvious system. Ron Kitaj's library – he did a frontispiece portrait of Dorn – contained many inscribed (and desirable) volumes of poetry. It now sat, as an obituary block, among so many others in this astonishing literary anti-mall. I brought items by Cal Shutter, Tom Clark and Michael McClure (whom we would be visiting later in the day) to the desk. The ever-helpful Nancy disappeared into the paper forest to search out – if not here, where? – the two mystery novels written by

Margerie Bonner in the shack on the Burrard Inlet. Meanwhile, I added Elizabeth Bowen's *A House in Paris* in its splendid pictorial dustwrapper to the pile, a nostalgic gesture: I recognized the pricing and initials of Martin Stone. I had admired, around 1978, this same item, displayed on his stall in the Camden Passage Market. I would return it to London. Businesses end. This death and the dispersal through auction house of the whole magnificent, insane Peter Howard bibliophiliac landfill was the end of a business in the widest sense. The last grace note of the pre-internet world of bounty hunting, visionary maniacs like Howard, Greg Gibson and Martin Stone.

Stephen Gertz, a friend of Peter, drawn into the web like so many, describes meeting him for the first time: 'He was standing in one of the aisles and looked like an aged, unkempt and unshaven derelict marooned far too long, surviving on a diet far too short on calories.' Another millionaire vagrant, another man of the road. For years, in Hackney, we subsisted on their benevolence.

I looked at the young Cal Shutter at Malibu, the beach-bum poet on the white throne. I looked at the intense McClure, in his gunfighter pomp, posing with fellow outlaws in North Beach. Shutter's numerous and fugitive booklets, in limited editions, some with serious price tags, dressed a couple of shelves. While the poet, a mile or so down the road, crept out at night with a begging bowl. Martin Stone, under a jaunty pork-pie hat, like a convalescent jazzman, smiled from the wall in a fading Polaroid.

Anna collapsed in a chair; the early start, the failure to snaffle a rock cake, the nightmare playback of our life among dead books, had taken a heavy toll. Nancy returned in triumph with both Bonner titles. I was dizzy with gratitude and turned, in trepidation, to check the prices. The pencil markings were my own. I had parted with both items, unread, many years ago, when Peter invigilated my stock. The cycle was complete. I could chauffeur Margerie back to Hollywood.

Recovering over a proper bowl of minestrone soup in a good out-of-the-way Italian restaurant, we checked the map to plot a way into the hills above Oakland, to find the McClure house. Ed Dorn was never quite comfortable in San Francisco. When he returned to Seattle, he had to abandon the faithful vehicle that carried his young family backwards and forwards across the States and down to Mexico (a predictable gastroenteritic disaster). The car was no Beat Generation Hudson auditioning for future movie fame, but a Morris Minor, which Dorn had failed to register. He left the papers with McClure and headed north by bus. Which felt right: after his day job as driver for a local Mafia boss, Ed shared luggage-handling shifts at the Greyhound Bus Terminal with Allen Ginsberg. And thus met – and bonded with – Jack Kerouac. There was much talk, interrupted by Jack's habit, soon taken up by the Dorns, of breaking off to stand on his head. When he grew tired, he unrolled his sleeping bag and settled on the floor. At weekends, the gatherings would reconvene at Mill Valley in Marin County. Dorn, who always had the sharpest of eyes for technicalities, loved Jack's way with a notebook: everything went down, the grit of spontaneous prose. Kerouac, for his part, squeezed Dorn for details of labours in the Northwest. He read and admired 'C. B. & Q.', the story published in the *Black Mountain Review*.

Michael McClure and Amy Evans McClure, the artist, have an elegant house in the hills. Consciousness slows on this deck as you gaze out over the trees, the secluded properties, the distant Bay. A steep green slope at the rear of the house is planted with Amy's 'spirit guides'; her sculpted horse heads, Buddhas and lean, totemic beings. The slim, silver-haired Michael moves on preordained trajectories across an uncluttered room to the balcony. He speaks slowly and with care, as if into a very close microphone. An actor curating histories of alliances and friendships that go all the way back to the Wichita Vortex. The film-poet Stan Brakhage is invoked. When I mention Gary Snyder, Michael produces an inscribed copy of Snyder's first book. Buddhist practice is important now and takes a large chunk of the day. In earlier times, Michael jogged. He did a regular three miles in Golden Gate Park. His sight, in one eye, is not good. His hands tremble, but he has no trouble locating the page he wants in Blake or Shelley. Kerouac's greatest book, he asserts, is *Some of the Dharma*. Witnessing McClure's rhapsodic play, *The Beard*, a sparring dialogue between Billy the Kid and Jean Harlow, at the Royal Court Theatre, back in 1968, was my last electrifying experience of theatre.

I took a wrong turn, coming off Oakland Bridge on our way back to the Holiday Inn. I could see the exit lane, but I couldn't get across to it in time. After chasing a number of wrong hunches into darker and darker places, we found ourselves stalled somewhere around San Bruno Mountain. I was all for junking the car and walking, letting the oils of my body compass take over. But we persevered through wastelots, docks, under concrete ramps, up steep and narrow streets without a lit bar or convenience store. I thought of Dorn, making his daily commute on 101, when he was assembling *Hello, La Jolla*. He trained himself to write with one hand tied to the wheel. 'A rather open scrawl while one's eyes are fixed to the road is the only trick to be mastered.'

We would catch a couple of hours sleep and start early, by 6 a.m., for the drive to Los Angeles. I decided that we'd have to take our leave of the scenic coastal route, and 101, and blast straight down Route 5, to give us time in Hollywood. And I remembered Ed's scribbled squib.

> Easy, Oakland,
> there's a roll-over
> in the hotlane

Hollywood

Fire is stopped by ice. It's always temperate and warm, but nobody notices. They don't step outside, they don't risk the sun's hurt. The horizon is iced too, it tinkles. Dollar bills come straight from the fridge. Palm trees are apologetic.

The money view from the bathroom, from our shower cabinet performance space – bigger, more brilliantly tiled, more Potsdamer Platz than my entire apartment on the Speer trip to Berlin – proved the final banishment of any notion of middle ground. The towers of downtown Los Angeles were an event horizon; hazier, dumber (a pointless bouquet of ill-assorted modernist props), less imposing than the standard helicopter-shot credit sequence for a new/old movie. The distance (drive time) between our hotel in West Hollywood and the corporate centre (that was no centre) registered as a grey-blue scurf left behind by a retreating tide. There was a freakish whiteness out there: the whiteness of a freshly laundered Klansman's hood. A necessary exaggeration in a town where exaggeration is the norm; inflate any claim by a factor of ten. And wait for the studio rewrite.

The Argentine novelist Rodrigo Fresán, now living in Barcelona, has a compelling image of J. M. Barrie in his early days in London, in a small room (he was a small man) near the British Museum. This is the critical moment in his life, when he realizes that what he does, and what he will do, and what he has always done, is to sit at a desk with his pen, his pots of ink and his papers. 'Better than any woman,' Barrie says. He stands at his window, in the smoky, sea-coal London dusk, in a wrap of comforting melancholia. And he counts the leaves of a London plane tree: one by one.

I looked down on Sunset Boulevard. If anyone in that moving stream cared to notice, among so many more seductive sights, a naked forked man, a writer from London, was clearly visible, framed and flattened like a throwaway Hockney. In this gallery of steamed mirrors and mirrors reflecting slices of other mirror, I was clamped and helmet-headed. An intruder on a set where taking a shower was a cultural statement or a reference to *Psycho*. I could understand the street only by photographing it: palm trees instead of lighting poles, billboard tributes to Elizabeth Taylor's space-blue eyes, underwear advertisements seven storeys high. From my spoilt viewpoint I could see the pipes, air-conditioning units, electrical hubs, and squares of native greenery beyond the remediation of Mexican gardeners. West Hollywood exploits this duality: searchlight novelties natives are too cool to notice against bougainvillea suburbs of professional dog walkers and bulging men dressed like cyclists who don't cycle. The visible (dull). And the unseen (super-surreal and worthy of investigation).

Sunset Tower Hotel, 8358 Sunset Boulevard. 14th floor. Choice of power shower or found-floating bath with rim of black candles. To convince clients that they are really here, the designers of the latest makeover have dressed the suite with table-sized books of pictures. Better, they imply, to stroke a couple of heavy pages of the soft city than to try to make sense of what is outside the window. *Los Angeles* as captured by Tim Street-Porter. Diane Keaton, standing in for Mike Davis (who was busy with *City of Quartz: Excavating the Future of Los Angeles* – with supporting quote from William Gibson), composes an introduction, some Davis-lite paradoxes. 'Living in a fantasy of a fantasy, based on a dream of a past that never was, is forgivable.' Diane recognizes that you can never, in this slide area, come to the end of the chain of thefts. 'The appropriation capital of the world, the wild west of the imagination, the dumping ground of every revamped hybrid ever assembled.'

This status product, like a folio of billboard images from the boulevard outside (and about the same size), is signed, and limited to 5,000 copies. It takes its considerable place in our three-book library alongside a volume on burlesque and fetish; provided, I assume, as an instructional manual for timid guests, an amyl nitrate prompt to up their game. After which, they can settle in a deep, Regency-striped chair, back to the clouds, for a virtual tour of *The Glamorous Homes of Vintage Hollywood*. With photographs by Eliot Elisofon. And whispered asides by screenwriter/novelist Gavin Lambert. The item is suede-covered and gravely respectful, granting access to the interiors you won't get on the Starline bus tour. Rock Hudson's statue-infested castle. Tony Curtis and his dog. Haciendas and manicured lawns under a fug of incipient Alzheimer's. Iowa Gothic and New England Colonial. 'An architecture of exile,' Lambert calls it. Exile from reality. The tennis parties are over. George Cukor's Mediterranean villa, just across the road from Sunset Tower – interiors by William Haines, bedrooms loud with Picasso and Matisse – no longer hosts lunches for handsome young actors, dinners for Truffaut and Andy Warhol. The walls of Harold Lloyd's Greenacres estate have cracked, gold flakes snowfall from the ceiling. The garden where he photographed pubescent girls in light summer dresses has run wild.

It would make sense never to leave the hotel. That's what Christopher Walken says that he does in London. Who needs it? Mike Davis defined Hollywood as the perfect synergy between gangster culture and the movie factories. A deluxe ghetto squeezed hard against *barrios* where nightmare is repackaged as idyll. To the constant scream of sirens. On my first morning walk I came across a high school boasting about the occasional attendance of the young Michael Jackson.

We were on the road out of San Francisco, with Anna at the wheel, before first light: into a fury of lane-jumping traffic. We made some bad decisions, heading east on 80, before doubling back, honked at, blinded by the rising sun. After an hour or so, we settled to a numbing procession of miles through agribiz plantations and a breakfast detour to a sleepy town with one Mexican filling station and a single coffee outlet where sallow authors polished screenplays beside a dollar shelf of paperbacks featuring a run of *New Worlds* magazine with stories by Moorcock, Ballard, Aldiss.

I drove the rest of the way and brought us to LAX, where the car could be dumped, by lunchtime. The idea of negotiating Los Angeles in the Impala darkened our time in San Francisco, to the point where we decided to get shot of the vehicle right away and to manage our brief Hollywood interlude on foot or by bus. In reality, although a river of sun-splintered metal swarmed on Interstate 5 (I-5), progress was faster and smoother than enduring a route out of Hackney to the Blackwall Tunnel. Californians *live* in their cars, while Londoners, immigrant or older-immigrant (like me), white-van psychotics, tailgaters in aggrieved elbow-horn entitlement, treat their smoke-saturated tin boxes as weapons of revenge against a world of thieving bankers and corrupt politicians. Every ride a scalp hunt.

The rental people barely glanced at the heap, our trip down the spine of the West was a very ordinary excursion. The Latinos had a deal going with what they pitched as: 'a personal limo service'. Which turned out to be a Nigerian multitasker with a Dalston grandma and a battered, low-sprung, Harrow Road cab with wedged electrical windows. What strikes me as we hit the San Diego Freeway is how new this landscape is, how trivial the human interventions.

Oil donkeys peck at low hills. We are in the Mexico of Hank Quinlan. Orson Welles created a convincingly sleazy border town out of Venice Beach for his Hollywood swansong, *Touch of Evil*. Death comes, with wheezing Shakespearean flourish, among the fouled ponds of the speculative oil field. Nodding donkeys, pumping away, day and night, take the place of actual animals. 'Your future,' as Marlene Dietrich said, 'is all used up.' In Los Angeles they dig for oil where other cities have allotments.

David Beckham, in the opinion of the cabbie, was more than an ambassador. He was *England*. Supernatural right foot. Carries a suit like a Vatican accountant. Every hair rethink is a cultural statement. Who else can fill underpants on a Hollywood Boulevard billboard *and* kiss hands with the Dalai Lama, Lord Coe, Tony Blair, Tom Cruise. That's ecumenical! The cabbie was a good judge. He could have been a basketball pro or a soccer star with Galaxy or Leyton Orient, if it hadn't been for the knee. Our man was a preacher, supporting actor, gourmet fusion cook. He had a steady gig driving an Old Jewish-Russian man around to collect dues from restaurants. He chauffeured a nice young kid, AIDS victim from a wealthy Miami Beach family, to the hospital. He did benefit runs for senior citizens funded by the city. When we shook hands, he left me his card: RAP-IDO. CLEAN BLACK SEDANS. FLAT RATES ANYWHERE. COMMERCIAL INSURANCE.

What happens next is mildly disturbing. But it conforms with the upgrade to business class for the flight to Vancouver at the start of our odyssey. The Sunset Tower Hotel had been recommended by our daughter, the one who visited Hollywood when she was travelling with a fated film on autopsies. The wrong corpses can sue. And bring down production companies and entire networks. The hotel had changed, evidently, from those more modest, transitional days in its lively history. But Anna found a reasonable deal for a last splurge before our flight home.

The mean setting for hospitality is a notch below hysterical. In taut-buttocked sepia uniforms, actors playing actors pose against restored sepia furniture and newer-than-new chocolate-brown drapes from the 1930s. Art Deco calligraphy defaces menus and mini-bar honesty slips like a runaway vineyard. 'You'd like to check in? Awesome.'

'Mr Sin-clair? We've upgraded you to a *junior* suite.'

In a blizzard of benevolence, with deskman and lobby artists behaving as if this beautiful blocky tower were indeed their home, the grope of underplayed civility (not servility) was *personally* directed. As if, again, I had been mistaken for someone else. A namesake. A person who had business in this town. A double. A smarter doppelgänger.

It is insinuated, a cough behind the hand, that when (not if) we take dinner, there will be some special guests. We are promised a surprise. Sleep-swallowed in the ocean of the junior-suite bed, after having swum a couple of laps of the candle-surrounded bath, before dissolving into hallucinatory visions of traffic on the boulevard, and endlessly recycling teases of silky models in black underwear, we decide, this one night only, to hit the hotel restaurant. And risk the awesome.

Every male who arrives pulls the maître d' aside to demand the best table. 'Of course.' A seminary of Armani theologicals in loose black suits, hair tricked and sculpted or scraped tight into pimpish ponytails; most, even in the airless intimacy of this dim red chamber, hide behind aviator glasses and replicas of the Ari Onassis fuck-off shades. The women who accompany them, if they are going to be signing the tab, also concern themselves with the geography of the grazing pit. They favour jeans, heels, baseball caps and cleaner pony-tails. All the diners look nearly like somebody from old television whose name you can't remember. Probably, like us, they are tourists. What is most surprising is the absence of surprise. Like Hull or Middlesbrough, squat hirsute men who want to sit outside, smoking and scratching, pay a premium to feed brittle young women who don't eat, but who toy, neurotically, with their iPhones and BlackBerries.

The people who make films, even films produced by dentists and money-laundering lawyers with vanity projects, are lunching, over mineral water, in a Peruvian place in West LA or a neighbourhood Korean restaurant in Santa Monica. Gary Walkow, who wrote and directed *Beat*, the only truly Mexican take on the Burroughs/Joan Vollmer legend, composed an account of the whole process: pre-production, shoot, aftermath. He called it: *As Bad As It Gets*. The virtues of his film were economic. An absence of budget meant economy of means, the simplest solutions. Plus: derangement, dysentery, international phone calls, volcanoes. The compact six-week shoot becomes a 500 pp documentary novel. Unpublished prose is more forgiving. As your own producer you are open to the risk of improving on history. Airbrushed self as blameless narrator: anti-hero, sole witness.

At the point where Jennifer Aniston is still up for the Joan Vollmer part that went to Courtney Love, Gary breaks bread with his producers. 'Roger was shorter than André, with curly hair, and a relaxed manner. Until he got upset. He lived up near Santa Barbara and wore blue jeans and ranch-style clothes to the office. André was tall and trim, a gym junkie. He wore out-of-date preppy clothes, and acted like an 80s hipster. He was very hyper and could speak at length without saying anything. He acted like he'd just snorted a couple of lines of coke in the bathroom – without leaving the room. He could channel this inner coke demon at will – or rather the coke demon channelled André.'

Walkow's typescript becomes as hypnotic as his film when he flies to Milwaukee to persuade the fabulously nutty Ms Love to come onboard. This apparent nuttiness is the badge of rock-hard realism: she really can take care of business; her business, herself. She won't give up a drop of blood for her film insurance drug test. The crew from DoP down will be Mexican, but Courtney comes with her own wardrobe and make-up people. Walkow would like nothing more than to retreat to his room to watch *The Criminal Life of Archibaldo de la Cruz*. And to fantasize about being John Huston shooting *The Treasure of the Sierra Madre*. But he has to field agitated calls from Roger and André. He has to charm Courtney. The only place in the world to relocate a stretch of authentic Beat history, from the stabbing of Dave Kammerer in New York to the shooting of Joan Vollmer in Mexico City, is a strip of ground not far from Lowry's Cuernavaca. When Burroughs wrote to Kerouac from Mexico City in March 1950, he boasted that he was 'virtually a Mexican citizen'. He couldn't think why he hadn't made the move years ago. 'I have a pistol permit (to carry), by the way, so I don't have to take nothing off nobody.'

To speak to Love, even when he is lodged in the same hotel ('a grandiose relic of the Gilded Age'), Walkow has to go through her personal assistant in Los Angeles. They step out to eat – or, in Courtney's case, drink: scotch and water. Gary sports his best black shirt, but he doesn't fool her. He won't be making sniffy runs to the bathroom. 'The dinner wasn't about food. First she wanted to sit outside and smoke. Then she wanted to sit inside and smoke.'

Love is both the ideal post-Beat Diva (she gives that word a capital) and a riposte to the perceived boys-only misogyny of the original early-1950s period. 'I had this boyfriend who had me read the Kerouac diaries and he told me that's how he wanted to live his life. And I thought it was so pathetic that I dumped him.'

Thirsting for a mineral water, but obliged by circumstances to risk a beer, Gary improvises: 'People have this idea that the Beat Generation was about riding these cars back and forth across the country, but if you made a movie about that it would be boring.'

'My bio-dad hung out with all those old Beats,' Love replies. 'He was the Grateful Dead's drug dealer. I thought they were pathetic. What I don't get about the relationship in your script: Bill takes morphine and Joan takes speed – why are they together?'

'They both drank.'

'That's good. I could use that. Druggies like Burroughs because he was a successful junkie. A successful junkie who lived to a ripe old age. That's why my dead husband liked him.'

'Mexico will be great,' Walkow promises.

He shows Courtney research shots of Parícutin, church ruins in a lava field. He promises a wide-angle lens. He gets his location man to tape a bunch of consecutive images together in a panorama that looks like something Burroughs might have produced in Tangier. They discuss turkey vultures. And Mayan death cults. Countdown calendars.

Two and a half hours later, Gary gets back to his room for a Perrier on the producer's credit card. The phone rings.

'I forgot to tell you my William Burroughs story,' Courtney says. 'Every rock star used to make the pilgrimage to Kansas to meet Burroughs and sit in his orgone box. And then he'd charge you a thousand bucks and sell you one of his shotgun paintings, which are pure trash. But my dead husband, Kurt, he went to Lawrence and recorded this album with Burroughs. It was Kurt fucked up and riffing on guitar and Burroughs droning on top. Maybe that's why I feel jangly about your script.'

*

The Sunset Tower Hotel, with its Moorish-Egyptian jukebox façade, its high bands of Aztec relief carvings, its palm trees and eyebrow-shaped pool, had a human narrative of equal exoticism. It began, like the humbler Marine Court in St Leonards, East Sussex, as a set of private apartments. Howard Hughes kept two (at least) for concurrent mistresses. John Wayne lodged a cow on the balcony. Frank Sinatra. Marilyn Monroe. Errol Flynn. The usual Kenneth Anger *Hollywood Babylon* album of conservative excesses.

In a timid hick town financed around the concept of the remake, and the unchallenged dogma that things are always better second time around, revamped vamps give you a smarter picture of where the body is buried. Forget Jean Harlow and Monroe: *Mamie Van Doren*. Who was not Dutch but Swedish (née Joan Olander). Mamie was as strong and career-fixated, in her day, as Courtney Love. She visited Sunset Tower on many afternoons with status-compatible escorts. She auditioned potential husbands. One of them, creosote-dark, beetle-browed, stocky and violent, was her co-star in a primitive Albert Zugsmith exploitation movie, *The Beat Generation*. Steve Cochran. Cochran, she reported, was an energetic but 'frighteningly erratic' lover. Mamie's Proustian confessions, ghosted by Art Aveilhe (it's easy to imagine him sopping up many hours of hardcore Hollywood gossip), were published as *Playing the Field*. A field the size of the Giants' stadium. It included: Rock Hudson (premature ejaculation over borrowed crinoline after arranged studio date), Howard Hughes (tennis shoes, later Kleenex boxes), Cary Grant (declined: too dull, chicken basket drive-in movie or LSD seance), Sinatra (declined: too long talking percentages with Italians), Steve McQueen (pillhead insatiable), Burt Reynolds ('high on jive but low on substance'), Warren Beatty (declined: can't compete with that level of self-infatuation). And ordinary regiments of the ones who don't really count: agents, producers, bandleader husbands, baseball-pitcher husbands, talk-show hosts (as booking tax). And Nicky Hilton. The ghosted Van Doren autobiography belongs on the business shelf in the airport, with those Seattle corporate memoirs and tips on how to play the market. The hallucinogenic folding and unfolding of waxed and burnished limbs, beds made and remade by hirelings, is the medium in which the deal is suspended. The cast list is small. Like Chelsea in the 1960s. All possible permutations work themselves out. It's intensely local and in-house. Like a flock of sheep serviced by a few reliable rams.

Mamie is refreshingly Swedish and free from gush: she is a working mother; she likes to eat, dance and accept compliments. She sees herself as the end of an assembly line of blonde bombshells: after Harlow, Marilyn – and her nearest rival, Jayne Mansfield. And she is well aware of the black-edged list: the suicides, victims of Satanism, highway decapitations. She is a cheerful loser, she'll never be a legend: she's still out there, doing the clubs in South America.

Marilyn, encountered, dressed down, taking a solitary meal behind dark glasses in New York, warns her: 'Keep away from politicians.'

There is a stand-out bad-journey photograph in the portfolio. Mamie was in Rome: Marilyn asks a favour. Will she go down to Sicily, the volcanic islands, to pick up an award? This is a David, Italy's Oscar, for Marilyn's performance in one of the biggest turkeys of her career, *The Prince and the Showgirl*. Mamie is the ideal substitute, the platinum Xerox. And how Homeric is the competitive positioning for the camera; in-sucks of breath, chests out, as the screen goddesses line up. Mamie squeezing the award by its thick base. Anna Magnani crushing it, one-handed, around the legs. Gina Lollobrigida losing it in the froth of her crinoline skirt.

The coming collision is inevitable: Mamie Van Doren (Nordic blonde, enhanced) will meet, and couple with, Steve Cochran (dark Irish, born Eureka), in an apartment in Sunset Tower. Under satin sheets. In the atomic flush of a dying twentieth-century industry: Hollywood. Both performers, male and female (archetypally so), are bobbing along in the shallows below the Plimsoll line of recognition: scandal celebrities, repro stars, alternative choices, reliably workaday (with a shot of basic sex appeal). If Cochran wanted an *and* in the credits – as with 'and Michael Caine', 'and Robert Mitchum' – it would have to be in television. Cochran was a type, a

Mitchum type (*Confidential* magazine notoriety), without the presence, the displacement. The nerve: to deliver what seems like nothing. He would never achieve Mitchum's performance in *The Friends of Eddie Coyle*. So, like Mamie, he enjoyed the perks; he took his collateral pleasures. He slept with co-stars as a matter of courtesy, either to advance his career or to exploit his billing: upwardly mobile, horizontally obliging.

Mae West, Jayne Mansfield, Mamie Van Doren, Sabrina: he mined the golden ones. Negative / positive: a balance for Cochran's saturnine humour, the insolence in which he traded for his reliable cameos: two minutes in a loud chalk-stripe suit exchanging gimlet glares with Dana Andrews (and winning) in Wyler's *The Best Years of Our Lives*. The voluptuous women, by the dictates of the time, teetered on the edge of transvestism; they overdid it like male impersonators. But there were also strategic affairs with Joan Crawford, Merle Oberon, Kay Kendall, Ida Lupino. Steve had notions of becoming a producer, taking control of his destiny; making a movie about a run south of the border. He was disillusioned with the bits as hoodlums, disposable black hats in westerns. He has a solid part in Peckinpah's *Deadly Companions*, but he can't manage that sharky grin, the athleticism of Burt Lancaster in *Vera Cruz*. He is somehow the wrong size, too short-necked and heavy for the horse.

Mamie and Steve are on greased rails. They are speeding towards Sunset Tower. But first they have to shake down on the set of *The Beat Generation*, which is written by Richard Matheson and produced by Albert Zugsmith: in order to ride the media frenzy – *Time*, *Life*, Steve Allen – two years after the publication of *On the Road*. Zugsmith stumbles on a fecund package: 'the weird "way out" world of the Beatniks'. Diced with serial rape, terminal film noir. Zugsmith worked wonders on minimal budgets. He did everything from *Sex Kittens Go to College* and *The Incredible Shrinking Man* to a strained collaboration with Orson Welles for *Touch of Evil*.

Mamie recalled a visit to Sunset Tower with the trumpeter Ray Anthony, who made a brief appearance in *The Beat Generation* (and a briefer one as her husband). 'Our own ragged breathing was the only sound in the apartment over the noise of the traffic far below on Sunset. A tingling of electricity coursed through my body.' The intimate grapplings with Cochran were closer to the ugliness of the film with which they were both involved. 'Steve became increasingly rougher, until one night he very nearly beat me up.' They parted. Until Zugsmith put them together again for *The Big Operator*. 'But I've never been good at a relationship the second time around,' Mamie said.

The best of Steve Cochran, however disagreeable he found the experience, is his collar-up, fists in pockets, tramp through the cold mists of the Po Valley for Antonioni in *Il grido*. The pilgrimage towards suicide (never return to the point of origin) is definitive. A brief exposure to the charisma and power of a European auteur changed something. Now Cochran determined to author his fate. He picked a crew – six healthy Californian females – and set sail on his forty-foot schooner, *The Rogue*, south towards Acapulco. They could thrash out a script and perhaps – like Gary Walkow (and *Beat*) – find Mexican money and budget technicians.

I was alerted to this episode by the account Paul Auster gives in his 2010 novel, *Sunset Park*. Here was just one of the strange coincidences that occurred as I assembled material for what might eventually become a book. No sooner was a chapter sketched out than the phone would ring with a potential character offering supportive evidence: a diary, an unpublished typescript. Tales of other voyages were coming at me from all directions.

Mamie Van Doren, her career flatlined, has a moment of existential crisis on a yacht. 'I looked westward past the dim outline of Catalina, out towards the open ocean.' All she has to do is drift. 'Happy ladies do not go on solo cruises and drop tears into the already salty Pacific.'

Neither do they sign on as deck crew for Steve Cochran. In Acapulco, the six Californian starlets mutinied and stayed ashore; to be replaced by three Mexican females, aged fourteen, nineteen and twenty-five. Young women with no nautical skills or experience. They were seduced by the possibility of roles in the film, executive producer status.

John Buntin, author of *L. A. Noir*, a useful history I found in a bookshop on Sunset Strip, near Whisky a Go Go, where Mamie partied the night away, described the gangster Bugsy Siegel's marine odyssey. He chartered a boat 'to look for buried treasure off the coast of Ecuador'. Siegel, in some bizarre confusion of Errol Flynn pirate pictures, *Treasure Island* and Conrad's *Nostromo*, initiated what Buntin calls 'the strangest yachting party in the history of Hollywood'. Guests included the future British Prime Minister Anthony Eden and Jean Harlow's father-in-law.

Am I being carried away? I hope so. Rodrigo Fresán, friend of Roberto Bolaño, said: 'We writers are experts at creating and fostering coincidences, the things Chesterton called "spiritual puns". Our lives and the lives of characters depend on them.'

Auster's novel describes a person with a first-class plane ticket and a choice of films: 'ancient fluff from both sides of the Atlantic'. He opts for *The Best Years of Our Lives* and registers Steve Cochran. And by way of Cochran he is drawn into the mythology of the bad journey: 'The shadow worlds that run parallel to the world we take to be the real world, the not-said and the not-done, the not-remembered. Chancy territory, perhaps, but it could be worth exploring.'

Now they are afloat, far from shore. Cochran's yacht is heading for Costa Rica, where they will scout for locations. Nobody knows what the script contained. Was it another John Huston-influenced adventure? *Treasure of the Sierra Madre* with Cochran in the Bogart part? *Night of the Iguana*? Cochran and Mamie Van Doren in *Under the Volcano*? Or Cochran and Courtney Love in *Beat II*, daughter of *The Beat Generation*? 'He was a rich and famous actor,' as Don Carpenter said in *Hard Rain Falling*. 'You see him all the time, these days, having serious conversations with dogs and sadly killing Indians.'

They sail into a hurricane. They come through it. Steve collapses, suffering from an acute lung infection. He dies of oedema, an effusion of fluids into the interstices of cells or body crevices. There is no rush for an autopsy. *The Rogue* drifts, unmanned, for fourteen days off the coast of Guatemala; the stiffening corpse in the jaunty cap accompanied by three young Mexican women. They are rescued on 26 June 1965 (one day after Cochran's birthday). The working title for the script was *Captain O'Flynn*.

Walking was the only way to reconnect with the solitude of Malcolm Lowry in Los Angeles. His father had him trapped in the care of an attorney (his local paymaster). The relocation followed a series of increasingly desperate telegrams to Liverpool describing events in Mexico City.

BRITISH CONSUL STATES LOWRY SUFFERING EPILEPSY AND ALCO-HOL UNDERSTANDS OWES THOUSAND PESOS THEREFORE CANNOT LEAVE WANTS TO GO SAN DIEGO CALIFORNIA PLEASE INSTRUCT.

Lowry sleepwalks. And coming early – 'A *walk*? Awesome' – out of Sunset Tower, I make an attempt to pick up his traces. I set out to find the fatal bus stop at the intersection of Western and Hollywood Boulevard where Malcolm met and embraced Margerie Bonner.

The Speer circuit resists. It's nothing like Vancouver, Forks, Cannon Beach, Port Orford, Red Bluff, Grass Valley, San Francisco. Long shadows of palm trees. GIRLS! GIRLS! Everything closed. Everything suspicious of pedestrianism. When Dylan Thomas was here he behaved as badly as was expected, pissing into Charlie Chaplin's plant pot and groping Shelley Winters. I can't remember if he got together with Mamie. She doesn't mention it. Dylan spoke, frequently, of his ambition to date an 'ash-blonde' movie star.

The vagrants, door-sleepers and shopping-cart homeless encountered on my walks were uniformly agreeable, making their requests, when they did, simply and directly without time-wasting bullshit stories, or metal-mouthed aggression. Until now. As I stepped, in apologetic English fashion, over a pavement bivouac (the only one in town), a midnight cowboy in leather hat reared up. 'Didn't I tell you to stay the fuck away from me?' He was a ruined Warren Oates, using the fly-smeared head of Alfredo Garcia as a pillow. His anger had a blade that went beyond performance. The empty streets turned to sand. Brain-damaged from too many fake barroom brawls for Andrew V. McLaglen (he wasn't old enough for Ford), he recognized me as some other self; someone who had been here before. The one-line bit exhausted him. He lost his spine and subsided on his Indian-blanket sleeping roll.

On this stretch of Sunset Boulevard, Gloria Swanson, Billy Wilder's vampiric diva, morphed into a bad-journey swansong. Into *Swandown*, the Andrew Kötting film. The pedalo voyage that was calling me back to England, to the sea at Hastings. Seeing the heritage real estate HOLLYWOOD letters on the hill above Griffith Park, I remembered Kötting's visit when he was chasing his father's inflatable effigy across the globe for the *Deadad* project. A *Carry On* remake of *Hamlet*, with the ghost (mute) as the chief character and Hamlet (his son) as a muscular clown. Kötting frolicked in the park, besuited like his rubberized father. Having failed to teach the deflated blow-up to surf at Venice Beach, Andrew pumps the wrinkled condom-skin to giant size in Griffith Park. 'A Mecca for the movie maker and industry to which he wished I'd aspired.' When the camera rolls, Kötting (channelling Kerouac) stands on his head. If a Hollywood career had been the aim, father would have understood this foolishness.

The first heart attack came at forty-two. Mark, Andrew's brother, depicts a physically powerful, angry man, his dead dad. A respected businessman reserving blows and obscenities for home. The young boy welcomed the daily return from the office up west by hiding in a cupboard, 'shaking like a dog, with a brother's breath in my ear'. One morning, after watching the bowler hat pass along the privet to disappear among other commuters, he sneaked to the deep freeze to scoop out a chocolate 'lovely' ('chocolate with fake cream on top'). His mother had been beaten and folded inside. 'Don't say a word,' she warned.

Later that day we stood on Steve Cochran. His star was set into a paving stone on the east side of the 1700 block of Vine Street. A cosmology of absence. A cemetery with no bodies. Extinguished gods and undying goddesses. Paw prints of immortal monkeys, dogs. Hoof marks of the horse part of western double-acts. And humans on all fours offering cleavage to the flashing bulbs.

Like all good tourists we took a ride in a small open-top bus through the dormitory suburbs of Beverley Hills and Bel Air. We gaped at the architecture of pride, nervous front inflated by unreal wealth and the certainty that it could all disappear as quickly as it came. A catalogue of copycatism, botched quotation; other people's good taste expensively acquired. Spanish colonial. Fall of the Roman Empire. Gothic bungalows for morphine-addicted Hungarian vampires. The landscape was not Surrey, not St George's Hill; it could revert, overnight, after fire or earthquake, to barren desert.

Behind these secure gates, Michael Jackson died. W. C. Fields sat at the end of his drive with an air rifle, hoping to bag a few snotty kids. Peter Falk, his faculties in the long twilight, was housed with a pack of dogs. Kirk Douglas was holding on. Julia Roberts was an absentee. No place on earth has so many immaculate tennis courts and sparkling pools: unpeopled save for the occasional Mexican gardener. The occupiers are elsewhere, Santa Monica, Santa Barbara. The hills are alive with divorce-settlement real estate. Bus stops for the curious. Who are never permitted to step off the bus.

Lowry wrote scripts nobody wanted. Kerouac sent letters to Marlon Brando inviting him to option *On the Road*: Marlon to play Dean Moriarty and Jack as Sal Paradise. No response. Brando wouldn't consider a character whose name combined his coming Method rival, little Jimmy, and the evil genius of the Sherlock Holmes legend. Hollywood is good only for literary swansongs, booze prose. Hardboiled sentiment: Faulkner, Scott Fitzgerald. Hammett, Chandler.

On Rodeo Drive, Japanese tourists in swan-white trench coats are posing for digital smears, outlet by outlet, designer boutique by designer boutique, alongside brand-name signs. The Blockbuster warehouse is holding a closing sale of DVDs. Thousands and thousands of dead movies and I can't find one of remote historic record or interest. They don't have *The Beat Generation*. Or anything by Gary Walkow. Or Andrew Kötting. Or Rossellini. Time to go home.

*

Today I passed Los Angeles and tramped on southward in the direction of the Mexican border. Merciless sun on dusty roads. My soles burned on the hot ground, for months without rain. What a strange walking tour, from Europe across Asia to the Bering Strait and to America – with kilometre stones to mark my doleful passage.

So wrote Albert Speer on 5 September 1965. He had been brooding on the Kennedy assassination and concluded that it was indeed the work of a single marksman. A very American affair, he snorted. Attempts on Hitler's life were plotted with 'the precision of a General Staff operation by circumspect, coolheaded people, year after year'. And they failed. 'That is the real tragedy,' the slippery hypocrite concludes. Leaving his insane travelogue as an obituary.

We took our last breakfast by a breeze-ruffled pool, before heading back to LAX, and serpentine queues, searches, delays. No more mistaken-identity upgrades. Trying to check in online, we had to wait while a Toronto man, thirty years this side of the Atlantic, scrolled down the Man U score. Like Cal Shutter, he treated me to a lengthy analysis of the enigma of Wayne Rooney, genius and priapic basketcase. The real problem was that short move down the M62 from Liverpool to Manchester. Schizophrenic from the start.

'Orange juice?'

'Please.'

'Fresh from the tree?'

'Great.'

'Tea or coffee this morning?'

'Coffee, please.'

'Awesome.'

Ash

I would never get on a pedal boat built to look like a swan.

– Roberto Bolaño

America Ground

Unblemished Chilean skies. And lung-scouring air. The dry heat of an arid sea of sand, its ridges and maimed rocks. From the edge of space, if by some miracle you perched there like that Austrian stuntman, funded by energy-drink corporations and peddlers of aftershave, about to become a human bomb, a media event, the Atacama Desert would register, among oceans of blue, wraps of swirling mist, as the only brown zone. A patch of dried blood. A scab on the liquid eyeball that stares right back at you. The insanity of that heretical leap is a coda to a journey running from the visionaries who imagined a basket pulled by flights of swans voyaging to the moon, through the fireworks and bunkers of Wernher von Braun and Speer, to the adventurism of the American trespass of 1969, the episode described by an English poet as 'squalid astral picnicking'. It is all a promo for a sugar hit. Speed made literal by the man in the nappy.

A dust of unborn stars and flakes of used skin shimmers through shafts of sunlight in deserted barracks, abandoned observatories. Star-watching is resistance. I wanted to go further south than Speer, to straighten out his endless, self-cannibalizing circuits of the Spandau garden; the rocks now defaced by whitewashed numbers. The border was crossed at Mexicali. 'It is a dreary region,' Speer wrote, 'with here and there preposterous cactus like plants, trees from the backgrounds of Expressionist movies. At the end of the last segment of my life there is nothing left but statistics, production figures.'

He stands in the garden. Only Hess remains. Coal is being unloaded from an army truck and heaped into an enormous glistening mound. 'So much,' Hess said. 'And from tomorrow on just for me.'

The narrative extracted from all those bad journeys made Chile seem like the place to which I should aspire but never achieve. No skies as pure as the dome above the Atacama Desert. Where the dialogue between origin and extinction is manufactured by monk-ish, rumpled men, and women with the courage to sift the gritty sand for years, hoping for fragments of bones from the disappeared. A foot in a ruined boot becomes a venerated relic. At this distance from the centres of wealth generation, capitals of greed, the out-lines of the story are smoothed and given force.

My travels were over. I retreated with my notes and photographs to the coast. From London I brought a box of books by Roberto Bolaño, to which new titles were added by the week. After dark, I watched DVDs. The impulse to explore further in the real world, to invent a morality from obstacles, was subsumed in memory-fugues of advancing age and cultural disaffection. Journeys to the end of the light became nostalgia for earlier more heroic periods. Became *Nostalgia for the Light*, a film by Patricio Guzmán. Guzmán uses the time it takes for light to reach us from distant stars as a metaphor for interrogating the recent past, the horrors of the Pinochet regime. If a star-mirror could be created, would it not be possible to read, or to keep alive, events from history? We could solve crimes, witness battles, watch pilgrims straggle across hostile territory, by going far enough out to catch the still-travelling match-flicker of our dying earth.

Such innocent, animate faces. The way they respond to the unseen interviewer. Chileans are the heart of Guzmán's film. You begin to see what that long exile means. Friends and families recalled. An intimacy so specific in range of reference, in relation-ship to land, so unified by what had happened, that the individuals gathered for the film become more than themselves. They carry away dangerous cargoes, in tattered rucksacks and cases secured with string. To Mexico City, Barcelona, Paris, Berlin. Some of them find their way to Highgate, to the café in Waterlow Park where a bearded man in a contemplative slump is trying to set his coffee mug down in yesterday's ring. While drawing obsessive grids of vanished canals in a sealskin notebook. And picking at a story by the

Flemish writer Georges Rodenbach. An author sad enough to suit the bearded man's mood and the mood of the winter city of his chosen banishment.

Oscar X supplied me with contact details for scattered friends of Bolaño, themselves now on the move between Spain, Argentina and the USA. What was I looking for? I kept my shutters drawn, my back to the sea, and held Bolaño's novel *Distant Star* firmly in my hands. The cover was haunting: a bifurcating set of tracks, like those ancient migratory paths across the desert in *Nostalgia for the Light*, leading towards snow-capped mountains and a cloudless sky in which a poet-airman is making the white contrails that form the novel's title.

One of Oscar's associates, Marcelo Cohen, reviewed *Distant Star* on its original publication. 'I believe this is the first review of Roberto's work,' he told me. Cohen speaks of the requirement to keep characters with few specific psychological features 'visible throughout very long journeys packed with incidents'. When information is concealed, it does not strike him as fraudulent. Behind the picaresque Bolaño migrations, the eccentricities of unshaven poets who are losing their teeth, sleeping on floors, is the transformation of Chile from the brief flare of its revolutionary moment into a death camp, a wilderness of unmarked graves.

Cohen is wary of the 'sudaca' risk: the term Spaniards use for South Americans arriving in their country as part of the political diaspora of the 1970s. The achievement of Bolaño, above all others, is to find his necessary place: in the off-season resort of Blanes. 'It is a sunny afternoon, the summer season has not yet begun,' Cohen writes. 'In a sleepy bar, two locals gossip. Through the window is a view of silent houses, empty beaches. Only "sudacas" know that this is the best location in which to delay the worst, and only an immense writer could discover that this is the exact place in which the glory and the coldness of the world pass without hurry.'

Marcelo arrived in Barcelona twenty days after the death of Franco in 1975. He lived where Bolaño lived without ever coming across him. 'His name was not mentioned by my colleagues.' Back in Argentina, he read *Distant Star* in 1998. And was deeply impressed by the atmosphere of playful melancholy, the stoicism of exile, the acceptance of defeat. He wrote an enthusiastic but measured review. A year later, on a summer evening, Bolaño rang. He was sick in bed and he liked to talk. His manner, Marcelo reported, was 'attentive and concentrated'. They swapped recommendations for the best English poets to read. They talked for hours.

Hastings seafront is a good setting for projects to launch or die. From the seventh floor of a building constructed in the 1930s to look like the *Queen Mary*, while offering the select few a landlocked version of the cruising lifestyle (cruising to war, military occupation, concrete cancer), I watched a disparate group fail to inflate a rubber dummy. Nothing unusual about this scene on a Sunday afternoon, the St Leonards end of Hastings was a refuge for the culturally and economically displaced. Times had changed, through cycles of boom and bust, retro stores clustering together for comfort, economic migrants hooked over the railings waiting for their expulsion papers, since the high days when the resort could advertise itself as a ritz destination, an English Nice or Menton serviced by the 'American Car Trains' of the South Eastern & Chatham Railway PERFECT SANITATION. FIRST CLASS HOTELS. GOLF LINKS, CHARMING WALKS AND DRIVES.

The inflated monster, a grinning man in a tight suit, was the father of Andrew Kötting. It was my first taste of Andrew's working methods: round up the family, initiate some outrageous act of absurdity, achieve exorcism. Push on to the next adventure, quickly, before clouds of come-down depression blacken the sky. 'He was clear in his mind but mad in his soul,' Kötting said. 'An easy-listening man's man. When it dies, he dies.' There were twin inflatables, Dad and Dad's dad. And Kötting, his family around him (by order), pumping up the saggy skin of unappeased ghosts. A 'memory-magnet' re-enactment, he calls it. Against a sepia postcard taken many years before in the same place. The white boat-building never shifts. It has long since gone down at anchor. The pirates have departed. If you climb up West Hill, above the Norman castle and the caves, Marine Court becomes a real ship moored alongside an unreal shore.

The Kötting exploration, *In the Wake of a Deadad*, travels to the end of the light. (The cone beaming from a projector in the darkened studio.) Hastings to Chislehurst, to Wuppertal, to the Faroe Islands, to Hollywood and Mexico. It is remorseless, knockabout, compulsive. Like a posthumous midnight phone call from Bolaño. The deadad figure is carried by the strong son, who is accompanied, at various times, by his brothers, his sister, his daughter, Eden. He needs no passport, clean shirt or underwear (he goes commando); freeing his briefcase for a ballast of Hamburg pornography.

I meet Kötting. He tests me on a cross-Channel swim (he swims, I pass the sick bucket). I test him with a circumambulation of Hackney (he refuses to swim around the borough). We plot a new voyage, Hastings to Hackney by swan pedalo. As part of my preparation I watch the *Deadad* film. There is nobody else in the gallery. Andrew hauls the effigy of his father to Mexico: 'in order that he might meet other dead'. Like Ambrose Bierce. And Joan Vollmer. And Neal Cassady. And John Hoffman. And Malcolm Lowry. Who is not there, in body, but earthed in Ripe, a few miles down the road from Hastings. Hoffman, the missing poet from the Six Gallery reading, the one ventriloquized by Philip Lamantia, wrote of running into daylight, where he would at last meet his double. He died in Guadalajara, but it was not far enough. He spoke to Lamantia of his desire to go south again. He wanted to 'build a raft and make it to Ecuador'. Or Peru. Or Chile. High deserts where men carve animals into rocks.

Kötting dresses Eden in a skeleton-painted body stocking. They drive from Mexico City to Pátzcuaro. At the side of the road, in a place where angels and other funerary ornaments are offered for sale, Andrew drapes himself in his father's deflated pelt. 'I stand inside him trying to take in *his* significance and everything that has led to me being here.'

They take the ferry to the island of Janitzio for the night of the deadad. Surrounded by marigolds and small, sputtering candles, Andrew lies down, legs apart, arms stiff at his sides, hands open, eyes open, never blinking, on the wrinkled skin of his father, on the Mexican grave. 'Just the sounds of the night of the Day of the Dead for company.' The father never stops laughing, showing his great white teeth. In the warm, red-gold glow of the marigolds, the mescal, the chocolate, the fruit. 'Death enters into everything we undertake,' said Octavio Paz, 'and it is no longer a transition but a great gaping mouth that nothing can satisfy.'

The swan pedalo voyage was no more than the anniversary of Kötting's Mexican ferry crossing. Pedalo becomes its anagram: *pelado*. Which means, as Lowry in his free-associating nightmare knew, a 'peeled one'. A man so drunk he has no skin. I wanted our film to be Homeric. I wanted to follow Odysseus as he makes an illegitimate raid on the land of the dead, where the pale flares are human souls. To have converse with them and to return.

We pedalled under a harvest moon, a few miles beyond Tonbridge, candles held up, nightlights on the stern of the swan. The camera crew were tired, weary of tracking us; the rib pulled away into the dark. Emerging from a passage of overhanging trees, we alarmed a flotilla of swans; white shapes moving apart, then coming back together, leading us towards the place where we would tie up for the night. And where Andrew would sleep, while I went with the line-producer and the boatmen to Chatham.

The peeled ones, Lowry said, in some obscure way, are in control of events. They wait for you in the worst bars.

In 1822 around 4,000 citizens of Hastings – nobody was counting – marched on Priory Meadow (once the chief harbour of the Cinque Ports, later a cricket field) for an open-air banquet, a feast; medieval in scale and delirium, Elizabethan in poetry and song, revolutionary in rhetoric. The people, so they deluded themselves, had defeated (again, again) a corrupt council. They withstood the reflex land piracy of the aristocrats who controlled this coastal geography, everything that surrounded them: Lord Cornwallis (Lord of the Manor), the Earl of Chichester (owner of the Castle), Sir Godfrey Webster (Battle Abbey Estates). Politicians and lawyers, with far-seeing generosity, allowed the squatters on this spit of sand given back by the sea, after a series of great storms in 1287, to sign leases for their own expulsion. They had seven clear years, with the honour of paying rent to the Crown, before every shack and upturned boat, every flint shelter, brewhouse and piggery, would be torn down; so that Mr Patrick Robertson, a wealthy merchant domiciled in London, after paying a ground rent of £500 per annum, could launch his grand project and convert the old libertarian squatter town into a fit resort for the gentry. Robertson visualized a gaudy reef of buildings running west along the seafront: hotels, places of assembly, a Bath for the bathchair colonels and their neurasthenic ladies. He tried to strike a partnership with Decimus Burton, who was already at work inventing St Leonards, an exclusive estate of villas, parks and terraces on the western fringe. There was loud talk of 'legacy' and 'heritage' (terms that nobody could distinguish with confidence). They took dynamite to the White Rock that once protected the entrance to the harbour.

Local historians (and I asked a number of them) are unable to put a name to the man who raised the flag and led the march from Priory Meadow. It was the Stars and Stripes, Old Glory; fifteen white stars winking against a night-blue sky, as dazzling as anything seen by astronomers above the Atacama Desert. Around the streets and over muddy ropewalks the procession surged; drums and fifes, tin plates, bagpipes made from bladders of pigskin. WE OWE ALLEGIANCE TO NO CROWN. The D-shaped scoop of land, gifted by the sea, declared itself: *The America Ground*.

Cabined in Marine Court, the concrete liner, I acknowledged the futility of my American tourism, this incontinent expenditure of words: Hastings was the true America Ground. The one described by William Blake in 1793 as *America: A Prophecy*. Blake hazarded his own removal from London, by settling on the coast at Felpham in September 1800. He took a cottage belonging to a man called Grinder, host of the Fox Inn, for a rent of £20 per annum.

'There was a beach where Blake's wife and sister liked to bathe, and where he had his first Vision of the Light,' wrote the pioneering

Blake scholar S. Foster Damon. 'A mile away to the east, behind a tongue of land, lay Bognor, just being built up as a fashionable watering place.'

Charles Olson sought out Damon. In August 1968 he acquired a copy of *A Blake Dictionary*. Damon published poetry under the pseudonym 'Samuel Nomad': *Nightmare Cemetery*, sixty-six sonnets from beyond the grave. In 1954 his play, *Witch of Dogtown*, was performed in Gloucester.

The America Ground, to the east of Priory Bridge, was a self-sufficient state, perhaps the only one living according to the precepts of the Declaration of Independence. As interpreted by William Blake. The flag, so I was told by an ancient mariner, sifter of legends, in his Old Town cave, where they know the value of everything and the price of nothing (computer doesn't work), affronted and terrified the Corporation to the point where they demanded that the shield of Hastings be superimposed, along with a Union Flag to balance the block of stars. The original flag, the one paraded around the bounds, was later presented to the borough in a gesture of reconciliation. Or surrender. But the confederate spirit lives on today in Green Man bonfires, pirate parades and biker-war replays. Most of these manifestations cherished and recorded by Andrew Kötting and his tribe.

By 1800, with Blake settled in Sussex, the America Ground, as if anticipating another poet, a stiff-backed future immigrant from across the Atlantic, was calling itself a wasteland. A shambles. Romantics focused on sliced boats; on hulks rescued from the Condemned Hole, where confiscated vessels, damned as unseaworthy, were kept. Ships taken by the excisemen were sawn in half. Paperless vagrants, fisherfolk, runaways, sturdy beggars, discharged militia, godless drinkers living in a state of concubinage: they clustered on the beach, the marshy meadows.

'They took possession without leave or licence.' Eliza Cook, the Chartist poet, on a visit from Southwark, made an entry in her journal. 'What is called "The Desert" was in old times no desert at all, but a piece of broken ground with patches of green turf and rocks.'

Tents made from hide were pitched against a grounded fleet of cut and upturned boats.

As much in evidence as the Steinbeck camp was the entrepreneurial drive of premature Fords and Rockefellers: the Hastings Breeds laid out ropewalks, operated lime kilns and coal stores. Thomas Thwaites had a tallow warehouse. John Gallop ran piggeries and poverty-row tenements. William Wellard butchered. Thomas Squire slaughtered pigs to order. Sewage ran into Priory Stream. As did the blood and fat of penned animals. Labourers working on the new construction projects bivouacked where they could, in tepees and hutches made from driftwood. And all this was America Ground. A confederacy of dunces.

> I see a Serpent in Canada who courts me to his love,
> In Mexico an Eagle, and a Lion in Peru;
> I see a Whale in the South-sea, drinking my soul away.

Blake is the prophet of Lawrence, Lowry, *Moby-Dick*. American smoke infiltrates our cloudy night. 'Albion is sick! America faints!' When they demolish the huts and hives, a number of the expelled Americans (Indians of England) take up the shells of their houses and wrestle them, by handcart or on their backs, to St Leonards. Kötting's Gensing zone, behind the man-made cliff of the present Marine Court, is where they relocate, dig in: Shepherd Street, North Street.

Rodrigo Fresán responded to my request for information about Bolaño. (I spent far too long trying to make something of a snapshot of the late Chilean eating an ice cream on a Spanish beach; head tilted, hair ruffled. In company with an unsmiling man and two smiling women. 'Bolaño always ends up turning his readers into detectives,' the blog asserts.)

I am shocked to discover that Fresán has read my books; he acknowledges one among the sources for his novel *Kensington Gardens*. Many, many sources. And this London is the wrong London, to the west. The novel is a brilliant hallucination unpicking J. M. Barrie and his lost boys, by way of the shattered prism of England's brief psychedelic moment.

'I'm afraid I closed the Bolaño Room in my Palace of Memory a couple of years ago,' Rodrigo said. 'Mental hygiene issues. I received twenty emails a day asking about his ghost. And I'm afraid I never wanted to be a medium.'

As a gesture of consolation, Rodrigo attached an early profile he'd composed around his friend, author of *The Savage Detectives*. And he told me a little about the book he was currently working on, a novel in which Mr and Mrs Malcolm Lowry share walk-on roles. 'I'm also reading everything by him, including very strange material.'

At the onset of winter in 2001, Fresán is in Barcelona. 'It's cold and there are clouds and there'll be rain.' Before climbing aboard the commuter train for his return to Blanes, Bolaño, for the first time in his life (or at least that's what he swears), steps into a Kentucky Fried Chicken outlet. Fresán accompanies him, he's hungry. They have visited La Central bookstore, where Bolaño picks up some books he needs, or might need, for his novel *2666*.

'Have you noticed? Everybody's here.'

The fast-food chicken operation is like midtown Hastings, where all the bruised exiles wash up, reconvene, pretend they are still in the game. Harsh strip lighting makes them into neon vampires. A club anyone can join: for South American immigrants. You recognize them, Fresán says, by the way they count out the exact change. 'The almost reverential silence of their chewing.' The only protagonist of Bolaño's books is literature itself: 'the territory of risk'.

I devour Rodrigo's novel, laying aside my Lowrys and Olsons: it's absorbing, this thesis, how we can slide back into the labyrinth of fiction and recalibrate it to suit our present purposes. I have no particular interest in Barrie or Kensington Gardens, but the richness of the fictive stew persuades me. 'They put me on a plane and took me to a house in a place called Tapalpa, in the mountains of Mexico, where an active volcano throbbed. From up high you could see horrible enormous black birds, like men dressed as birds – turkey vultures – crossing the sky on the horizon.' Looking for a rendez-vous with Lew Welch?

Where does the neurosis end? Rodrigo reveals in a postscript the most alarming fact of all. 'In the first part of Bolaño's *2666*, that's me and my wife, in Kensington Gardens.' If you cross the line, what then? How can you continue without the services of the predatory author?

2666, as you can imagine for yourselves, is lifted from my Bolaño shelf; a gold brick with a cover design mixing bands of Gustave Moreau with eye-catching digital numbers ticking down the sec-onds to apocalypse like an atomic clock. The author in his rear-flap identity photo is corvine, lacking spectacles, a political prisoner again. A redundant football manager heading for Kazakhstan.

My repeat Bolaño journey, now with a single location in mind, is a breathless rush. I remember coming through Hyde Park. I remem-ber a man on the bench in the Italian Garden. I remember the snake. But Rodrigo's cameo must have been blanked by my distaste for Peter Pan and his feeble statue. Now here he is. We never met in life; much better, much safer, in literature.

'They sat on a bench by a giant oak tree, Norton's favourite spot . . . As dusk fell, they watched a young Spanish-speaking couple approach the Peter Pan statue. The woman was very pretty . . . The man beside her was tall and had a beard and moustache and pulled a notebook out of his pocket and jotted something down.'

Then comes the snake.

'There aren't any snakes here!' said Norton.

The man's name is Rodrigo. My email correspondent is lodged in Bolaño's great book. (He writes books of his own, one of them constructed around this location.) I can walk there and meet him at any time. *He has no time, he can't deviate.* The woman sees a snake, the man is preoccupied with his notebook. The third person, the one with a significant role in the narrative, is Norton.

As dusk fell . . .

I knew from what Oscar X told me at our first meeting in Waterlow

Park that Bolaño, in the early days of his Barcelona exile, was an addicted reader of comics, graphic novels. Was it possible that he had come across my book *Slow Chocolate Autopsy* – and that, as an admirer of Dave McKean, whose drawings and treated images lifted the collaboration, he had leafed through it? The protagonist, a man who can move through time but not place, is Norton: 'Prisoner of London.' My book opens: *Norton, no question, was there in the garden when the incident occurred.*

Unlikely. I'd like to believe it. It would make an attractive equation: Santiago, Barcelona, London. But my Norton was a lift, I found him in a novel published in sensationalist form as part of an Ace-Double. *Junkie: Confessions of an Unredeemed Drug Addict* by William Lee (otherwise: Burroughs). 1953. I got my copy signed in Lawrence, Kansas. The Burroughs legend opens: *My first experience with junk was during the War, about 1944 or 1945. I had made the acquaintance of a man named Norton.* Norton very soon vanishes from the page, he's the devil's advocate: he introduces Burroughs to junk. He forces him to write. To write his way out of the fix. To make the bad journeys with a copy of Céline in his luggage.

'Norton felt a desire for change. To get away. To visit Ireland or New York,' Bolaño wrote.

The Chilean's stroke of genius is to make Norton a woman; young, intelligent, sexually adventurous. The other Norton, the time-chained spectre of Burroughs, is sullen and mean. He thinks he looks like George Raft. 'Norton was trying to improve his English and achieve a smooth, affable manner. Affability, however, did not come natural to him.' This Norton was not even Norton. His 'real name was Morelli or something like that'. Bolaño's Norton is educated, a free spirit. Everything mine is not. Gender migration never in the script.

In the mirror-world of metafiction, Liz Norton discovers Rodrigo Fresán. She is not stuck in Kensington Gardens, she reads *Kensington Gardens*, a 'story of shadow identities and suicide'. She reviews *Kensington Gardens*, favourably and at length, for the *London Review of Books*. She makes reference to all seven Fresán novels, six of which remain untranslated. (She does not digress into the symbolism of 7.) To be English, in the eyes of the Barcelona writers gathered in the Kentucky Fried Chicken outlet, is to be a savage detective: Sherlock Holmes let loose, with intent, on Georges Perec, Walter Benjamin, Malcolm Lowry.

Norton – who is always referred to by her surname – notices that Fresán has a highly developed sense of London, achieved by an intense programme of reading. Among many other sources, she references J. G. Ballard, Ford Madox Ford, Peter Ackroyd, Barry Miles, Michael Moorcock. *Mother London* leads her to Kensal Green, that mysterious suburb of the dead with its obelisks and broken temples. She commends Fresán's discovery of the angel tree. A memorial statue divinely impregnated. 'At some point, a hermaphroditic seed fell into a fold of her stone robe and set down roots.' Rodrigo must have stalked ground beyond libraries, she supposes.

That angel statue reminded me of Pound. 'The tree has entered my hands . . . The branches grow out of me, like arms.' And the painting *Apollo and Daphne* by Pollaiuolo. I was astonished that among so many angels, so many trees, Fresán found his way to the one photographed for my London book *Lights Out for the Territory.* 'The dead,' Fresán wrote, 'become the fictions of those of us who survive them; we subject them to the indecency of deletions, additions and revisions . . . we end up rewriting that other zone.'

In an afterword to *Kensington Gardens*, Fresán confesses: he does not know London at all, he never left his hotel near Heathrow. Bolaño inserted him as a gesture of friendship. The angel tree, contrived in Santiago and Guadalajara, came from an image in a paperback book.

The English sea rewrites itself; at night we listen to the drag of tide on the shingle, by day the traffic. From my balcony in Marine Court, I watch the parade: the Duvet Man, naked in grubby swandown, and the drinkers ducking into alcoves to avoid another police sweep. A solitary asylum seeker walks to the edge of the waves, foaming scum on his boots, to smoke like Bolaño, or lick at a lardy ice cream.

I have not seen or heard another soul in this building, the concrete plague ship. But I imagine all kinds of occupants; writers who don't write, but who while away the long hours watching DVDs of Steve Cochran movies like *Private Hell 36*. Other monitors – you hear the sound as you pass down muffled corridors – are playing in empty rooms. Steve is a killer cop for Don Siegel. His investigations lead him to a lounge singer who breakfasts on vodka (an obvious Marine Court applicant). She is performed by Ida Lupino. With whom Steve, of course, initiates an affair. The character's name is Lilli Marlowe. And Marlowe is where *Slow Chocolate* . . .

Stop. *Cut*. Fresán explains how his invented hero 'is tired of all his adventures and all the odysseys he's embarked on in vain'. I sympathize. 'He can hardly even remember what he's chasing after, what he never reached.'

If, as I'd like to believe, and as I *can* believe in the context of this book, Bolaño is still alive, still active, where better than St Leonards? The hulk of Marine Court like a ghost ship silvered in ice. (There is another, more upmarket vessel from the same period, in Puerto Rico.) No requirement to visit Blanes or Vulcano, Hastings majors in exile and displacement. *Roberto is somewhere in my building*. He had been readying himself for this, ever since that first novel, *By Night in Chile*. What did he say? 'It was no accident that his house had appeared to me shortly before in the guise of an ocean liner!'

The copy of *2666*, the only book solid enough to stop my loose stack of uncorrected typescript blowing over the balcony when the door opens, is turned away from me. The numbers of the title are reversed, *2666* becomes *9997*. 9997 COBE (Cosmic Background Explorer) is a main belt asteroid. It orbits the Sun once every 4.06 years. *Earth-9997*, closer to Bolaño's practice, is a Marvel Comic in which 'Death is given the job of manning the collective pool of reality.' Captain America and his wild bunch of superannuated superheroes have gathered to conquer the aliens. 'With the advent of alternate realities, somebody has to take these fragments and put them together.'

I have a letter, received that morning from Cal Shutter, waiting on my desk. 'You are not an American,' Cal said. 'You will never understand Americans. You want to see Olson and Dorn from their trips to England. Forget it, man. You'll never begin.' And I knew now that he was right. I was cured of my interests and obsessions. Cured by confrontation. Cured by the light on the sea. Their intensities would never be mine.

Andrew Kötting is preparing to liberate Edith the swan pedalo from under her blue hood, her chains on the shallow Pleasure Beach pool, beside the silent fairground. To manhandle her across the shingle. *Deadad* is no longer part of this; you can put away the wrinkled rubber skin into one of the caves beneath Marine Court. Andrew calls the inflatable: Bigman. The bear. Maximus. As Charles Olson in Gloucester shaped his own mythology around the curse of inherited size, pillaging historical sources for analogues. Until he stands alone. Above the crowd. Figure of Outward. 'The sea stretching out from my feet.'

Kötting's film *Swandown* takes fire when I leave it, when I come ashore at Trinity Buoy wharf, by the lighthouse, to rush across town for my flight to Boston. Then the story begins to say what I couldn't say, about the condition of this part of London; it demonstrates invasion, enclosure. It mourns, in true Homeric fashion, our parting.

When Ed Dorn writes about Gloucester – which I am approaching again on a wet road, with Henry Ferrini and Greg Gibson, as they detour to find Olson's apartment – he casts his projection of Bigman: 'I want him to walk by the seashore alone/in all height/ which is nothing more than/a mountain.'

It is that season, darkness coming early, storm systems from across the Atlantic. Kötting, in wetsuit, kicks through the breakers; straight out to the buoy, then west towards Bulverhythe and Bexhill. He tells me that he is swimming to Cornwall. He leaves me his much-travelled yellow bag. And a pair of boots without laces.

Acknowledgements

Especially to Anna Sinclair for her turns at the wheel and her company on the road between Vancouver and Hollywood. To Muriel Walker for allowing me to quote from the diary she kept during the filming of *Vulcano*. And for the use of photographs from her archive. Andrew Kötting's dynamic absences in water and mud on the swan-pedal from Hastings, his onboard chatter, were a constant and nuggety provocation.

With thanks for research materials, hospitality and inspiration, to: Valentina Agostinis, Ammiel Alcalay, Peter Anastas, Anonymous Bosch, Bryan Briggs, Brian Catling, Angelica Clark, Tom Clark, Marcelo Cohen, Georg Diez, Jennifer Dunbar Dorn, Kim Duff, Gareth Evans, Henry Ferrini, Rodrigo Fresán, Deb Gibson, Gregory Gibson, William Gibson, Benedetto Lo Giudice, David Herd, Tanya Hudson, Nicholas Johnson, Mark Krotov, Gerrit Lansing, Amy Evans McClure, Michael McClure, Linda Moorcock, Michael Moorcock, Miguel Mota, John Richard Parker, Chris Petit, J. H. Prynne, Paul Quinn, Kevin Ring, Christopher Roth, Lisa-Marie Russo, James Sallis, John Sampas, Robert Sheppard (and the Liverpool Firminists), Paul Smith, Gary Snyder, Susan Stenger, Colin Still, Philippe Vasset, Gary Walkow, Carol Williams, Patrick Wright, Oscar Zarate. I would like to express my gratitude, as ever, for editorial care and design inspiration from Simon Prosser, Anna Kelly, Anna Ridley and Sarah Coward at Hamish Hamilton.

My rapid-sketched portraits of Charles Olson and Edward Dorn owe much to the pioneering biographies of Tom Clark. *Charles Olson: The Allegory of a Poet's Life* (New York, 1991) and *Edward Dorn: A World of Difference* (Berkeley, 2002) have been source books on this long journey. I quote from them with the author's permission.

It was invaluable to view *Polis is This: Charles Olson and the Persistence of Place*, the documentary by Henry Ferrini and Ken Riaf, as well as two other Ferrini films: *Lowell Blues: The Words of Jack Kerouac* and *Poem in Action: A Portrait of Vincent Ferrini*. I'd like to thank Henry Ferrini for making them available.

Thank you to Lane Morgan for permission to reproduce the photo of Charles Olson, 1945, Enniscorthy Farm, Keene, Virginia (copyright © Rosa Morgan).

Gary Walkow's Mexican-shot film, *Beat*, was more use than anything I came across in the serious-budget mainstream. I quote from Walkow's substantial unpublished account of this production, *As Bad As It Gets*, with his permission.

Film portraits of Gary Snyder and Michael McClure, shot by Colin Still, were a great help in fixing my Pacific Rim topography. Miguel Mota's documentary, *After Lowry*, was the perfect complement to his guided tour of Dollarton. *Malcolm Lowry*, the biography by Douglas Day, proved a thorough and reliable guide. Albert Speer's *Spandau, The Secret Diaries* (London, 1976) was a haunting companion, a dark shadow. Andrew Kötting's entire oeuvre was snacked and sampled, from film to CD to drawing to live performance and deepwater swim. *Swandown* and *In Search of a Deadad* (book and film) were of particular relevance

I would like to thank Gregory Gibson for permission to quote from *Walk in Progress*, his privately printed account of the epic trudge down the Connecticut River 'by a man who finds himself getting old, but not too old to walk'. Rodrigo Fresán's novel *Kensington Gardens* came along at just the right moment and was supplied by the generosity of the author. My thanks for his permission to quote from it. I'm grateful to Gary Snyder for allowing me to quote his poem 'For/From Lew Welch'. And to William Gibson for the glitter and shine of the quotes he permitted from *Spook Country*. Nick Baron, from the depths of the Lenin Library in Moscow, has allowed me to publish the letter from Alec Bernstein (Alexander Baron) to Muriel Walker.

Some of the material on Gary Snyder, Edward Dorn and Gregory

Corso was first published, in earlier forms, in the *London Review of Books* and in chapbooks issued by Kevin Ring's Beat Scene Press. I also quote from my own *The Kodak Mantra Diaries*, originally published by Albion Village Press in 1971 and reissued by Beat Scene Press in 2006.

IAIN SINCLAIR

HACKNEY, THAT ROSE-RED EMPIRE

Hackney, That Rose-Red Empire is Iain Sinclair's personal record of the area of north-east London where he has lived for forty years.

In this 'documentary fiction', Sinclair meets a cast of the dispossessed, including writers, photographers, bomb-makers and market traders. Legends of tunnels, Hollow Earth theories and the notorious Mole Man are unearthed. He uncovers traces of those who passed through Hackney: Lenin and Stalin, novelists Joseph Conrad and Samuel Richardson, film-makers Orson Welles and Jean-Luc Godard, Tony Blair beginning his political career, even a Baader-Meinhof urban guerrilla on the run. And he tells his own story: of forty years in one house in Hackney, of marriage, children, strange encounters and deaths.

'An explosion of literary fireworks' **Peter Ackroyd**, *The Times*

'Gloriously sprawling, wonderfully congested, one of the finest books about London in recent decades' *Daily Telegraph*

'Iain Sinclair's twisty love-letter to Hackney . . . the book London's most unusual borough deserves' *GQ*

'Remarkable, compelling, bristles with unexpected, frequently lurid life. On Sinclair's territory there's nobody to touch him . . . a gonzo Samuel Pepys' *Sunday Times*

IAIN SINCLAIR

GHOST MILK

Beginning in his east London home many years before it will be invaded by the Olympian machinery of global capitalism, Sinclair strikes out near and far in search of the forgotten and erased.

Burrowing under the perimeter fence of the grandest of Grand Projects – the giant myth that is 2012's London Olympics – *Ghost Milk* explores a landscape under sentence of death and soon to be scorched by riots. This is a road map to a possible future as well as Iain Sinclair's most powerful statement yet on the throwaway impermanence of the present.

'Brilliant, superb. Anger drives the book forwards. Sinclair has gone from cult author to national treasure' **Robert Macfarlane**, *Guardian*

'Wonderful, sharp, amusing, grippingly atmospheric. One of our most dazzling prose stylists' *Daily Telegraph*

'*Ghost Milk* reads like a meld of Allen Ginsberg, comic books writer Alan Moore and an anarchists' message board . . . Sinclair is original, observant, a wonderful phrase maker' *Evening Standard*

He just wanted a decent book to read ...

Not too much to ask, is it? It was in 1935 when Allen Lane, Managing Director of Bodley Head Publishers, stood on a platform at Exeter railway station looking for something good to read on his journey back to London. His choice was limited to popular magazines and poor-quality paperbacks – the same choice faced every day by the vast majority of readers, few of whom could afford hardbacks. Lane's disappointment and subsequent anger at the range of books generally available led him to found a company – and change the world.

'We believed in the existence in this country of a vast reading public for intelligent books at a low price, and staked everything on it'
Sir Allen Lane, 1902–1970, founder of Penguin Books

The quality paperback had arrived – and not just in bookshops. Lane was adamant that his Penguins should appear in chain stores and tobacconists, and should cost no more than a packet of cigarettes.

Reading habits (and cigarette prices) have changed since 1935, but Penguin still believes in publishing the best books for everybody to enjoy. We still believe that good design costs no more than bad design, and we still believe that quality books published passionately and responsibly make the world a better place.

So wherever you see the little bird – whether it's on a piece of prize-winning literary fiction or a celebrity autobiography, political tour de force or historical masterpiece, a serial-killer thriller, reference book, world classic or a piece of pure escapism – you can bet that it represents the very best that the genre has to offer.

Whatever you like to read – trust Penguin.